NEWSPAPERS CAREER DIRECTORY

Second Edition

NEWSPAPERS CAREER DIRECTORY

Second Edition

The Career Directory Series

Editor-In-Chief: Ronald W. Fry

The Career Press Inc.
PO Box 34,
Hawthorne, NJ 07507
1-800-CAREER-1
(IN NEW JERSEY: 201-427-0229)

The Career Directory Series

Newspapers Career Directory, Second Edition
ISSN 0889-8499

Text edition (Paperback)   ISBN 0-934829-35-7
$26.95

Text edition (Hardcover)   ISBN 0-934829-45-4
$34.95

Text editions of this Directory may be ordered by mail or phone directly from the publisher. To order by mail, please include price as noted above, $2.50 handling per order, plus $1.00 for each book ordered. (New Jersey residents please add 6% sales tax.) Send to:

The Career Press Inc.
62 Beverly Rd., PO Box 34,
Hawthorne, NJ 07507

Or call Toll-Free 1-800-CAREER-1 (in New Jersey: 201-427-0229) to order using your VISA or Mastercard or for further information on all books published or distributed by The Career Press.

TABLE OF CONTENTS

SECTION II: DEPARTMENTS & AREAS OF SPECIALIZATION

SECTION III: THE JOB SEARCH PROCESS

SECTION IV: JOB OPPORTUNITIES DATABANK

SECTION V: APPENDICES

ACKNOWLEDGEMENTS

Our Heartfelt Thanks To:

• The many contributors who, while fulfilling their own significant job responsibilities, somehow found the time to write the articles—those invaluable bits of advice—we believe are the core of this <u>Directory</u>. We commend them for the concern they've shown for you—the aspiring professionals some of them may even eventually hire!

• Their staffs, who often helped with the research, dealt with our editors to make sure all the materials arrived on time and handled the many details endemic to such an undertaking. (And an *extra* special thank-you to Kristin Taylor, Sheila Gibbons and Chuck Blevins at Gannett Co., Inc. and Mary Crowsen at Knight Ridder, Inc.)

• The American Newspaper Publishers Association and its Educational Foundation, especially Roz Stark, Terry Dickerson-Jones and Peter Romano, and the executives at the numerous specialized associations within the field, especially: Paula Markiewicz (International Newspaper Promotion Association), Bob Kasabian (International Newspaper Financial Executives), Lee Bollinger (Association of Newspaper Classified Advertising Managers), Pat Kelly (Society of Newspaper Design), Susan Schoebel (International Newspaper Advertising & Marketing Executives) and Lee Stinnett (American Society of Newspaper Editors). These professionals recommended most of the sterling roster of top executives we assembled to write the articles and advice in both editions of this <u>Career Directory.</u> They and their staff helped with suggestions, criticisms and advice.

• To make this brand-new second edition as comprehensive as possible, we added a number of new topics (and authors). Unfortunately, this required that some excellent articles written for the first edition be dropped, solely to keep this <u>Directory</u> at a manageable size. Our thanks to those professionals whose articles were omitted from this second edition—for their help from the beginning of this project, their recommendations regarding additional topics and authors for this new edition and their kind understanding of editorial necessities!

• Many other top executives were unable, because of time constraints or other pressing commitments, to add articles to this year's edition, though many then worked with us to get other authors, looked over galleys or suggested important new topics. Our thanks to them all— and a warning that they will be the first contacted for the third edition!

• The many newspapers and publishers that provided the detailed information—more than ever before—on employment and internship contacts, training programs, and, most important, entry-level job opportunities. (See the *Job Opportunities Databank* for this exclusive data.) We thank each of them for helping us gather this information for you.

• The many people at The Career Press and our supplier companies who worked long hours compiling this data, editing articles, proofreading and doing all the other things necessary to complete a volume of this size and complexity. We thank all of them for their time, efforts and invaluable contributions: Dick Start, John Fitzpatrick, Carol Setzer, Jim Horn, Harvey Kraft, Scott Zipper, Abby Wittlan, Roberta Kopper, Tam Mossman, Tom Stein, Joe Zipper, Carol Start, Bill Killpatrick, Cy Chaiken, Michelle Gluckow, and all the folks at Words at Work, Book Mart Press, L'Escape Artistes and the staff of the New York Public Library.

Thank you—all of you—my friends.

Ronald W. Fry
President
The Career Press Inc.

Getting The Most Out Of Your Directory

Since the magazine publishing industry has always been what employment counselors call a "glamour" industry, it's not surprising that, as usual, there is an ample supply of qualified candidates and a shortage of actual entry-level jobs.

This Newspapers Career Directory, now in its second edition, was specifically created to help *you* break out of the pack hunting for one of those jobs. (If you are instead interested in magazine or book publishing, we also have separate volumes on those industries, both now available in brand-new third editions.) It won't just tell you how to get a first job at a newspaper—because *how* to get a job is only one aspect of the complex learning process you will need to go through, a process that includes learning about yourself, the newspaper business in general (it *is* radically different from magazines or books), and key papers and job specializations in particular.

It's a process of discovering *what* you want to do, *where* you want to do it, and then, and *only* then, *how* to break down the publisher's front door. This Directory is, therefore, a compendium of *all* the resources you'll need to make the *series* of decisions necessary to get that first job ...or to give you a better understanding of the newspaper business so you can move on from your first job.

And it's written by the pros—25 of the top people in newspaper publishing today. Articles and advice written specifically for this volume and directed specifically to *you*.

But why shouldn't we include information on books and magazines, too? Aren't *they* involved in "publishing?" Doesn't that make them pretty similar? Not by a long shot. Although some of the departments and job descriptions *sound* similar, these publishing worlds are as different as any other industries, despite their all having "publishing" in their names. Being an editor at the *Los Angeles Times* won't help you learn the ins-and-outs of Random House and won't prepare you very well for editing *Architectural Digest* either. Even given these differences, some have tried to lump all three industries into a single "publishing career guide." The result, unfortunately, is a book that gives short shrift to all three industries. (The other problem in virtually all such volumes we've seen is that they're invariably written by a freelance writer who's never worked for a book publisher, magazine or newspaper!)

If you're sure you want to be in "editorial," but don't know the differences between the editorial functions at a magazine, newspaper and book publishing house, the three different publishing volumes will help you explore all three industries before you make the mistake of breaking into the wrong one! There is not significant movement between these industries, so knowing the differences and moving in the right direction from the very start of your career are extremely important.

HOW TO USE THIS DIRECTORY

Anyway, to return to those of you interested in *newspaper* publishing. We've attempted to organize this Directory in such a way that reading it is a logical, step-by-step, educational progression.

Section I (chapters 1-6) offers an overview of the industry—where it came from, where it is, where it's going—as well as three brand-new articles on newspaper internships, how to get a job working for the Associated Press (or other major newswire service) and the opportunities for minorities.

Section II offers more detailed discussions of the major areas of job specialization (in the order in which they appear)—Circulation (at both large and small papers); Design (at small and large papers and a brand new article on editorial cartooning); Editorial (at large and small papers and a brand-new article by a young reporter on what it's really like); the Financial side of the business; a brand-new article on opportunities in the growing area of newspaper Librarianship; Production; Promotion (large and small papers); a brand-new article on the Research area; and Advertising Sales (five articles covering every area of sales, from classified and retail sales to handling national accounts). The nineteen chapters in this section were written by top leaders in each field, professionals already doing what you would *like* to be doing.

After studying these sections, you should be well on your way to deciding exactly *what* you want to do—Section III will help you figure out *how* to go about getting your first chance to *do* it. It includes a detailed Job Search Process that will take you through evaluating yourself and potential employers, preparing resumes and cover letters, the interview process and, finally, sifting the job offers.

Section IV is your *Job Opportunities Databank*, including listings of hundreds of newspapers throughout the United States. Most of these listings include information on internships, training programs, key contacts, even actual and expected entry-level job listings.

This information is exclusive to this <u>Directory</u>, gathered through our own surveys of these publishers.

Finally, Section V consists of two appendices—(A) industry trade organizations and (B) trade publications—more important information to make sure you get exactly the right first job in newspaper publishing.

DISAGREEMENTS AND REDUNDANCIES

You'll discover as you read through the many articles in this volume that <u>the authors don't agree on everything!</u> In fact, you'll find certain instances where they rather vehemently *dis*agree, including their basic advice on breaking into the business, whether to work for one of the big papers or start at a smaller daily or weekly and more.

What's going on here? How do you know who to listen to? Frankly, no one has all the answers, let alone all the *right* answers. Such occasional disagreement is only to be expected given the varied career paths and experiences our contributors have gone through in so many different departments at so many varied papers. We also think it's important that *you* realize there isn't always one way in, one way to do a job, one place to work, one way to think. We have occasionally inserted "Editor's Notes" into the body of articles to refer you to other chapters or sections where you can find related, though perhaps contradictory, advice or information.

On the other hand, you will occasionally find repetitious advice—on interviewing techniques, how to break in, etc.—from article to article. (Reviewers especially please note!) <u>We are aware of this duplication and have purposefully not edited out such repetitious advice.</u> Why?

Not everyone will read every page of this book—the young man who fancies himself the next Gill Fox might never make it through the Production or Circulation articles. Someone just "thumbing through" may entirely miss an important piece of advice if it's in only one section or chapter.

And second, although we believe the extensive job search process included in our staff-written Section III "covers all the basics," if the advice is sound and correct, we're sure it can't be repeated often *enough*.

THE GOAL WE SET...AND ACCOMPLISHED

When we published the first edition of this volume in 1987, students we queried indicated an intense need for a <u>guide to resources</u>—articles and advice on every aspect of the newspaper business by the practitioners out there doing the work, listings of major publishers (with then unavailable information like who to talk to, potential openings, educational requirements, specific titles, etc.), the trade organizations to contact, the trade magazines to read, etc.

The overwhelmingly positive reaction to the first edition of this volume proved that we had achieved our initial goal: To produce the most comprehensive, all-inclusive guide to newspaper publishing for entry-level people ever published.

We feel confident that with this second edition we have succeeded in the more difficult goal we set for ourselves this time: To make the best book on getting into the newspaper business even better.

Most of all, we hope it helps *you* get exactly the job you want in this exciting business.

Good luck!

SECTION I

Overview Of The Newspaper Business

CHAPTER ONE

The Mission of Newspapers

By

Alvah H. Chapman, Jr., Chairman & CEO
Knight Ridder, Inc.

In the early 1960s, most of the newspaper companies in America were privately-owned, family-managed businesses. Newspapers were frequently managed by third and fourth generation family members. Professional qualification was *not* always a major part of the job criteria.

But with changes in ownership came shifts in leadership and professionalism: The key jobs today are *not* going to the son or son-in-law of the owner, but to the best-qualified professional manager, editor and publisher.

Newspapers have revised and updated their content with more special sections in the areas of business and local news. Technology has advanced to allow for better color reproduction. Computers enable editors to use more and better graphics.

THE UNCHANGING MISSIONS OF NEWSPAPERS

But one thing has *not* changed during my years in publishing. That is the special mission —the special trust—belonging to those given the privilege of publishing newspapers.

Mission #1: Serve Our Citizens And Government

Simply stated, a primary mission of our American newspapers is to give our readers the vital, often complex information needed so that, as citizens, they are better equipped and prepared to live safer, more meaningful lives.

Newspapers should also serve (and I think they do) our democratic system of government. Citizens should be informed about the business of government in a democracy.

Without newspapers to explain government, to report politics and politicians, to discuss taxes, to question justice and governmental regulation, and, in our editorials, to examine, criticize, and praise, the democracy that we know today simply would not exist.

It is only through knowing the truth and making our own decisions that we can continue to maintain a free society.

Mission #2: Make A Decent Profit

It's a fact of business life: If a newspaper doesn't make a decent profit, its editorial view will inevitably become a prejudiced one, subservient to the agency or outside business that sustains it.

To be free, the newspaper must be beholden to no single individual or group. And it must succeed in the marketplace.

We are sometimes charged with showing favoritism to an advertiser or a major institution in a community and yielding to internal pressures from such groups. This is rarely the case. Let me cite an example:

In 1985, a Pulitzer Prize for Public Service was won by the *Fort Worth Star-Telegram* and reporter Mark J. Thompson. In a series published in the *Star-Telegram*, Thompson revealed that nearly 250 U.S. servicemen had lost their lives as a result of a design problem in a helicopter built by Bell—the second largest employer in the Fort Worth area. This led the Army to ground almost 600 of their helicopters, pending Bell's modifications.

Reporter Thompson had gone to Washington, found evidence of this problem, and obtained confirming documents. He also was able to get an internal document in which an employee of Bell discussed a suspected problem with the helicopters. Though Bell and the Army were aware of the internal memo, no action was taken until the *Star-Telegram*'s series was printed.

When the newspaper printed these stories, the Army then investigated. Its findings confirmed what the articles had stated. Subsequent suits by families of soldiers killed in the helicopters have been won in court.

Twelve hundred people (mostly Bell employees) cancelled subscriptions to the paper. The company refused to let carriers service newspaper sales racks on Bell property and sent letters to other businesses suggesting an advertising boycott. Bell felt that the paper shouldn't pick on them since they were such an important employer in the community.

But the series was published despite the attempted boycotts. Unquestionably, lives were saved by this courageous and professional newspaper action.

Mission #3: Offer Insights

The newspaper, in addition to providing news and commentary, has another historic mission—to offer insights into life around us.

Who would be happy if there were no comics, or humor columns, or sports and amusement sections, or crossword puzzles, or even an astrology column?

From its beginnings, the press has entertained as well as edified. We realize this so very much when our editors inadvertently omit the Sunday crossword puzzle or decide to drop a long-running comic strip in favor or a new one. Our telephones and mail boxes literally bristle with protests.

Mission #4: Publish Advertising

A fourth mission is the newspaper's role in supporting the free economy in America—through publishing advertising and bringing together the buyers and sellers of goods and services.

Just as news, opinion, entertainment, and general information are important ingredients in satisfying reader tastes, so is advertising a key factor in a successful newspaper. Newspaper advertising is sought out by readers. And pity the poor newspaper in a competitive environment that does not have a full array of department store ads or a full complement of classified.

This nation's economic development would suffer without the force of newspaper advertising to move goods and promote services. There wouldn't be as many jobs. Our standards of living would be lower. Our choices of goods and services would be lessened.

Mission #5: Safeguard Personal Liberties

The press must pay close attention to government. In this function, it should sound the alarm whenever citizens' rights are infringed. The press must protect especially the little persons in our society, standing up for them and their liberties in time of crisis, however unpopular that stand may be. They have and can afford no other voice to plead their cause. Let me cite one example from my own experience.

Phenix City, Alabama, a city of 30,000, was in absolute political bondage in the mid-1950s. A group of racketeers, funded by the proceeds from an illegal numbers game and prostitution, had literally taken control of the local government.

For years, some friends of mine—business people, church members, good Americans — tried to correct this problem. One Election Day when these people tried to vote, they were brutally beaten as they approached the polls. Two reporters from the neighboring *Columbus* (Georgia) *Ledger* were also beaten as they attempted to cover this event.

With no success at home, the Phenix City Reform Group ran Albert Patterson, an honest local attorney, for State Attorney General. His election as the state's chief law enforcement officer signaled the imminent downfall of the ring that had helped put Phenix City in a vise.

But Albert Patterson was murdered before he could take office.

The State of Alabama was in shock. Two days later, a press conference was called by the Deputy Sheriff and Chief Prosecutor of Phenix City. They announced the "greatest manhunt in Alabama history" for the murderer of Albert Patterson.

Reporters for the *Columbus Ledger* attended that press conference and could get no answers to their questions about suspects, investigations, procedures, and so forth.

The next morning, the Atlanta, Birmingham and Montgomery papers headlined "Greatest Manhunt in Alabama History." But the *Columbus Ledger*, after a night of painful agonizing and soul-searching, headlined, "Manhunt Greatest Fraud in Alabama History."

Newspaper pressure mounted,, and within a matter of weeks, the governor had declared martial law. Every judge and every policeman, along with the sheriff and his deputies, were removed. Within 90 days, some trials were held and many guilty pleas were entered. The result: hundreds of indictments were issued and scores of individuals in that community, including the ringleaders, went to prison.

A courageous newspaper and a responsive governor restored freedom to the 30,000 Americans of Phenix City, Alabama.

I know that story well because my father was the president of that newspaper and participated in the agonizing decision of how to handle the story of the press conference.

And incidentally, the *Columbus Ledger* won a Pulitzer Prize for Public Service for that series of stories.

THE CHALLENGES WE NOW FACE

Newspapers are being challenged as never before in our history. The suburban newspapers want our readers, the U.S. Postal Service wants our preprints, and radio, television, and magazines all want our advertisers. But the bottom line is that newspapers are responding to these challenges in a remarkable and exciting fashion.

We have come through a technical revolution in the last 25 years in which we've changed from a cumbersome, expensive production system to a much more efficient one based on electronics, computers and film. We would not have the flexibility to deal with the complex marketing requirements of our advertisers and readers were it not for these innovative production techniques.

We have, in the past 35 to 40 years, moved from being a business largely managed by family members to a business managed by professionals. These professionals recognize and deal with the conflicting requirements of readers, advertisers, employees, communities and shareholders; and we do so by giving the fullest additional commitment to our First Amendment responsibilities.

In short, the business of publishing newspapers is in good shape; its future outlook is quite promising.

It is a dark world out there. But in our nation, the flame of freedom is largely undimmed. It is obvious, but inescapable, that good newspapers, conscious of their First Amendment responsibilities, add fuel to support this flame.

This perspective may help to explain the special passion which motivates those of us who are privileged to work in newspaper publishing. It is a mission satisfied only as we strive for professionally-edited, well-managed newspapers of excellence.

ALVAH H. CHAPMAN, JR.

A third generation newspaper executive, Mr. Chapman was born in Columbus, Ga. He lived for several years in Bradenton, Fl, where his father published the *Bradenton Herald.*

He graduated from The Citadel in 1942 with a B.S. in business administration. In World War II, he served as a B-17 bomber pilot and squadron commander, completing 37 combat missions. After the war, he joined the staff of the *Ledger-Enquirer* in Columbus, becoming business manager in 1948.

In 1953, he became executive vice president and general manager of the *St. Petersburg Times;* he left in 1957 to become part-owner, president and publisher of the Savannah newspapers.

Mr. Chapman joined Knight newspapers in 1960 and, two years later, was named vice president and general manager of the *Miami Herald.* He became president of the *Herald* in 1969, a position he held until 1973, when he was named president of Knight Newspapers.

When Knight Newspapers and Ridder Publications merged in 1974, he became president of the newly formed corporation. He was named chief executive officer in 1976 and chairman of the board in 1982.

CHAPTER TWO

The Future of Newspaper Publishing

By

Nancy J. Woodhull, Vice President/News Services
Gannett Co., Inc

News and information have become the hottest commodities of this century. People are willing to pay more than ever before for more different types of information; and they're willing to try a variety of methods—radio, television, electronic transmission from computer to computer, etc.—to get that information quickly. Despite all this change and technological advances, no other medium commands the authority that a newspaper does (and always has). The newspaper is what we call "the medium of record"—the medium everyone turns to for the full, complete account of a news event.

I'm extraordinarily optimistic about the future of newspapers. The wonderful thing about a newspaper is that a reader can get the facts and then hold onto them, referring back to them as often as necessary. Readers' reliance on newspapers for comprehensive coverage forces newspaper reporters, photographers, and editors to be more thorough and accurate. Consequently, the newspaper is a product one comes to trust.

I believe newspapers will keep that special place among an information-hungry public well into the 21st century—provided those who enter the journalism field can meet the challenge of communicating about a complicated world in simple, straightforward terms.

NEWSPAPERS ARE GOOD BUSINESS

Today's newspapers are enjoying a favorable financial climate. Newspapers have regularly been showing operating profits of 20 percent or more of their revenues—a performance figure that has made them attractive acquisitions for larger media companies.

Gannett Co.,Inc., where I work, is the U.S.A.'s largest newspaper publisher. It owns 90 daily newspapers, including *USA TODAY*, and 39 non-daily newspapers. It also has diversified into radio and television broadcasting and outdoor advertising. But since its founding in 1906, it has been best-known as the owner of newspapers in small- and medium-sized communities all across the nation. But in 1985 and 1986, Gannett purchased some of the country's most distinguished newspapers, all published in larger cities: the *Des Moines Register*, the *Detroit News*, The *Courier-Journal* in Louisville, Ky., and the *Arkansas Gazette*. Gannett's newspapers and broadcast properties are linked by the Gannett News Service wire, so that news enterprise from all Gannett reporters can be picked up and published or broadcast by Gannett editors nationwide.

Quality journalism is an advantage of chain ownership. Another is the opportunity it offers to individuals who want to grow in their profession. Writers, editors, production experts, illustrators, graphic designers, and circulation and advertising specialists can move from small to middle-sized papers, acquiring the experience that could someday help them get to the likes of the *Detroit News* or *USA TODAY*.

For some time, many beginning journalists headed immediately to "the big city" to write for their first jobs, hoping for their big break. Now there's a trend back to the traditional practice of getting early experience on small and medium-sized dailies. Personally, I believe that's the best training path for entry-level reporters, because you get to do more different kinds of things and learn how to make your own decisions.

I started at a small, 50,000-circulation daily in New Jersey. I was a reporter, an editor, did layout—just about everything. It gave me a great feeling for what's involved in getting out a newspaper. I urge you to consider a similar route. You'll become more familiar with the non-editorial departments (such as display and classified advertising and circulation), simply because things are so compact, which will make you better prepared to take on more responsibility when you eventually move to a larger newspaper. That breadth of knowledge is important: If your eventual goal is to be an editor or publisher, you need to learn more than how to produce solid reporting; you need to learn how to make a newspaper profitable, too.

TOMORROW'S JOURNALIST

Journalists in the 21st century will have to think more "broadly" and be more creative. Even a rookie will be expected to be much more multidimensional. Why? Because newspaper readers—that diverse group of people who devour information and expect us to explain how developments in science, business, leisure and entertainment, health and social issues will affect them—demand it.

Newspapers used to be our automobiles, our TVs, our telephones, what we used to use to keep track of our friends in the next town. But now that we have those things ourselves, we don't need the newspaper as much to tell us *what* happened; we need newspapers to explain to us *why* things happened as they did and how that will affect us.

People want their newspapers to be more responsive, to provide information they could use to interpret the world around them—not just the reporter's or editor's world, but the one in which many different kinds of people live.

Today and in the future, it will be important for editors to have the ability to see the big picture, and for reporters to regard themselves as more than wordsmiths who can turn a smart phrase.

This is what you should expect if you want to make a place for yourself in the U. S.'s 300-year-old newspaper publishing business:

- You must be multidimensional.

- You must relate to your readers.

- You must be willing to constantly explore new ways of presenting information, ways that will help your readers act on the information you've provided.

- You must have a curiosity about people and the systems they set up in which to live and work.

- You must be a proficient writer and grammarian.

The last of these criteria can't be emphasized enough. Many students have lost or failed to develop what writing ability they have. They don't really know the basics of grammar, punctuation, or syntax. Journalism desperately needs people with these capabilities. Love of language and the ability to use it expertly will be essential to the future of newspaper publishing and all types of communication.

THE NEWSPAPER TEAM FOR THE YEAR 2000

I've focused here on how journalists can prepare themselves for the challenges of the future, but there are many other people on a newspaper's team besides reporters and editors who contribute to a paper's success—the publisher, advertising director, circulation manager, production director, controller, human resources director, etc. All key people in the newspaper enterprise.

All of them will be as intensely involved as the people in the newsroom in keeping the newspaper in first place as the medium of record.

Publishers are responsible for the paper's profitability and for its effectiveness as a community institution. They will have to spend even more time getting to know different community groups so the newspaper can be tuned into business trends, civic and educational needs, and government and politics.

The advertising director will have to know how to find new markets among the newspaper's readers and compile the research that will convince advertisers that selling to those markets will help their businesses. The ad director also will have to be exceptionally aware of the competing strategies devised by developing media like cable TV, pay TV, and cable shopping programs—as well as those of radio, commercial television and magazines, the more "traditional" media—and be prepared to counter them.

Keeping old readers loyal and attracting new ones is a job that falls to the circulation manager. That person will be challenged to track lifestyle habits, transportation patterns, real estate development, and commercial growth to find out where current readers are and where new ones can be found. The circulation manager is not just responsible for delivering the newspaper—he or she is also responsible for identifying new markets of readers.

The stereotypical production manager used to be a gruff old guy who stood over typesetters, paste-up artists, and printers to make sure the paper actually got out. Today's production manager presides over computer-driven typesetting equipment, advanced technology that makes it possible to receive color photos taken thousands of miles from the composing room, and satellites that beam images of newspaper pages to printing plants across town or hundreds of miles away. Tomorrow's production manager will have to utilize ever-newer technology in an effort to continually improve the appearance of the newspaper and the speed with which it can be put together and distributed.

The controller will be looking at how the newspaper can perform its functions in the least expensive way possible. He or she will be a key strategist in developing ways the newspaper's profits can grow in a business environment in which there are an increasing number of competitors selling news and information.

The human resources (*aka* personnel) director will be responsible for seeing that women and diverse ethnic groups are represented at all levels of decision-making—in the newsroom, in sales, and in administration. This person's success will be measured by how well and how fairly the newspaper is staffed.

Everyone on this team will have an important role to play in the future of newspaper publishing. Each will be required to be a multidimensional professional with energy and vision inside them and a good education behind them. They will need to grow as managers of people and projects, as well as specialists in their area of journalism.

And most importantly, they'll need to adapt to the changes of the Information Age. What's so different about the world we're heading towards in the year 2000? Geography no longer really separates people. We don't physically have to be somewhere to participate in an event—because journalists will bring it to us. Television and radio have shared in the advantages of immediacy that advanced technology has made possible. But only a newspaper can deliver a breaking news story that lasts, that can be reread and savored, and followed each day as details unfold.

The newspaper is—and will continue to be—the medium relied on for the *whole* story.

NANCY J. WOODHULL

In her current position, Ms. Woodhull is in overall charge of Gannett News Service, along with fulfilling her concurrent duties as president of Gannett New Media Services.

She began her newspaper career as a proofreader on the *News Tribune* in Woodbridge, NJ, in 1964. She left to become a reporter for the *Detroit Free Press* in 1973, moved to the *Rochester Times-Union* in 1975 as night city editor (later managing editor), and to the *Democrat and Chronicle,* also in Rochester, as managing editor in 1980.

In 1982, Ms. Woodhull was one of the seven original planning editors of *USA TODAY* and was named managing editor. She became vice president/news of Gannett New Media Services in 1984 and senior editor of *USA TODAY* in 1985.

In 1986, she was named president of Gannett New Media Services, and, later that same year, senior editor of Gannett News Service. She was promoted to her current position with the latter in January, 1987.

Originally from New Jersey,. Ms. Woodhull now lives in McLean, Virginia, with her husband and daughter.

CHAPTER THREE

Is There A Future For Minorities In The Newspaper Business?

By

**Earl M. Thompson, Asst. Advertising Manager/Sales Development
Dayton Newspapers, Inc.**

Whenever I am introduced to anyone as being with the local newspaper, he or she assumes I'm a reporter. After 18 years, it gets a little tiresome. When my wife and I go to a party, someone usually says, "Watch what you say in front of Earl, it might end up in the paper." More often than not, this assumption is simply false, especially for blacks, who currently do not hold a proportionate share of newspaper managerial, reporting, sales or production jobs.

There are many "invisible" careers in the newspaper business, all of which can be very rewarding—<u>circulation representatives, accountants, advertising account executives, artists, photographers, computer programmers, purchasing agents and personnel, marketing or research staffers.</u> These are some of the key areas that are invisible to the public, but intrinsic to the running of the business. And newspapers *are* a business! Without a healthy profit margin, a newspaper cannot carry out its responsibilities to the community—to report on what's happening today, what happened yesterday and what's ahead for the future.

If you are a minority, I would advise you not to have tunnel vision about a career in the newspaper business. Prospects are tremendous, providing you don't think "working for a newspaper" is synonymous with working as a journalist. If you are a marketing, finance or computer science major, check out a career in print.

Newspapers will be around as long as Man continues his love for the printed word. And newspaper people come from all backgrounds.

WHAT CAN A BLACK/MINORITY EXPECT?

My first inclination is to say not much! My second inclination is 'to say maybe, just *maybe*, there is some hope. But you must always remember one fact of life: America's newspapers are owned by whites. Some are family-owned, some publicly-owned, but either way, they are still controlled by whites.

Though some newspapers in the '60s and '70s advocated equal opportunity, this turned out to be little more than lip service at many papers—management staffs remained mostly white. Today newsrooms and advertising departments have approximately 3% minority staffing; circulation departments have not done much better.

As we come to the end of the '80s, we are beginning to make some changes—nearly twenty years after the newspaper industry told everyone else what to do. Better late than never. Hopefully, tomorrow's young, talented minority person will be able to concentrate on developing his or her skills and talents and not have to fight the battle of equality every step of the way. I say this with an honest feeling of great hope, though I have to admit some reluctance because of the lack of progress thus far in the industry.

ARE YOU READY?

With the above caveats in mind, it's safe to say the newspaper business is not very different than many other industries—the talented, competitive and well-connected will get ahead. So getting an education is only part of your struggle; you must also be talented, have a strong desire to compete, and above all, get connected to someone who is willing to invest his or her knowledge and time in you. In other words, find a mentor. To get ahead, display your talents daily, and above all, be prepared for the disappointments that surely will come. But keep fighting back. Those of you who keep your goals in sight will reach them

Those goals, at least initially, should be realistic and obtainable. Understand what it is going to take to reach them. Find someone with whom you feel comfortable, to whom you can talk and confide in, someone who will be honest with you. For if you are to compete, and compete effectively, you are going to have to know your strengths and weakness.

Without this knowledge, it becomes almost impossible for you to compete in a competitive environment. Watch out for your detractors, for they will surely be there. Learn to listen, watch what you say and to whom you say it. Always remember that you will encounter persons who want you to fail. Don't be afraid of them—it's all part of the competitive environment you've thrown yourself into.

Now, back to understanding your strengths and weakness. This is where a mentor will pay off. And believe me, you *will* need a mentor. In fact, if you are a black, you will need *two* mentors—one black and one white. Your black mentor will be able to help you stay in focus and in balance. Your white mentor will teach you the art of corporate politics, an art form to which your black mentor may not have been exposed, but one which *you* must learn if you are to survive in corporate America.

KEEP LEARNING—IT'S IMPORTANT

Never feel that you know as much as you think you do or that you need to know. Be willing to continue your education. Whether or not you go back to college to get your MA, MS or MBA, you must be prepared to attend workshops and seminars throughout your career. And subscribe to and study the professional journals in your area of specialization. *(Many of these are listed in Appendix B—Ed.)* Never stop learning—a little learning *is* a dangerous thing.

And remember: You're not doing all these simply for the sake of "learning"—workshops and seminars give you an opportunity to "network!" Having an MS, MA or MBA will not automatically guarantee you a managerial job, a directorship or publisher's position. In fact, there are many publishers, directors and managers without such advanced degrees. But if self-growth is important to you, that should be reason enough for you to want to keep learning. Knowing as much as you can about your business will keep you from a lot of compromising positions.

WHAT TO EXPECT FINANCIALLY

You're fresh out of school, lack experience (except for a summer internship), but still want the new BMW...right now. Forget it! I am not saying that you will *never* be able to afford a BMW. I *am* saying, however, that few, if any, <u>entry-level</u> salaries will allow you to afford such luxuries. So be realistic when you talk to recruiters about your initial salary expectations. Check around and get a feel for what others are paying in similar career fields before you ask for the moon.

It's difficult to become very rich in this business, but you can make a good living. Just remember that superior job performance and experience are the prerequisites for great opportunities and huge paychecks! As in any business, you must pay your dues and prove yourself. In general, reporters and ad executives can expect to earn salaries in the $25,000 - $30,000 range after a few years with a proven track record, at least in fairly large metro areas. Top salary figures for line people, exclusive of management positions, usually taper off around $35,000 or so at present. Management salaries, of course, are much higher in most cases.

Many minority candidates I have interviewed seem to have problems negotiating their own worth. Don't—I repeat, *don't*—be afraid to negotiate salary and benefits with your employer, though, again, I remind you to be realistic. This is where a mentor can be very helpful.

WHERE TO START

Where do you find that first job? I would recommend a medium-sized paper. This will allow you the opportunity to get more hands-on experience right from the start. Most smaller papers are located in small, often rural areas of the country. The evidence currently available does not indicate a lot of career opportunities for blacks in these areas. There are exceptions, however, so investigate first. As I've said, times are changing.

THE BOTTOM LINE

I have tried to cram a lifetime of experience into this article. It is meant to do one thing—to give you a realistic viewpoint as a minority of what *can* be a very rewarding career field...if you are prepared to deal with and meet the challenges that lie ahead. Then maybe, just maybe, one of you will end up being the publisher, general manager or even the editor-in-chief of one of the nations major metropolitan newspapers. I sincerely hope so.

GOOD LUCK!

EARL M. THOMPSON

Earl started as a Circulation Representative at Dayton Newspapers, Inc., supervising the distribution and sales of the evening edition. He was the second black to become an account executive in the Advertising department and, in 1982, the first black promoted to assistant retail advertising manager. He manages a staff of eight sales people and oversees product and sales development of some of the newspaper's specialty publications.

To earn his degree, Earl attended Central State University in the evenings full-time while holding down a full-time job during the day. Since graduation, he has attended numerous advance management seminars and workshops.

He has been active in his community, serving on the board of directors of Wesley Community Center (a self-help center), has served as president and vice-president of several community educational councils, and as president of the board of directors of the Dayton Newspapers/WHIO Federal Credit Union. Earl is currently the President of the Dayton chapter of the Black Presbyterians Caucus and a member of the National Chapter. He is a member of the Dayton Newspapers, Inc. Affirmative Action Committee, the NAACP, the SCLC and the Speakers Bureau for the Task Force on Minorities in the Newspaper.

CHAPTER FOUR

Internships: Key Preparation For Your Future In Journalism

By

**Mary Kay Blake, Director, News Staff Recruiting/Newspaper Division
The Gannett Company**

How valuable is an internship to someone trying to get into journalism?

Let's put that question another way: How good a beginning do you want your career to have?

WHAT A NEWSPAPER INTERNSHIP WILL DO FOR YOU

Internships are invaluable. They can:

- Give you a chance to see what your chosen profession will really be like, day-in and day-out.

- Provide you with experience in your chosen field even before you graduate into it.

- Offer a solid portfolio of published work which you can show potential employers.

- Help you learn how to organize time and juggle projects.

• Match you with a number of present and potential mentors, each of whom may contribute to your professional growth. (Everyone in a newsroom—not just your supervisor—can help you learn about life on a newspaper.)

• Develop strong work habits and daily discipline meeting deadline.

• Connect you with editors and colleagues who may choose to use their firsthand knowledge of you and their contacts in the industry to help you find a full-time job at graduation.

• Turn into a job. Many an intern has moved right into a professional role—or graduated and then gone into one—at the newspaper where he or she interned.

Most of the young people I know who are being hired in the newsrooms of daily newspapers these days have three credentials: a degree in journalism (often combined with a second major); extensive experience on campus publications (usually but not exclusively the college daily); and at least one newspaper internship.

It's possible, of course, to land a job without all three of these bits of background; I suppose there even are people who find that first job without *any* of them. But you'll find the search a lot easier and the newspapers that are interested in you a lot more numerous if you've prepared yourself for the profession in these three ways.

A VARIETY OF INTERNSHIP OPPORTUNITIES

What kinds of internships are there? Probably as many as there are newspapers. Indeed, if one of the established formats outlined below doesn't fit into your schedule or the kinds of newspapers you can connect with, see how creative you can be in devising a unique program of your own that you can present to an editor. It'll show your creativity and the kind of ingenuity that is always of interest to an employer.

Among the established types of internships are these:

Full-time professional newsroom work for a specified period: It's usually three months (or 12 weeks) and usually in the summer. But the stay can be shorter or longer, and it could be any season of the year. Some newsrooms now have an ongoing, year-round internship program, often set up through a local or regional college.

Part-time work for a specified period: This kind of program usually lasts a semester and involves 10-20 hours or newsroom work per week. Again, however, flexibility is a key factor and the hours could be fewer (generally not more) and the time period shorter or longer.

Rotating internships: These involve work in several newsroom departments—two weeks in features, two weeks on the copy desk, two weeks in sports, etc. Some are very structured and allow for little or no deviation; more often, however, your interests help decide which areas you will work in.

Paid internships and credit internships: In the former, you work for a weekly or hourly wage. In the latter, you earn college credit for the experience. Some newspapers offer both kinds, usually dealing with local colleges on the latter and students from farther away (who have to then find and pay for local housing) on the former.

Pre-professional and professional internships: The latter involve reporting, editing and photography roles and usually go to students between their junior and senior years in college (though they *have* been landed by younger students or graduates who want/need another credential or a bridge to a job.) The former usually are support roles and involve research work, support work, clerical work and newsroom exposure, but not usually at the professional level.

FINDING ONE THAT'S RIGHT FOR YOU

Work with your school's placement office. Be persistent: Ask to be on interview lists for any possibilities.

Write lots of letters on your own to as many newspapers as you can find *(using sources such as the Job Opportunities Databank of this Career Directory, Internships, Volume 2: Newspaper, Magazine and Book Publishing—also available from the Career Press—and the Editor and Publisher Yearbook, all of which should be available in most libraries—Ed.).* Include with your cover letter a clear and concise resume and 6-12 examples of your work (neatly presented—not scraps of paper cut and pasted).

Be sure to have a trusted friend or colleague proofread your resume and letter. I know editors who immediately toss aside any applications that contain typos, misspellings, incorrect names or, worst of all, misspellings of their own or their newspaper's names.

Be willing to look beyond the "name" newspapers—too many students already are vying for the scarce internship spots. Look for the good mid-sized newspapers (those under 100,000 circulation) where you will be an integral part of the entire operation. You'll get broader experience there anyway.

Start early—some newspapers select their summer interns by January 1st.

Be flexible. Make sure the newspaper knows that if summer isn't a good time for it to have you as an intern, you could arrange your schedule to work during another season. (More and more students are taking the option of summer school and winter internships, in order to be available when the openings are.)

Try for part-time or stringing work at daily (or even weekly) newspapers in your hometown or the area around your school. Sometimes such roles lead to internships; they at least will provide clips and contacts to use in further searches for a spot. And they demonstrate your eagerness to gain experience.

Work on campus publications—again, they provide helpful clips. And the experience helps show an editor that you can organize your time well enough to handle both classes and work.

AND WHAT TO DO ONCE YOU HAVE

Even before you begin the job (or arrive in town if it's not your local paper), make sure you are reading <u>daily</u> the newspaper of whose staff you soon will be a part. Ask for a mailed subscription if you're outside it's local area It will help you become familiar with the newspaper, its style and staff; it also should help you begin to learn about the town and get your work off to a faster start.

Be curious and aware. Don't limit your learning to the department(s) to which you're assigned—spend some of your off-time in other sections. See what happens in features. Check out a busy Friday night in sports. Learn how the copy desk works—and what happens to copy in composing. Ask to sit in on daily newsroom meetings or weekly editorial board sessions. Observing the kind of interaction that occurs there (or doesn't) can help you better understand the newspaper—and whether it's one you'd like to join once you graduate.

Take a slightly different route to work every day—you may spot story ideas you (and other staffers) otherwise would bypass. That kind of enterprise often leads to good reader pieces—and strong investigative ones.

Ask lots of questions. Ask your editors what they like (and don't like) about their work. Ask your colleagues what kinds of editors they like to work for. Ask both about other newspapers they've worked for—and what made those newspapers great or not so great.

Push for feedback. Learn from the comments. And ask for specific reviews of your work. Don't settle for "it's fine." An editor may not have a lot of time to spend with you daily. So try to find out what he or she liked (or didn't like) about your leads one day. Ask about your transitions the next day. And whether you sought enough sources or asked them the best questions the day after that. Bit by bit, you'll begin to learn the techniques and skills that separate the great journalists from all the others.

Offer to work on longer-range stories in between your regular assignments. There usually are five or ten minutes (or more) of "down" time every time you're waiting for someone to call you back or a clip to be culled from the library. Use that time to begin building the research and phone-call blocks for another story—or several stories. Keep each in a separate queue or notebook; keep building on them bit by bit. You'll end your internship with more clips than those who sat around waiting for assignments and learn some very valuable time-management and juggling skills that are crucial to all good journalists.

Remember that an internship is much like your education: You will get out of it what you put into it in terms of effort, energy, enterprise and enthusiasm.

If you think it will be a good experience—and seek every possible opportunity to make it one and to grow in and from it—you will find every moment of it worthwhile, now and in your very promising future.

If you wait for assignments, don't ask questions and don't seek out new areas to explore, you might as well spend your time and energy in another way.

And probably in another profession.

MARY KAY BLAKE

Mary Kay Blake, 40, has worked in newsroom recruiting and news staff development roles for Gannett Co., Inc. for ten years. For nine years before that, she worked in newsrooms as a copy editor and reporter. She is a graduate of the College of St. Francis in Joliet, IL (B.A. with honors in English).

Her current role involves overseeing an extensive college-recruiting program for Gannett's 90 daily newspapers, including *USA TODAY*. (The company also includes 39 non-daily newspapers; *USA WEEKEND*, a newspaper magazine; Gannett News Service; eight television stations; 16 radio stations; and the largest outdoor advertising company in North America. Gannett also has marketing, television news and program production, research, satellite information systems and a national group of printing facilities. Gannett has operations in 40 states, the District of Columbia, Guam, the Virgin Islands, Canada, Great Britain, Hong Kong, Singapore and Switzerland.)

Mrs. Blake also coordinates the consideration of Gannett newsroom staffers for other positions in the company and leads the search for "outside" talent to bring into the group, although she notes that her role as recruiter is increasingly augmented by newsroom staffers and editors throughout the Gannett group who bring promising prospects to her attention so she, in turn, can share their credentials at newspapers as openings develop.

She is married to a journalist. Her husband George is editor and vice president of *The Cincinnati Enquirer* (also a Gannett newspaper).

CHAPTER FIVE

Take It From The Top...

By

**Greg Stevens, Vice President North-West Operations
Scripps League Newspapers, Inc.**

Being publisher or general manager of a small to medium-sized newspaper is tremendously rewarding, usually fairly lucrative, continually interesting, educational and broadening. It's certainly the best job *I've* ever had.

Nowadays, most newspapers are members of "newspaper groups." This means that they are owned by publicly- or privately-held (family-owned) corporations. Almost always, the day-to-day operating, news and content decisions are made *locally* by the management team at the individual newspaper.

As these are the only types of newspapers I've worked for, they're the only kinds I can talk about. But, as I say, most newspapers are no longer run by well-heeled entrepreneurial types who own *and* run the operations themselves. They're run by publishers and general managers who have been appointed by the newspaper's ownership to be in charge of the total operation. Like a Sears store or a steel plant or shipbuilding company.

When you're the publisher or general manager of such a newspaper, you are the boss. This means that the managers of all the various departments in the newspaper—advertising sales, the business office, circulation and the editor (who is only responsible for the *news* in the newspaper, *not* the whole operation)—all report to you. And you, in one way or another, report to the corporation that owns the paper, since you are responsible for the quality, the profitability and the short and long-term goals of that newspaper.

In every operation, only one person can really be the boss; but then, not everyone *wants* to be boss. I know quite a few talented, hardworking newspaper professionals who have no desire at all to be managers, let alone publishers responsible for the whole operation. They don't think being in charge would be worth the stress and tension of decision making. Or they think it would be lonely at the top.

Also, a newspaper has a variety of specialty departments within it: There are News and Editorial, Display Advertising, Classified, Circulation, Composition, Printing, Computer Science, Business Management, and more. Each of these specialties provides very different functions for and within the newspaper operation. Many people who enter newspaper work as one kind of specialist or another never *want* to leave their specialty. And that's fine, too.

SO WHAT'S DIFFERENT ABOUT THE PEOPLE AT THE TOP?

Of course, almost all people who get to be publishers or general managers of newspapers were at one time "specialists" themselves. But unlike those people who don't think being in charge would be right for them and unlike those people who are so dedicated to their newspaper specialty that they never want to stop practicing it...*some* newspaper people think that it would be a whole lot of fun if *they* had the chance to call the shots, chart the course, and make the decisions.

For someone who is already employed at a newspaper, the first step in this direction is usually taking charge of some function within his or her own department—the reporter who takes a shot at an assistant editor's position, the ad salesman who goes for an open advertising manager's slot, etc.

Publishers are usually selected from eligible department heads by corporate officers. In most cases, these officers were once successful publishers themselves (and before that, newspaper specialists of one kind or another), so they know what to look for. They will want someone who understands the operation of the total newspaper and has genuine respect for the importance of all the specialties that must work cooperatively to write, sell into, produce, and distribute a good newspaper.

As a publisher or GM, your ongoing responsibilities to the corporation will be in terms of relative numbers: circulation gained or lost, advertising space sold for how much per inch, and so on. All the revenues generated by the newspaper's income centers every month will be depleted by the paper's "outflow"—the operation's payroll and expenses—leaving (you hope) a difference on the plus side, which, after taxes, represents the newspaper's profit. The profit is usually shown on a balance sheet on "the bottom line." (That's where that common expression comes from.)

So any individual who aspires to the publisher or GM titles will need to demonstrate a general respect for business, an appreciation of the importance of earning a profit (nothing good happens to any business or its employees without a healthy percentage of profit), and the desire and ability to learn and understand the business mechanics that support the operation of the situation briefly described in the preceding paragraph.

You won't have to train to be an accountant; it's just a matter of being able to orient yourself to the goal of the profitability of the operation.

That's *not* ALL you have to be or care about to be a good publisher. As a matter of fact, if the preceding *was* ALL, you might as well be the boss at any old business, rather than the publisher or GM of a newspaper. But other than the above "musts" for being an effective publisher, there's a wide latitude.

I know outgoing, friendly publishers who have earned the respect and love of their managers and employees. Many of them are active in the Chamber of Commerce and attend all the business mixers and ribbon cuttings.

On the other hand, I also know more reserved, bookish publishers who are more comfortable dealing with accounting ledgers and readership surveys than directly with the employees, readers or advertisers.

I know GMs, formerly ad salespeople, who still like to make calls on major accounts with the advertising staffers. And publishers—former editors—who retain the authority and title of "editor" after their ascension to the top because they want to make sure they have the final say about what's in the paper on a daily basis. Some continue to write a weekly opinion column.

There are humorous publishers, very serious ones, old and young, male and female...

WHAT THESE PEOPLE DO EVERY DAY

There are so many different types of publishers, running their day-to-day operations with so many different management styles, that it's hard to say what a publisher's "typical" day would be like. But if I tried to outline some of the things an "average" publisher might do over the period of a work week, it would probably include the following:

- Meet with members of the community on an informal basis—at a service club meeting, Chamber of Commerce function, or over morning coffee in town.

- Meet with each of your major department heads at least once, maybe for 30 minutes to an hour. Discuss departmental operations, take notes, refer to notes from your last meeting. Stay in touch with what the departments are accomplishing—their goals, problems, conflicts with other department heads, and so on.

- Review the records your business department gives you on advertising and circulation sales; compare these figures with (A) what you budgeted for the current time period and (B) what the numbers were for the corresponding period last week, last month or last year. Get a feeling of "where you are," business-wise.

- Participate in a discussion with your editor on publishing an editorial opinion on a local issue of public concern (or write one yourself).

- Take paperwork or business reading home on two or more evenings and/or over the weekend.

And so on.

When you are the publisher or GM, you have a lot of meetings. You talk to a lot of people. You probably send a lot of memos to confirm understandings and set directions.

Communication is pretty important; otherwise the department heads can start pulling against one another. (The departments' purposes and priorities are in some cases very different—almost *opposed*, in a few cases, like advertising and the news department.) Your job is to make sure all these separate teams are pulling the wagon in the same direction...and that it's a direction that's good for the product and the health of the company.

BUT THEY GET PAID WELL

Remember, you *are* the boss. And as such, most publishers are paid a nice salary, plus a bonus based on the earnings of the newspaper.

Publishers of weekly newspapers generally make less money than the publishers of daily newspapers. Again, there is a great deal of variance between publishers' salaries, but I would say a young publisher of a weekly that's turning a profit will earn about the same money as a seasoned reporter or ad salesman at a pretty large daily newspaper. In 1987, this means between $35,000 and $60,000 per year.

There are over 1,700 daily newspapers in the U.S., the majority of them with circulation under 50,000. Dailies with a circulation from 10,000 to perhaps 30,000 subscribers would pay their publishers between $50,000 and $90,000. Perhaps more. Perhaps a *bunch* more. There are much larger newspapers, to be sure, but perhaps only several hundred in the country.

In addition to salary and bonuses, there are the benefits and "perks." Some are written, such as stock purchase options (which often pay dividends in excess of your payments to buy them, thus resulting in extra income for you), many are unwritten. The publisher or GM of a local newspaper occupies a pretty respected position in the community: There are invitations to grand openings, attendance at educational (and fun) newspaper conventions in other cities, and much more.

As I said right at the start of this article, it's the best job I've ever had.

HOW TO MAKE IT TO THE TOP

If you're considering a career in the newspaper business and think you might want to "aim for the top," what should you do to maximize your chances of becoming a newspaper publisher or GM?

1. Take courses in school that will give you basic business skills; work on your "people skills" on your own. Learn how to communicate convincingly, verbally and in writing. Fortunately, there are a lot of "self-help" books out now that can help you enhance your personality, influence people positively, budget time, and prioritize effectively. They can't hurt, they're easy to read, and they help!

2. Get started at a mid-sized daily newspaper. Where the paper is too small, the staff is often too lean to afford the recommendation that follows next. Where the paper is too large, the departments are often separated by significant barriers. The starting pay may be a bit better at the latter, but the presumption is that you're supposed to just "do your job" and not bother people in the other departments. So the result is less opportunity for you to learn other newspaper specialties or be noticed outside the walls of your own department.

3. Become active in the community, "representing" the newspaper—on your own time —on some public committee or working board. The Chamber of Commerce Western Days Committee or the Salvation Army Pancake Breakfast...it doesn't matter. Exposure to "community improvement" contingents will flesh out your impressions of how the community perceives the paper.

Many newspaper specialists never consider whether they'd like to be managers until the possibility of becoming one is offered or otherwise revealed to them. Whether or not newspaper management is really for *you* is pretty hard to decide from the outside looking in. But the situation does give a real edge to someone who gets on the inside and decides early on to shoot for the top.

I suppose the key really is whether being at the focal point where all the major pieces of a newspaper's operation interact really excites you. If you were the football player who just *knew* that if *you* were the coach or the captain, you'd make the right decisions and the team would win...or if *you* were always in the middle of things on the Sorority annual project, planning and organizing everything...you have the basic stuff of management and are probably a natural.

I hope this perspective has been of some assistance. If you *do* decide on a newspaper career...and *do* decide you want to go for the management ladder...I wish you the best of luck.

GREG STEVENS

Greg Stevens, 42, is general manager of *The Napa Register*, a six-day daily newspaper serving 22,000 subscribers in Northern California's Napa Valley. He also has regional responsibilities assigned by Scripps League Newspapers, and the publishers of six other daily and weekly members of that group report to him.

After college and a stint in Vietnam, he started out in the newspaper business with a portfolio of editorial cartoons and a desire to learn. He hired on at a small, 13,000-circulation daily in Southern California as "staff artist and advertising services representative." Attracted by the advertising side, he acquired some accounts to handle for the paper on his own. He practiced his own advice, learning how to take news photos, write features and operate production equipment on his own time. Three years later, he was offered a department head position at his paper's larger "sister paper," with responsibilities for promotion and marketing, and gained expertise in these areas over the next four years.

In 1979, he joined the Scripps League group by accepting a marketing position with Hawaii Press Newspapers on the island of Oahu. Shortly afterwards, he was appointed assistant publisher. In 1982, he became publisher of a twice-weekly rural newspaper in Sonoma County, north of San Francisco. In 1983, he received a promotion to assistant publisher of the daily *Napa Register* in neighboring Napa County, where he has lived and worked since. In early 1986, he was appointed general manager of the *Register* and vice president of North-West operations for Scripps League Newspapers, Inc.

CHAPTER SIX

Opportunities At The Associated Press

By

Jack Stokes, Director of Recruiting
Associated Press

The Associated Press is the world's oldest and largest news-gathering organization. It is owned by its American newspaper and broadcast members, who share its costs and benefits. This unique cooperative structure also means that member newspapers and broadcast stations share their local news with The Associated Press as part of their membership agreement.

AP was founded in 1848 by six New York publishers who wanted to cut costs. Since then, it has grown from a small domestic staff and a single foreign correspondent in Halifax, Nova Scotia, to 1,600 reporters, editors and photographers, working 24 hours a day, every day of the year, in the United States and abroad.

Based at its international headquarters in New York, AP has 142 domestic bureaus and 84 foreign bureaus serving news outlets in 115 countries. From a system designed to benefit a handful of newspapers, it has mushroomed into a service for more than 15,000 newspaper and broadcast outlets around the world. One billion people a day hear or read AP news.

WHAT THE ASSOCIATED PRESS DOES

The **General Desk** in New York is the main control point for domestic news and the supervisory desk for The Associated Press worldwide. Each U. S. state bureau has an AP wire specifically for state news. The state bureaus send stories to the General Desk where editors decide which stories are important enough to put on the main national wire.

All the major news that is reported by AP staffers overseas comes into the **Foreign Desk** in New York, where the editor and his or her staff supervise assignments and news coverage around the world and edit foreign news for domestic news outlets.

World Services is responsible for AP's news and photo delivery to all newspapers, radio and television stations outside North America. Located in New York, the World Desk edits and distributes news for 10,000 media outlets worldwide.

The mission of AP's **foreign correspondents**, who answer to both the Foreign and World Services desks, is to report news that originates outside the United States. AP bureaus abroad also distribute world news within their respective countries and transmit their own news to other nations, including the United States.

AP's national **Sports and Business departments** are based in New York along with AP's **Newsfeatures** department, whose writers produce weekly Sunday news and human interest features.

The largest **reporting bureau** in The Associated Press is located in Washington, D.C., where a 150-member staff of national writers, editors, regional reporters and photographers keeps tabs on all aspects of the federal government and national politics.

AP's **NewsPhoto operation** is based in New York. Hundreds of staff photographers around the world record the joy and tragedy of life. With the technological breakthroughs achieved by AP engineers, pictures can be transmitted around the globe in minutes on AP's vast international picture network. AP began the modern age of newsphotos in 1935 with the introduction of WirePhotos, the first service to transmit pictures daily by wire.

Part of the NewsPhoto operation is the newly expanded **Graphics department** where editors and artists use AP-developed computer-based technology to edit and transmit graphics to newspapers and transmit news graphics over the newsphoto network.

In addition to serving newspapers, The Associated Press has a separate operation for the needs of broadcasters. AP **Broadcast Services**, with headquarters in Washington, D.C., is the home of scores of anchors, editors and reporters for radio and television. The full range of news services for thousands of broadcast outlets includes scripted news reports for radio and television, radio newscasts and video reports. The radio newscasts are part of **AP Network News**, the full-service, commercial-free radio network of The Associated Press. The television reports are part of **TV Direct**, a joint venture with Conus Communications.

On the state level, bureaus have broadcast editors who provide member stations in their areas with regional and local news in the form of scripted news reports on the printed broadcast wires.

AP has been a leader in the field of communications for 140 years, pioneering many innovations that are now taken for granted. A hundred years ago, AP was first with the news, using the pony express, carrier pigeons and Morse code. In 1875, AP established the first permanent leased news wire, and in 1935 made journalism history with the successful transmission of daily pictures over the AP WirePhoto network.

In the late 1960s, AP introduced the CRT (Cathode Ray Tube)—or VDT (Video Display Terminal)—and allied computers to the newsroom, revolutionizing the way news is edited and transmitted. More recently, AP has developed computer-based photo and graphics editing and transmission and the industry's first satellite news and photo delivery system.

AP's **Communications department** is responsible for the continuous transmission of the AP's vast flow of news and pictures. The 500 technicians, engineers and chiefs of communications around the world deal with technology ranging from teleprinters to satellites. A research and development center in East Brunswick, N.J., helps keep AP on the cutting edge of news technology.

THE QUALIFICATIONS YOU NEED TO WORK AT AP

In such a diverse, news-oriented company, there are as many career paths as there are staffers. But it all starts with your *first* job with The Associated Press, because the news cooperative is a promote-from-within company—most of the senior management at AP headquarters in New York started out in the news ranks.

So how do you become an AP newsperson? You can apply by contacting the AP bureau nearest you. Bureau listings are in the *Editor & Publisher Yearbook*. If you meet the qualifications, you'll be asked to fill out an application and take the vocabulary and news writing tests. An interview is also required.

Applicants for full-time, regular news jobs should be college graduates with a minimum 18 months of full time news experience on a daily newspaper or broadcast station.

For people who lack the 18-month minimum experience requirement, AP has a limited number of temporary openings which sometimes lead to regular positions. The application procedure is the same—contact your nearest chief of bureau.

If you're interested in broadcasting, you can apply directly to AP Broadcast Services at 1825 K Street N.W., Washington, D.C. 20006-1253. The 18-month minimum experience requirement applies. The Broadcast News Center occasionally hires less-experienced people for temporary openings. All applicants should have experience with tape editing equipment and other standard tools of the broadcast industry.

Photographers should have 18 months to five years of experience on a daily newspaper, shooting news pictures, meeting deadlines and getting a feel for journalistic photography. Applicants must be able to produce technically excellent pictures and cover a wide variety of news. It's also important to have a good background in color photography and an interest in communications technology, such as how pictures are transmitted around the world.

IT'S NOT LIKE WORKING AT A NEWSPAPER

Working for the world's largest news service is different from working for a newspaper. One major difference is the pace of work. AP people face constant deadlines because, unlike newspapers, there is never a final edition. Many AP bureaus operate 24 hours a day and handle news for both newspapers and broadcast stations. Since AP has bureaus all over the world, the scope of its news coverage is wider than most newspapers.

AP newspeople generally cover a wide variety of news, raning from sports to disasters.. Experienced AP newspeople are expected to be well-versed at working in the field and being on a desk. Desk work entails working in the bureau and editing stories written by staff members or contributed by member newspapers and broadcast stations. Editors also report stories, mostly by telephone, and write them. Reporters in the field go to news events and write or call in what they have learned.

There are many avenues to explore in the AP after mastering the necessary bureau skills. Advancement opportunities for editorial personnel include news editors' jobs, one-person correspondencies and large correspondencies, which include supervising other staff members. Other career paths include the foreign service, Washington, capital bureaus, chiefs of bureau and assistant bureau chiefs.

Notification to staff members of vacancies in such positions are generally made via AP's nationwide job posting system for key jobs beyond the entry level. Job posting spells out what the position entails, the qualifications needed and the procedure for applying for the posted openings. All of these jobs are filled regularly from the best of the staff of The Associated Press.

JACK C. STOKES

Mr. Stokes joined AP's Department of Human Resources in November, 1987, after serving in a variety of news and executive positions. Before his appointment, he had been deputy director of corporate communications. He began his AP career as an intern for two summers, joining full time after graduating from Long Island University with a journalism degree in 1973.

After Working in AP's New York City bureau, he transferred to the national broadcast department in New York in 1974 and was named night supervisor in 1982.

In 1983, he was named deputy to the general broadcast editor, responsible for scripted news services produced by AP. After Broadcast Services moved to Washington, D.C., in late 1983, he took over administrative, payroll and personnel matters for that division.

He lives in Brooklyn, N.Y.

SECTION II

Departments & Areas Of Specialization

CHAPTER SEVEN

Circulation: The Newspaper's Most Misunderstood Soft Drink

By

Harold F. Woldt, Jr., Circulation Director
Newsday

Remember the Dr. Pepper "most misunderstood" advertising campaign? Well, that slogan aptly describes the perception many people have of Circulation. After all, an editor edits, a marketer markets, production produces, and a compositor composes. So, one would think, it's only logical to assume that a circulator circulates.

Let's end this riddle: The Circulation Division of a major metropolitan newspaper is misunderstood because most people, including those who work for the newspaper in other areas, are simply unaware of the diverse and changing day-to-day functions carried out by this vital and dynamic division. If you are a student of pure marketing, then you will be pleased to know that the functions of sales, distribution, re-packaging, public relations and finance all exist within this one division. A division that is intimately involved with the newspaper as a product. This product must ultimately find its way to the doorstep of a very important person—the subscriber—or into the hands of a reader, who must be able to purchase the newspaper at retail points-of-sale.

A career in any department of any newspaper can be an exciting and rewarding experience. But a career with a major metropolitan daily, especially within the Circulation Division, can satisfy even the most insatiable appetite for hard work, an abundance of diversity, and a new challenge every day.

THE RESPONSIBILITIES OF CIRCULATION

In its most basic definition, Circulation has the responsibility for the daily and Sunday distribution and sale of the newspaper. There are, however, many more functions to be performed, both before and after distribution takes place. At a large metropolitan newspaper, Circulation personnel interact with all departments, probably more so than the employees of any other division. Typically, the Circulation Division is divided into several sub-departments—Home Delivery, Single Copy Sales, Promotion and Marketing, Transportation, and Administration. A brief explanation of each of these and their potential interaction with other divisions within the company will clarify further why Circulation affords such a diverse career path.

Home Delivery manages distribution to single-family homes, usually through a network of employees and/or independent contractors.

Single Copy Sales, on the other hand, supervises the sale of the newspapers via retail establishments and newspaper vending machines.

The *Transportation department,* as the name implies, oversees delivery to both Home Delivery distribution points and Single Copy Sales locations. Usually, this is accomplished through either a company-owned or leased fleet. At a large newspaper, this fleet may include several *hundred* vehicles and a fully-supported garage replete with a maintenance staff.

Promotion and Marketing develops the various sales tools and programs aimed at maximizing sales and service for Home Delivery and Single Copy personnel. Usually some form of Telephone Sales staff is incorporated into this department.

Administration must keep accurate records of Circulation sales activities and usually performs payroll functions, customer billing, customer service, budgeting, ABC-reporting and, depending upon the newspaper's sophistication, computer data base management.

So no matter what your background, no matter what your interest (save for a highly-specialized or technical area), there are numerous opportunities within Circulation.

ENTRY-LEVEL POSITIONS

Entry-level positions at my newspaper are available in all of the aforementioned departments. There are, however, a few prerequisites that you should have before considering a career in circulation. You must be willing to *work*; the days are full, often demanding, always challenging. Anyone looking for a comfortable routine should *not* consider circulation management. Self-motivation, a sense for marketing, an analytical mind and curiosity—mixed with a genuine enthusiasm for change—are all valuable assets. You must enjoy and get along with people—our department has well over 500 full-time and an equal number of part-time employees. They all have to be pulling in the same direction, as each is a valuable member of the team and must feel that his or her vote counts.

While titles for entry-level positions vary from one newspaper to the next, some of the most common are **district sales manager, single copy sales representative, telephone sales supervisor, training supervisor, transportation manager, fleet supervisor,** or **circulation analyst**. District sales managers and single copy sales representatives encompass the largest number of employees within Circulation. Their primary function, as noted earlier, is to supervise the sale, service, collection and distribution of either home-delivered papers or retail sales. We have a number of men and women with varied skills and credentials who perform these functions; and while a college degree is a definite enhancement, many of our circulation personnel have been hired without a degree.

The compensation you can expect for any of these positions depends, to a great extent, on where the newspaper is located—big city, small town, East Coast, Midwest, etc.. In general, staff functions tend to pay a bit less than line management and/or supervisor positions. In our market, an entry-level position within the Administration department starts at a minimum of $23,000. District sales managers and single copy sales representatives often begin at a salary in excess of $25,000. If an individual has an advanced degree or particular area of specialization, starting salaries may approach $30,000 or more. (While there are over 1,700 newspapers in the country, these salaries are usually pertinent to those in the top 20 metro markets.)

Superior performance usually results in rapid advancement within the Circulation Division—it's not uncommon to see employees with three to five years experience earning between $35,000 and $45,000. (Remember: These salaries are for the New York market.) These are just a few of the entry-level management and supervisory positions available at a large newspaper.

CIRCULATION'S RELATIONSHIP WITH OTHER DEPARTMENTS

The two departments upon which Circulation is critically dependent are Editorial and Production. There is almost daily discussion about the editorial content of each day's paper and how it will be produced and packaged.

Circulation's management team works closely with the newspaper's Research and Marketing departments to stay in touch with the inevitable changes that occur in a dynamic market. Where in the market is the paper positioned? Who are its readers and non-readers? What is the best method to secure new readers? And how do we do this in the most efficient possible manner?

Historically, even at large newspapers, circulation sales were procured through youth carriers. This method of selling is changing and changing rapidly. While telephone sales remains a staple of the order procurement process, newspapers are now utilizing more direct mail, free-standing inserts, and television and radio offerings. As a result, it demands closer ties with Marketing and Research (as well as Editorial and Production).

Because of the sheer number and the broad diversity of people who work in Circulation, there is an absolute necessity to be thoroughly versed on human resources policies and procedures. This means periodic consultation with the Human Resources staff.

The Circulation Division is a revenue-producing entity and, therefore, must adhere to strict financial controls with respect to revenue and expenses. Often the control of this information is developed through computerized, on-line circulation and financial systems. Responsibility for the maintenance of these systems usually rests with the Circulation department, but fosters a close relationship with both Data Processing and the company Finance Division.

I think you will agree that Circulation functions like a company within a company. Its interaction with virtually all other divisions provides not only broad exposure within Circulation, but to the other departments and divisions as well. Thus, one can truly learn the newspaper business through a career in circulation.

GETTING INTO CIRCULATION—NOW'S THE TIME

There is probably no better time to enter the circulation profession than now. The technological age has finally come to circulation, and a more professional approach to marketing a newspaper is in demand. The importance of Circulation— financially as well as strategically— is critical to the newspaper's success. As a result, marketing-oriented executives, either through education or varied assignments within the newspaper business, are now moving into leadership roles. Publishers and presidents of newspapers realize now, more than ever, the value of having well-trained, highly-motivated circulation personnel.

Declining readership and the competition for readers' time require special attention and planning. Publishers are clearly aware that a healthy circulation base can increase advertising revenues (which are usually predicated on how much circulation a newspaper has or will have in the market).

Competition between existing newspapers today is strong, and, as one would expect, only the strong will survive. That strength will be enhanced through hiring, training, and developing the most talented and dedicated individuals. Circulation's time is truly now—it provides a diversity of career options at a time when money and attention are being increasingly channeled into improving the overall profession.

So, Circulation executives do a lot more than circulate a newspaper! While the vast majority of people outside the industry are still somewhat unaware of this fact, *you* at least now know that this business of circulation is diverse, challenging and financially rewarding.

The industry needs good people. When can we hear from you?

HAROLD F. WOLDT, JR.

Mr. Woldt assumed his current responsibilities in 1986; he became circulation manager of (then) *New York Newsday* in 1985. Prior to *Newsday*, he was vice president/ circulation director of the News and Sun-Sentinel Company (1981-1985).

He began his newspaper career with the *Chicago Tribune* in 1969 as a classified advertising representative. He became classified automotive staff manager in 1970, national advertising sales representative in 1972, city home delivery zone manager in 1975, national circulation manager in 1977, and circulation manager in 1980.

Mr. Woldt was the 1971 winner of the Chesser M. Campbell Award. He received his B.S. in journalism from Southern Illinois University in 1969. He is married and has one daughter.

CHAPTER EIGHT

Opportunities In Circulation
At Smaller Daily Newspapers

By

Nicholas T. Nicks, Circulation Manager
La Crosse Tribune

The Circulation department at most smaller daily newspapers has a wide range of responsibilities, including: (1) subscriber service; (2) subscription sales through the carrier system, door to door, direct mail and telemarketing; (3) distribution center production (counting, inserting and bundling papers); (4) home delivery; (5) single copy sales through dealers and vending machines; and (6) transporting papers to all carriers and single copy outlets. Generally, the Circulation department assumes full responsibility for the newspaper after it is printed. It is one of the three primary departments of any newspaper, along with Editorial and Advertising.

The District Manager Position

The most common entry-level position in the Circulation department is that of **district manager.** (Other titles for the same job description include **district sales manager, district sales advisor,** or **district advisor.**) This individual is responsible for service, sales, and collections, via a group of independent contractors or carriers (sometimes the carriers are employees). Whether they are youths or adults, independent contractors or employees, depends upon the individual needs of the particular newspaper and the market it serves. The district manager is also usually responsible for single copy sales in his or her area, which would include carrier recruiting, training and motivating.

A district manager's job is not a desk job. Although you can expect to have a work area (with a desk) in the newspaper office, much of your time will be spent working out of your car.

Since a daily paper is usually published seven days a week, and may be delivered either early in the day or late in the afternoon, you must not mind working unusual hours. Being responsible for recruiting, training and motivating carriers means you must be able to work when the carriers are available. That means early *as well as* late in the day.

A district manager's position may not be the most glamorous, but it is not without reward. A starting district manager can expect to earn anywhere from $11,500 to $22,000 the first year. Those at medium-sized dailies may expect to earn in the mid- to upper 20s after two to three years on the job. If you stay in the business, you could become circulation manager at a larger daily and earn up to $80,000 per year. Or even become a publisher of a daily paper.

Required Education And Skills

The ideal candidate for the position of district manager today has a B.A. or B.S. degree in business or marketing, relates well to people of all ages and personalities, is flexible, patient, and career-oriented. If the newspaper has youth carriers, then an academic background that includes courses in child and adolescent development and psychology will be helpful.

A college degree is *not* a must, but is becoming more and more of an asset and *is* required at some dailies. Another characteristic is the desire to make circulation management a career. Circulation management is far too challenging to hire someone who is just interested in having a job.

Opportunities For Advancement

An individual able and willing to learn the wide range of duties in the Circulation department would be ready for promotion to a middle management position at a medium-sized paper or to **circulation manager** of a smaller daily paper after two to three years. Medium size papers (25,000 to 75,000 circulation) usually have middle management positions known as **zone managers,** each of whom is responsible for supervising several district managers.

A successful district manager has the ability and experience to be successful in a wide range of other occupations. However, if you plan to move, be aware that would probably start in an entry-level position in that other field.

Internships And Part-Time Positions

Most small and medium-sized dailies do not offer internships, though many metropolitan daily papers offer marketing internships with a concentration in the Circulation department. But there are many part-time positions in Circulation that would give you a good start on a career.

Telemarketing offers experience in direct cold call selling; to be a successful telemarketer, one must learn all the features and benefits, customer service procedures, rates and the market area.

A part-time job in customer service offers training in service and subscription terms.

Some newspapers also employ part-time door-to-door **crew managers** or **coordinators**. These individuals must learn all the skills of the telemarketers, plus get involved in training and motivating.

Most Circulation departments rely heavily on part-time help. If you express an interest in a career in circulation management to the human resources manager of any daily newspaper, you would probably receive serious consideration for the next available position. You may even get hired on the spot.

NICHOLAS T. NICKS

Mr. Nicks has been in his current position since 1981. He is responsible for the Circulation department, Distribution Center and Pressroom at the *La Crosse Tribune*. Previously, he was circulation manager of the *Daily Times-Press*, in Streator, Illinois (1978-1981) and district circulation manager of the Dubuque (Iowa) *Telegraph Herald* (1971-1978)

He has served on the board of directors and as secretary/treasurer of the Circulation Management of Illinois Association, on the board of directors of the Central States Circulation Managers Association, and as editor of the latter's training and development publications. Currently, Mr. Nicks is chairman of the International Circulation Managers Association's "Leader" (monthly training publication for district managers) committee and on the University of Wisconsin's Extension's Steering Committee for Circulation Seminars.

Mr. Nicks received a B.A. from Loras College in 1971.

CHAPTER NINE

Newspapers: A New Field Of Design

By

Ron Couture, Managing Director-Editorial Art
The New York Times

Newspapering is a unique field all its own. Investigative reporting, news analysis, photojournalism and opinion have all been a part of reporting the news for years.

Journalistic design is, essentially, a new area of expertise that has entered this field and has, in many ways, brought about a stronger product for the reader. Improved typography, more informative charts, diagrams, and maps are the result of an awareness that design plays a major role in the making of a newspaper.

In order to work for a newspaper, artists must be intensely interested in news and able to find enrichment through the demands placed upon them. Working on tight deadline to produce a superior product is an especially rewarding and exciting experience, but it demands considerable fortitude. This is not a field of design that allows "artistic freedom" of expression, but, rather, a field of artistic integrity and factual presentation through design.

Entry-level positions in the art departments of major newspapers will vary slightly from paper to paper. But, for the most part, those with at least three to five years experience in publishing (or experience at a design studio that specializes in editorial design) have enough experience to open the door for an interview.

If you're talented, pay attention to detail, and are fast, accurate, and able to communicate —you have the bare essentials for a job. Extra pluses for a position include strong interpersonal skills, a keen sense of visual communication, and news judgement. Combine these with an acceptance of being on call 24 hours a day, and most likely, if there's a job opening, you have it.

Don't expect to work Monday thru Friday, nine to five, for a newspaper. Depending on your job, hours will vary to a great degree. If you're an art director, 10 or 11 a.m. to 6 or 7 p.m. or later is not unusual. If you're part of the art production staff—such as a map or chart artist—you might work 2 to 10 p.m. or 4 p.m. to midnight.

The Art department is essentially two teams of people. The **creative/design** team and the **art production** team. The creative team of art directors work directly with the editors of the paper; the art production team works directly with the art directors.

COMPOSITION OF THE ART DEPARTMENT

The Art department at *The New York Times* is not unlike those at other major newspapers; there's just more of everything. The "more" is necessary because of the immense product we produce—as many as 1,000 pages a week. My department is directly responsible for designing and laying out over 350 pages per week, which encompass the daily & Sunday newspaper, the Sunday magazine, magazine specials, and special news tabloid sections.

The staff of 61 is made up of **art directors**, **designers**, **art production personnel**, **map & chart artists**, **photo retouchers**, and **studio photographers**. All are specialists in their own right who mesh together to form a strong, interactive family.

ART DIRECTORS

Art directors are the creative core of the department. They come from a variety of backgrounds, but all have at least five years of publishing experience, usually as an art director of a major publication.

Their day is a mixture of meetings and creative direction. At 11 a.m., they meet with their editors and review the day's upcoming needs. Stories are reviewed and discussed —which page they'll appear on, how they'll be visually displayed, etc. The lead story is read, and concepts for illustration or photography are discussed. These concepts are drawn out roughly on a tissue pad to show how the initial page will look.

When the meeting is over, the art director starts the final planning of the pages. If illustrations are needed, an illustrator is called in to work on some of the concepts discussed at the meeting and to add a few of his or her own.

When the rough illustrations are finished, the art director reviews them and chooses the one which best exemplifies the story. The rough is placed on the page and presented to the editor for approval. This rough page shows the placement of text, headlines, photos, and illustrations.

(Because of volume, and the need to have fresh approaches to illustrations on a constant basis, *The New York Times* does not have a team of staff illustrators; all work is freelanced out. Other papers our size *do* have several staff illustrators and assign the overflow of work to freelancers. If you're interested in illustration, a fine arts degree or courses in commercial illustration, drawing, and anatomy will be necessary. Courses in magazine design would also be a tremendous help to you.)

Art directors also work directly with photographers and photo editors to select the best picture for the story. If a picture has not already been taken, the art director will discuss the photo assignment with the picture editor before that editor assigns it to a photographer.

The art director may see a particular angle or situation that will enhance the page or improve the story presentation. Perhaps instead of the usual 'mug shot', a picture of a person in action would draw the reader into the story. The photo editor then assigns the photo shoot to a photographer and works with the art director on selecting the final photo for the page.

To keep the paper stylistically cohesive, the art director must work within developed formats. While working with these formats, the art director is still expected to be imaginative, creative, and ready to explore new approaches and concepts with enthusiasm.

Formats for headlines, text, photo captions, and quotes allow the art director to quickly design and fit the stories on the page, but give enough latitude to be creative and inventive. Learning these formats, both stylistically and technically, on the text processing system is a must before designing any page of the paper.

After a page is approved by several editors (there may be changes at *any* point) the art director makes copies of the page. The copies are given to the editor, makeup editor, photo editor, and the art production staff of the Art department, where it is technically prepared to meet the printing requirements of the paper.

EDITORIAL ARTISTS

At *The Times*, editorial artists are divided into three specialized groups: art production, map & chart, and section artists. Their functions and expertise vary to a great degree, depending on the group to which they belong. (In most other papers, art production artists perform all of these jobs and may also lay out pages of the paper under the direction of an editor.)

Art Production Artists

Art production artists should have an art school or college background, with courses in magazine production, printing preparation, photo reproduction, color preparation, and, if possible, some computer courses.

I look for people with at least five years of experience in the art production field. These artists must know the printing requirements of newspapers and magazines and be able to produce clean, accurate mechanicals to be sent to the engraving department of the paper.

Although this area is slowly being taken over by computer technology, there will always be a need for hand-done work. If you're interested in computers *and* have an artistic eye, you might consider exploring this area of art (though computer technology will be changing the field so radically, it's hard to tell just where or what an artist should have for a background until systems are fully developed).

The work of an art production artist includes cropping photographs, cutting silhouettes, retouching photographs, and preparing final pieces of art that the art director has designed.

These pieces of art, prepared in a technical manner, are sent to the engraving department to be photographically assembled as one piece for the final page of the paper before it is printed.

Map & Chart Artists

Map & chart artists at *The Times* are perhaps the best-known in the field and have a worldwide reputation for accuracy and detail. The map archives are made up of over 50,000 volumes of reference material; approximately 20,000 pieces of finished art are on file.

Map & chart artists must have an art production background and at least eight to ten years experience. They should have a strong interest in history and geography and excellent inking and drawing skills.

News maps are usually done on a breaking news basis. The artist works directly with a news editor from a particular news desk, such as metropolitan, foreign or national. Editors give the artist information on the news event; the artist plots out the area on a tissue and plans where captions and labeling will go. When the tissue is complete, the artist displays it to the editor via close circuit television for approval.

It is imperative that the artist have an even temperament to accept the numerous changes that will undoubtedly occur during breaking news events. This may sound like a futile job, but it is the most sought after in the industry today. A map artist can gain a tremendous sense of accomplishment and fulfillment in producing such an important part of the news report on deadline.

Feature maps are done with an art director, since they require a stronger sense of design and may be part of a layout designed to include photos or illustration. In some papers, map artists illustrate the mountains and valleys of a map with contour drawing and hand letter the labels. But most papers today desire the cleaner look of typography.

Graphics Editors

The buzz word in newspapering today is "Information Graphics"—the result of the art director's and editor's efforts to explain a complicated topic in a simple, easy-to-understand way.

Graphic diagrams on topics such as science and medicine or how a nuclear disaster has occurred, have increased the need for top-notch map and chart artists.

It has also established a new editorship, the **graphics editor,** the link between the reporter and the map & chart artist. If you have a reporting background and are able to boil down detailed information, you may find this new type of position very rewarding, especially if you're also interested in art.

Section Artists/Designers

Section artists and designers are under the overall umbrella of editorial artists in our Art department. The section artist works with an art director on the larger sections of the paper. They usually have three to five years publishing experience as an assistant art director or designer working directly with editors.

Their primary function is to assist the art director in laying out the section's pages and producing the mechanicals for the section. In short, they are art production artists with a strong design talent, and they back up the art director during news emergencies. This is the only position in the department that could lead to an art directorship.

Designers also work in the magazine area of the department, laying out and designing pages and overseeing the paste-up done by the paper's composing room. All have had several years of experience in publishing before being hired.

Most major papers have entry-level positions in the Sunday magazine or the feature news sections. These people usually start off as a **design assistant** and step up to a designer's position after becoming familiar with the routine of the magazine and demonstrating their ability to make solid contributions to the product.

EDUCATION

There are many schools and art colleges around the country. Most have diploma or degree programs in art, design or visual communication. Although many companies don't require a degree, it's always a plus if you have one.

Unfortunately, courses in newspaper design are not commonly found, and when they are, they are often offered only as an adjunct to a journalism major.

Courses in publication design usually cover magazine design and book layout and offer an excellent foundation. Additional courses should be taken in writing, editing, marketing, advertising, computers (in general), and, if possible, computer graphics (relating to art production).

There is only one organization that is dedicated to fostering design and visual communication in newspapers—the Society of Newspaper Design (The Newspaper Center, Box 17290, Dulles International Airport, Washington, D.C. 20041). You may find it helpful to contact them for a listing of colleges or courses to take.

SALARIES

Salaries vary tremendously across the country, tempered by geographic location and union jurisdictions.

Larger city newspapers, which are mostly unionized, pay the most and have the largest staffs, making it easier to climb the career ladder from an entry-level position. Smaller city and town papers are usually non-unionized and pay less to start, but healthy increases in pay and responsibility are available if you prove yourself valuable.

Entry-level positions such as designers or map and production artists start anywhere from $18,000 to $20,000 and can go as high as $25,000 or $30,000, depending on initial experience and geographic area. More experienced (5 - 15 years) designers, map and production artists' salaries start at around $27,000 and can go as high as $50,000 or $55,000.

Art director salaries are perhaps the most variable of all. Experience, talent and interpersonal skills all play a strong role in determining both the job description and salary positioning. Most major papers have a starting art director salary of $40,000 to $50,000. As the marketplace becomes more competitive, salaries can move to as high as $65,000 or $80,000, depending on what paper you work for and the number of staff artists reporting to you.

THE DECISION

The field of newspapering can be an adventurous career and may mean moving from one publication to another, meeting new challenges, and working with new cohorts. It's a business that's ever-changing, always alive, and has its roots deep in our country's constitution.

It can be enlivening, educational, disheartening, and discouraging. And the most personally rewarding job you'll ever know.

RON COUTURE

Ron Couture joined The New York Times as assistant managing art director in 1977, became managing art director in 1979 and was promoted to managing director of editorial art in 1985. He oversees 18 art directors and a staff of 61 who produce the Sunday, daily, magazine, and special publications of the paper.

A native of Massachusetts, Mr. Couture has been editorial design director for The Boston Globe, a TV on-air designer for WGBH-TV in Boston, and has worked in several design studios specializing in corporate identity, packaging, urban planning, and architectural graphics.

Mr. Couture has been guest lecturer for the School of Communications at Boston University and has presented papers at many professional conferences. He has also directed workshops on newspaper design for the Newhouse School of Journalism at Syracuse University.

He has served as chairman of the Mount Kisco Architectural Review Board for the past eight years, is regional director of The Society of Newspaper Design, and is an active member of The Art Directors Club of New York, the AIGA, and The Society of Publication Design. He has won numerous awards in his field and has judged many leading design competitions.

Mr. Couture lives in Mount Kisco, New York, with his wife, Sandra, and their two children.

CHAPTER TEN

Editorial Art and Design At Smaller Newspapers

By

Ray Wong, Graphics Editor
The Tennessean

Art and design have finally been recognized as essential parts of the news gathering operation. At many smaller newspapers, however, this idea is just catching on; they are looking <u>now</u> for people with the skills to provide illustrations, informational graphics, and page design that will make their newspapers more attractive.

Design is not limited to pretty, colorful presentations, slick magazines and splashy billboards. In the newspaper business, whether the paper is large or small, good design is achieved by presenting information—the stories, photos, art, type, and the product as a whole (the newspaper)—in an easy-to-read, attractive manner. By doing so, the newspaper can become an integral part of its readers' daily habit for information.

DESIGN GOES BEYOND "LOOKS"

- It relates similar stories as a unit, organizing the paper so a reader can get through it quickly.

- It relates the headlines to the stories.

- It links the headline, the picture, the caption, and the story in a single unit.

- It puts the right typeface with the right story.

- It provides the proper, legible type size.

As you can see, design is more complex than it looks! A strong design tells the reader that this is a unique publication. It gives it an identity—no other newspaper looks like *this* one. It reflects the community, its life, its people and its culture. The newspaper, through its content, explains visually, as well as in words, the happenings that make a community tick.

The process of design dictates the kind of visuals needed (or not needed) for the story. The presentations may be big bold typography, a striking photograph, a soft illustration or a detailed map. Each of these, or some combination of them, can fully illustrate a story.

Design works when the illustration technique is right for the story. Should the image be in pen and ink, air brush, water color, pencil or a three-dimensional graphic? Should the story be illustrated with a map or chart? Can we make the chart or map more interesting by combining it with an illustration?

Design is looking at the white space—how it can make the eye move on the page from white images to gray images to dark images. Or vice versa. Using white space strategically in a design helps provide excitement and movement.

Design uses a legible typeface so readers can read the newspaper. It tries to provide more story in less space, without sacrificing readability.

Newspaper design is more than "looks." Looks are essential, but form follows function. And *that* axiom is the theme for all editorial graphics.

GETTING THE READER'S ATTENTION

The competition among all media to capture the reader's attention has created the need for a better-designed, more attractive product. Television is colorful, spontaneous and entertaining. Magazines are slick and beautifully reproduced. Billboards cry out for instant attention. Add to these the other countless forms of communication that bombard the reader every day...and you'll have an idea of the challenge confronting any newspaper designer.

Add in the increasingly limited time readers have to appreciate the newspaper, and you have the makings of a new set of guidelines for producing a newspaper.

As markets change because of different lifestyles, newspapers must also change to provide a publication that visually competes. Newspapers are responding by changing the way they are produced. They are taking a hard look at their people and production methods in an effort to help readers understand and use the paper more effectively.

The people to whom newspapers have turned to effect these changes are <u>visual communicators</u>—journalists who utilize their design expertise to produce an attractive package that doesn't sacrifice the fundamentals of good journalism.

The new technology of pagination (sending the entire newspaper from a computer terminal to the typesetter and, eventually, to the printing press) and the use of the graphic display terminal to produce art have expanded the duties of the designer and the artist. It is this technology that now enables the designer, the artist, the editor and the reporter to efficiently communicate the news to the reader. They're successful if the reader "bites."

A NEW FIELD AND NEW CHALLENGES

The field of graphics journalism is still in its infancy. Graphics staffs did not exist before 1980. Previously, graphics-oriented areas were not part of the news operation. The Art Department was part of the advertising staff; the Photography Department was a service department under the City Desk.

In the late '70s, declining newspaper readership, the reality of boring layouts and bulky newspapers, soaring newspaper costs, and lack of newsprint alerted editors and management to the fact that newspapers needed to try a new approach to keeping their readers.

Part of that approach was to upgrade the way the newspaper looked. Managements started experimenting with new designs, new ways to approach the news and new ways to "lure" the reader into the newspaper.

Dailies like *The New York Times*, *The Morning Call* (Allentown, PA), *The Minneapolis Tribune*, *Chicago Daily News*, *Washington Star* and the defunct *National Observer* were the forerunners in experimenting and eventually changing the way newspapers looked. Instead of just laying out their newspapers, they "designed" them. It was the beginning of a graphics revolution.

The newspaper industry hasn't been the same since late 1982, when *USA Today* was introduced. *USA Today*'s use of graphics, color and more-structured format has affected virtually every newspaper in this country. Its influence on design, packaging, color, maps, charts and its weather map have influenced many newspapers who have reassessed their graphic commitment to readers.

In addition to the aforementioned newspapers, the *Seattle Times*, *Hartford Courant*, *St. Petersburg Times*, *Orange County Register* and a host of others have joined the ranks of newspapers that have taken giant leaps to make themselves more readable and attractive.

The newspaper visual revolution has committed us to look for artists, reporters and editors who are visually attuned to the readers.

Future newspaper artists and designers will use computers to design. Computers will link the graphics person to the rest of the newsroom operation. On many newspapers today, this technology already exists. Artist and designers, as well as editors, will learn that these are tools to help the creative spirit, not short cuts to journalistic excellence.

NAMING NAMES

The newspaper business probably has more synonyms than any other business. This is even true for job titles. An **artist** can be a **graphic designer**, an **illustrator**, a **graphic illustrator** or a **graphic specialist**. The person in charge of the artists can be a **managing editor/graphics**, **assistant managing editor/graphics**, **graphics editor**, **art director**, **graphics coordinator**, **picture editor** or **photo director** (the latter two positions also are in the Photography Department).

The editorial artist's main responsibilities are to provide illustration, charts, maps, logo types, special typography and some page design on a daily basis. The artist usually works with the art director or a news editor in finalizing the art work. In the course of producing the work, the artist usually works with a reporter or writer to make sure the graphic works with or supplements the written copy. Many newspapers require the reporter to provide all the information necessary to produce a graphic.—the numbers for a chart, pinpointing a location for a map, etc.

Newspaper graphics fall into three areas. The most obvious is the impact graphic—an illustration or photograph whose main purpose is to attract the reader to the story. It contains little information, but gives the reader a sense of what the story is all about. Surrealistic images, silhouettes, and special design type fall in this category. An example of this type of graphic would be a side view of a large sliced tomato for a story on eating tomatos.

The situational graphic explains to the reader how something works or how a sequence of events occurs. This probably is the most difficult graphic, because it requires the artist to combine both words and an illustration in an attempt to depict reality in illustrative form. The more detail that goes into this illustration, the better the graphic. One example: a graphic showing how two airplanes collided on the runway at the local airport. To get all the information, the editorial artist needs to get the reporters, the photographers, the newspaper library and the editors working jointly to establish the sequence of events, the lay of the land, the types of airplanes involved and the circumstances surrounding the crash. Then the artist reconstructs the scene so the reader can see the event.

The informational graphic is the "bread and butter" type illustration in the newspaper — the maps and charts that dress up a story. Readers respond to a story that talks about a trend when they can *see* exactly what that trend is. This illustration usually is factual in nature and helps the reader quickly understand the story. It also provides an overview of the story so the reader doesn't have to scan the entire copy block.

An example could be a chart on the fluctuations of the U.S. dollar overseas and its effect on imports into the U.S. The chart would show the price of the dollar over a period of time and compare the number of imports in each of those periods.

Gathering the information required for such an illustration requires working closely with reporters to get the basic facts, the gist and tone of the story, and rechecking the information to be sure it reinforces the message in the copy.

The graphics editor or art director—the frontline people of the Graphics Department—provides the overall direction for the visual presentations. Assignments by reporters and editors usually are cleared through the graphics editor, who then assigns an artist to do the graphic. The graphics editor also can make assignments and provides the artist with enough information to determine the appropriate medium, whether to use color, how to size the graphic, etc.

In addition to management responsibilities—ordering supplies, approving overtime, scheduling and budgeting—the graphics editor also works with other editors on the display of art, doing the layout or designing the presentation.

The direction the graphics editor takes on any project usually determines how the newspaper will look. His input into the decisions of story play, headline display and page design will determine how attractive the page looks. This process can be hands-on or delegated to persons who handle the design.

Depending on the size of the newspaper, the graphics editor is usually the dominant authority of the visual end of the newspaper's editorial sections. Larger newspapers usually have assistant managing editors/graphics as the management head of the department.

Other responsibilities for the graphics editor include maintaining the design of the newspaper, setting policy on design and working with various section editors on long-term planning for their pages, as well as designing special sections, like fashion or style.

On *The Tennessean*, I directly control the visual presentation of the newspaper and oversee its layout. I also have responsibility for making policy guidelines on the display of art, typography and photography. The Art and Photography departments are under my direction, and I represent them in the Publisher's Council, which is made up of all the senior editors of the newspaper. *The Tennessean* has eight full-time photographers, three part-time photographers, a picture editor, laboratory manager (who handles the darkroom) and two full-time artists.

THE ART/PHOTO TEAM

Many artists like to use photographs as sources for their illustration ideas. The Photography department is probably the closest ally of the Art department in the newsroom. The two departments—Art and Photography—share some of the same problems that are related to being a service department, but they also share visually the same benefits of good design—enhanced display of their work.

The two areas work together on specific illustrations where detail is essential. The artist continually strives to make things as realistic as possible; when an artist can use a photograph to draw from, it adds to the reality of a story. Usually, photos are the preferred illustration for any story, because the realistic nature of a photograph—as opposed to the more symbolic nature of a line illustration—gives the reader a better feel for the subject. Fact just has more impact.

WHAT WORKS, WHAT DOESN'T

Of all possible printing surfaces, newsprint is probably the worst—it's coarse, thin and doesn't "hold" ink well. Consequently, some illustration techniques work better than others. Pen and ink, hard line, and thick lines work best for reproduction. When trying to produce softer images, air brushing is probably the best route. Pencil and hair line drawings are the least effective, because their nuances are lost in the printing process.

Many newspapers use Flurocolor techniques for that water color or air brush "look" for illustrations. Flurocolor is a process in which dyes produce the color and a special lens in the production camera separates it. Next to flapping color with acetate materials like Amberlith or Rubylith, Fluro is best able to provide a softer image and gives the artist more latitude in different shades and hues of color. (Flapping color uses the three basic process colors—magenta, cyan and yellow—to produce color in print. Various combinations of these three colors will produce the full color spectrum. Most artists in the business dread this mechanical work because it's tedious and prone to error.)

WHO WILL GET THE JOBS

Newspapers across the country are looking for qualified people able to produce an exciting, good-looking product. The large newspapers have vast numbers of people supporting the graphics process. On smaller papers, the artists may have to do a lot of the initial legwork of getting the information themselves before they can start on the boardwork.

Formal training for an editorial artist or graphic specialist should include a solid foundation of ideas and a broad perspective. Artists in the news world will be required to work on a broad range of topics—the better informed the artist, the better his or her work.

A good artist must understand the business of journalism. This enables the artist to understand why facts are important, why a story has to be presented fairly, why there are only two hours to produce the material and why the business of journalism is the way it is. Being first and foremost an inquisitive journalist helps the artist understand the importance of the material being produced.

Photography can also be a helpful subject for the artist or designer. The techniques learned from lighting, composition, using different angles, and providing a three-dimensional illustration can all be translated into a process an artist can use in his work.

Architectural courses give the artist a sense for detail. This is important in the understanding of the nuances of design work. Learning about architectural renderings also provides experience in perspective.

Besides these specific courses, a general liberal arts education is helpful.

Computers in the newsroom and the artist's graphic display terminal will require some knowledge of how computers work and ways the artist can integrate his work into the mainstream of the news flow. Many schools offer courses using graphics stations like Apple Computer's Macintosh, which can draw charts, maps and other simple illustrations.

Taking graphic arts technology courses can be helpful, too. A beautiful image on paper is wasted if it cannot be reproduced. Learning about printing processes, how production cameras work, and the mechanics of producing a newspaper can facilitate the artist's understanding of the possible techniques (and their limitations) that can be used to produce a good image.

Newspaper intern programs can give the artist looking for a career in editorial graphics a meaningful experience. Presently only a few papers in the country offer such programs, but, in addition to the detailed internship listings in the *Job Opportunities Databank* of this Directory, a list of these opportunities is available from the Society of Newspaper Design. Presently, there are only a few schools that offer programs in editorial graphic design. However, many schools do offer commercial or product design degrees.

The Society of Newspaper Design also holds an annual seminar on current topics in the design field. They have several educational programs that provide scholarships and direction for students to learn about newspaper graphics.

Newspaper artists and graphic designers face an exciting future. The challenges are there, the newspapers are there. Let's hope that the visual stimulus for good-looking, well-thought-out designs are here to stay.

RAY WONG

The Tennessean is a 150,000 daily circulation (260,000 Sunday) newspaper in Nashville. Mr. Wong's four years with the paper has resulted in a stronger visual presence for the newspaper, culminating with a redesign in 1985.

Before joining *The Tennessean*, he was the graphics editor for *The Clarion-Ledger/Jackson Daily News* in Jackson, MS for seven years. Previously, he was a picture editor for *The Toronto Star*.

Mr. Wong is presently a co-regional director for the Society of Newspaper Design and a member of the National Press Photographers Association. He has served on the faculty of numerous local colleges and on the professional advisory committee for journalism at Western Kentucky University.

Mr. Wong received his undergraduate degree in journalism from Arizona State University and a master's in photojournalism from the University of Missouri.

CHAPTER ELEVEN

For Jonathan Swifts Who Can Draw: The World Of The Editorial Cartoonist

By

Gill Fox
Freelance Editorial Cartoonist

Among the nine phases of professional cartooning—advertising, animation, caricature, comic book, editorial, illustration, magazine gag, sport and syndicate cartooning— editorial and political cartooning can be the most cerebral and satisfying. However, trying to find a position as an editorial or political cartoonist on a big, metropolitan, daily newspaper can be extremely frustrating and, because of the nature of the cartoon/newspaper business, require the most unorthodox methods.

FUNCTIONS OF AN EDITORIAL OR POLITICAL CARTOONIST

First and foremost, there *is* a difference between these two types of cartoonists: An **editorial cartoonist** is one whose art satirizes an editorial column. A **political cartoonist** chooses his or her cartoon subject from current events, without the inhibiting control of an editorial written by someone else. Throughout the rest of this article, however, I will use the term editorial cartoonist exclusively; you should assume that all such references apply to political cartoonists as well.

In a broad description of job function, a staff editorial cartoonist will produce two- to four-column cartoons with, hopefully, biting satirical observations for the editorial page. These cartoons generally appear next to the editorial to which they refer. The format is usually horizontal, though there are still a few artists who work in the old, vertical format.

The cartoonist is expected to produce anywhere from three to six cartoons a week (depending on whether the paper is a morning or afternoon edition) on deadline. The editorial cartoon is the highest form of impact graphics in newspapers, so the art should stop a reader in his tracks.

Obviously, the editorial cartoonist is an important member of any large newspaper's Editorial department. Though you'd never guess it by the seeming lack of respect they are afforded: Unlike the well-known jobs on a newspaper—publisher, general manager, editor, etc.—editorial cartoonists rarely appear on the table of organization. And only infrequently will you see an editorial cartoonist listed in a newspaper's masthead.

THE TRAINING AND BACKGROUND YOU NEED

Though a college education would be a great asset, it is not strictly essential for an editorial cartoonist. A national poll would undoubtedly uncover a substantial number of successful editorial cartoonists who lack college degrees. But this state of affairs will change as we move into the well-educated future. The ideal? If you can boast of a degree in both political science and journalism and possess a portfolio of good samples, you'd be in an excellent position to get an entry-level job against *any* competition.

But some personality traits are just as important as any education—you should be an obvious self-starter and obsessed by editorial cartooning. How do you recognize such an obsession? By your own actions: You probably started accumulating sample cartoons by working on some phase of cartooning for your high school paper and/or yearbook. You continued this work in college publications while taking courses in journalism and drawing. By then, you had developed a firm political philosophy of your own, but remained flexible enough to strike in either direction if it became apparent that your own convictions were wrong. Early on, in your love for the business, you sought out and cultivated the acquaintance of professionals to learn the eccentricities of the business and began pushing and probing for freelance work or a staff position.

And, of course, you need to have reached a certain level of skill in art. This is where your portfolio comes in—it's the proof that along with a solid education and demonstrated dedication, you have the talent to do the work. Your portfolio should be complete before you graduate from college or art school, though you could certainly begin saving samples long before. It should include a variety of neat, professional graphics that relate to newspaper illustration, including article illustrations, humorous spots and even some political cartoons that you did for various publications. While some of these samples could be rendered in felt tip or mechanical pen, I would expect that most or all—including second versions of these other renderings— would be drawn with traditional brushes and pens. Technique-wise, I would be looking for the ability to compose a picture with dramatic impact, regardless of the political philosophy expressed.

Getting Started And Getting In The Door

The quickest way to get your work reproduced in a newspaper is to approach the editor or, even better, the editorial page editor of a local or weekly newspaper. The latter is the one to see for an interview—he or she usually writes the editorials and is responsible for all the material on the editorial page and the page opposite it.

On the big metropolitan dailies, go to the Personnel department and, through them, arrange an interview with the art director of editorial art. He or she is responsible for humorous art for columns and articles on unusual subjects plus the cartoon art for covers of supplements and the pages opposite the editorial page. The use of this "spot art" has increased on the big dailies—it can be found throughout the newspaper. on People's pages, Women's pages, Entertainment pages, etc. Much of this art is assigned to freelance artists. However, the *New York Daily News* uses at least four cartoonists on staff. If you are lucky enough to land a staff job on a large daily, you would be in a position to volunteer to do the editorial cartoons when the chief cartoonist is on vacation or sick leave.

The Positives And Negatives Of The Business

For the past five years, I have freelanced political and editorial cartoons in the New England area, which includes papers with circulations from 10,000 to 1,000,000. When the big dailies are out looking for an editorial cartoonist, they will sometimes advertise in *Editor and Publisher*, a weekly magazine that reports on the newspaper business. The artist sends clips of his or her cartoons to the editor and through a slow process of elimination, the editor gets down to the two or three cartoonists he or she wishes to interview. This process can take as long as three months. I was eliminated by a professional at the *Providence Journal*. At the *New Haven Register*, I lost out to a young, inexperienced artist. In that case, there were 60 submissions—my samples got down to the last six before I was eliminated. It is a brutal business. You have to thrive on rejection.

However, it is not always negative. As a result of sample copies that I voluntarily sent to the *New York Post's* executive editor, I was given a freelance assignment for six political cartoons illustrating a series on waste in the Pentagon. The fee for these drawings was top scale.

There are things a young cartoonist should know that are peculiar to the contemporary field of editorial cartooning. In a close personal study of the five-state New England area, I have come to the conclusion that the professional political cartoonist must be prepared for periodic moves geographically. These moves are made for basically two reasons: to take a position as editorial cartoonist on a newspaper in a distant state or to move up from a small paper to a big metropolitan paper in order to gain increased income and exposure. From everything I've seen, a series of such moves in one's professional life are definitely the rule, not the exception.

The Typical Day Of A Staff Cartoonist

The traditional editorial cartoonist—salaried and on the editorial staff—usually starts his or her day early, listening to the morning radio and TV news reports, reading news magazines and the daily papers, etc. He or she attends an editorial meeting at about 10:00 where the issues for that day's editorial column are discussed by the editors. Between 11:00 and noon, he or she does some quick thumbnails (simple, rough sketches)—from one to four, depending on the artist—which are then shown to the editor. If it's a lucky day, he or she will have one approved and, by 1:00, be working on a finished drawing. The time it takes to finish the cartoon will depend primarily on the complexity of the art. It can be done in two to four hours, depending on the individual and his or drawing style.

THE WAGES OF SATIRE

A Short History Lesson

In order to appreciate the levels of remuneration and the potential at the top, you need to know some of the changes that have taken place in the field in the last 55 years.

From 1930 to 1970, large newspaper syndicates contracted their own syndicate political cartoonists. These artists did five or six cartoons a week on outstanding national and international issues. This material was then distributed to the small and medium-sized newspapers that could not afford their own staff cartoonist. Usually, big metropolitan dailies had a salaried editorial cartoonist on staff who produced material on national, state, regional and local issues. These staff cartoonists were not nationally syndicated.

Between 1965 and 1970, more smaller dailies (circulations from 40,000-75,000) began to employ staff editorial cartoonists. Around the same time, a few of the top editorial cartoonists on the big city dailies signed with syndicates to nationally distribute three or four of the six cartoons they did every week for their mother papers. The big dailies liked the arrangement because their newspapers' names got national exposure under the artists' signatures. Of course, the artists loved syndication because they substantially increased their income, getting residuals for cartoons they had already been paid to do.

Taking a cue from this development, the editorial cartoonists on smaller dailies began signing syndication contracts; in the last ten years, this movement accelerated. A syndicate on the West Coast, for example, distributes the work of eleven editorial cartoonists in a single package that is sold on a weekly basis. Most of the big syndicates are now distributing between two and six cartoonists, selling their work individually. These dual developments have completely eliminated the old-style, resident, five or six-cartoons a week syndicate cartoonist.

End Of The Line

The statistical odds of making it to the top of editorial cartooning are astronomical. Let me create a composite of three artists currently at the pinnacle of the editorial cartooning profession: He's 40-50 years old, college educated and started cartooning for school and university publications. He's on the editorial staff of a large (250,000 to 1,000,000+ circulation) daily. He has won at least one Pulitzer Prize and many lesser newspaper awards. His drawing and writing skills are superior. His salaried income is roughly $50,000 to $75,000 a year, but he earns an additional $50,000 to $100,000 a year in residuals from the syndication of his reprints in 150 to 500 newspapers nationwide. He is also in demand for illustration assignments from national magazines, other publications and, in some cases, for newspapers as well.

And Where The Journey Starts

Now for the bottom of the field. Let's start with freelancing, because this is how you accumulate professional samples. I'll use the papers in Connecticut as an example. When I was teaching cartooning at Fairfield University, I had a 45-year old student who had been doing one political cartoon a week for a fair-sized Connecticut daily (75,000 circulation). The paper had been using his art for about one year. He was receiving $10 per cartoon. When he asked for a $5 raise, the editor stopped using his cartoons.

In my own experience around the state, I have found editors of papers with 40,000-50,000 circulation who might go as high as $25 per cartoon. But if you ask for $35-$50 per cartoon, they won't bother to call you back. They will even brag about using the cartoons of rank amateurs and college students on local issues, paying them $10-$15 per cartoon. This prompted me to ask one senior editor in Connecticut why he wouldn't dare use a rank amateur to write an editorial, but seemed to have no problem using one for the equally-important editorial cartoon. His reply? He claimed not to know .the difference between good and bad artwork.

On the positive side, there is one chain of highly successful weekly newspapers in Connecticut that will pay $50 per cartoon to an experienced professional. The top rate for a weekly in the state is paid by a Gannett-owned paper—they are paying $75-$100 to a professional cartoonist for one cartoon a week. And he's been doing it for at least five years.

The big circulation dailies in Connecticut, such as the *Hartford Courant* and the *New Haven Register*, are more in line with their pay scales, which I believe is between $25,000 and $40,000 a year for an on-staff cartoonist who produces five to six cartoons per week. A top daily in Rhode Island pays between $32,000 and $35,000 per year for a staff job. The *Hartford Courant* also buys and pays an equitable rate for op-ed and article illustrations—between $75 and $150 each.

In New York City, the big dailies—and this is because of the Newspaper Guild—will pay a freelance cartoonist as much as $1,000 for a single week's work. The Guild's salary rate for a staff artist is between $800 and $1200 per week.

After Editorial Cartooning

If an experienced artist decides to leave editorial cartooning, his or her experience and skills would serve him or her well in any of several other specialized areas of cartooning— illustration, children's books, a syndicated feature or caricature. Keep in mind that building an income from freelancing requires a very disciplined individual. In order to make such a move to another area of cartooning or art, you would need to carefully study and analyze the various areas in which you wish to work and render at least four to six professional samples for each category.

One last piece of advice: If you really want to break into this field, contact members of the Board of Governors of the Society of American Editorial Cartoonists for more information on this unusual business. I would also try to find a videotape of the 1987 Editorial Cartoonists Convention in Washington, D.C.

GILL FOX

Mr. Fox began his career as art director/artist for three of six editions of the *European Stars and Stripes*, including the Paris edition, during and after World War II. He has been an editorial cartoonist for the *Paris Post* (European edition of the *New York Post*), Long Island newspapers, *Westport News* and *Greenwich News*. He has also freelanced cartoons to the *New York Post*.

Mr. Fox drew a syndicated panel—"Side Glances"—for the Newspaper Enterprise Association for twenty years. A series of environmental cartoons.he drew was nominated for the Pulitzer Prize in 1980. He has also produced many national advertising campaigns for Smith Bros. cough drops, Real Lemon and the 1984 "Flick Your Bic" campaign, among others.

As an illustrator, he has worked for Hearst's *American Weekly, Medical Times* and the children's book division of Random House. He taught cartooning at Fairfield University for two years as part of their Continuing Education Program.

CHAPTER TWELVE

My Life As A Young Reporter

By

Anthony Giorgianni, Reporter
The Hartford Courant

Imagine having the opportunity to explore things you've always wondered about, but never really had the time to investigate or experience: Spending the day at an air show, asking the pilots what it's like to travel in a high-speed, tight formation. Visiting a courtroom, watching attorneys argue complex legal issues that will determine the fate of someone accused of a serious crime. Or going to supermarkets and buying dozens of items, just to confirm your suspicion that consumers are being charged more than they should be.

That is how news reporters spend most of their day: learning. The rest of their time is spent trying to interpret what they've learned and deciding the best way to present that information to the public.

The reporter's world is certainly one for people who like to take things apart, examine how they work and then put them back together—we are given lots of opportunity to do just that. The opportunities come from editors at the newspaper itself; from routine or unexpected news events; from laws that guarantee the public access to government records and proceedings; and from sources, many of whom will want to expose sensitive information. And from your own imagination and curiosity about the way things operate.

DAY-TO-DAY ACTIVITIES

As a new reporter, you will often begin your day by gathering information on a subject about which you plan to write. Where do such stories originate? An editor may assign you to cover a press conference at which the mayor will unveil the new city budget, which carries a major tax increase. While monitoring the city's police radio frequencies, your newspaper learns that a homicide has just occurred and sends you out. During your routine visit to the town planning and zoning office, you are tipped off that a major shopping mall developer has been asking questions about a wide stretch of undeveloped land in town. Perhaps a local school has been cited for building code violations and your subsequent inspection of state and town records reveals a disturbing pattern of such violations. Or an attorney telephones you about a lawsuit he filed against a chemical company that, the attorney claims, has been exposing workers to dangerous substances.

The exact subject matter you will write about will depend to a great extent on the beat you are assigned to cover regularly.

If you cover a town, you may be responsible for many areas, including town departments and policy-making bodies like the police department, planning and zoning commissions, the school board, the town council and the mayor or other chief officer. You probably will be involved in covering town political elections and the townspeople themselves, writing feature stories on interesting personalities.

You could be a business reporter or a sports writer. Or a statewide specialty reporter, covering the environment, education, law enforcement, the courts, labor or state politics. Or cover the federal government, the Supreme Court, Congress, even the White House. Such specializations will require you to develop an expertise in the area for which you are responsible. You will have to know how government departments operate and what laws pertain to them.

LEARNING HOW TO LEARN

Gathering information about some subjects is very easy. In the case of the mayor's press conference, for example, town officials probably will be eager to explain the spending package in detail...and community leaders and special interest groups will be eager to criticize it. You will have lots of information, some good quotes and a story that will appeal to just about anyone who uses city services and has to pay taxes.

Covering the homicide probably will be more difficult. Concerned about protecting evidence or scaring away suspects, police will release only the barest details. Neighbors, family members and co-workers may be too frightened or upset to talk. They may even react angrily to your questions, regarding them as ghoulish or insensitive. Yet your editors will be pushing you to come up with an explanation for the crime, to learn about the victim's life and, if it isn't released, the cause of death. You probably will feel frustrated, even angry yourself, as you try to do a job in a hostile and often sad environment.

That is not the only problem you will face in your efforts to gather information for a story. Sometimes you will have to explore extremely complex issues. And unlike the leisurely-written term papers you are used to producing for college courses, the report you'll have to prepare for today's or tomorrow morning's edition is probably due in a few hours...at most.

The Challenge Of Beat Reporting

When I was assigned to cover *The Hartford Courant's* consumer and utilities beat in 1986, I realized how challenging some issues can be. Suddenly, I found myself having to write stories about an electricity rate increase that had been proposed by the state's major power company. Due to the effect the increase would have on homeowners and businesses, the subject was page-one material day after day—an exciting prospect for any reporter.

Yet I found myself confronted with issues so complex and unfamiliar that they began to look frightening. Just about everyone knows how confusing filling out a federal tax return can be. Imagine dealing with various methods of tax computation for a multi-billion dollar nuclear power plant. And that was only one of the topics that came up in the utility rate hearings.

Gathering the details and trying to interpret them was problematical enough; assembling them into a story that wouldn't send readers into a stupefied coma was the second challenge I faced. It was even more difficult because I was new on the beat and had to familiarize myself with "utility jargon," a specialized vocabulary known only to a microcosm of utility officials, state and federal regulators and a select group of Wall Street financial analysts.

It took hard work, but after examining and re-examining all the pieces and considering and reconsidering explanations from those on both sides of the issues, things began to finally come together. I suddenly began understanding those complex issues.

The Rewards You'll Cherish

That's when journalism is most exciting. I had used all my resources—my education, analytical abilities, patience and outside research—to break through a monumental barrier. And once I understood it all, I was able to examine the arguments made by both sides, interpret them and ask the hard questions, the ones that readers would have asked if they had had the time to investigate and learn the way I had.

Through that process, I had learned a lot about how things operated, about things I never even knew existed. More importantly, it was not hypothetical, not something I was reading about in a book. I was participating as a member of the public, representing the public and its right and need to know.

Of course, there were other ways in which I could have learned about how utility rate cases are decided. I could have taken college courses after work or attended the meetings of state utility regulators. But, in truth, I probably never would have found the time. Even if I had, I certainly would not have had the access my press credentials afforded me had I been a college student researching the subject.

Even if I had taken the courses or attended the regulators' meetings, I would not have known that incredible feeling of accomplishment that came when I saw the newspaper on the newsstands and the front page story with my name at the top. More significantly, I probably never would have realized that complex utility issues could be so interesting and challenging had I hot been exposed to them because of my work.

Seeing your name in your own paper is a joy, and sometimes you'll even see your story picked up by other newspapers, by television and radio. You'll hear people you don't even know discussing it.

Even more gratifying, your story may cause some change. For example, your investigation exposing corruption may result in criminal indictments of the participants or the enactment of new laws to protect the public. Your story about the victims of a house fire may bring an outpouring of donations and other offers of help.

And The Frustrations You'll Endure

Of course, reporting is not always exciting. As you prepare to attend your fiftieth local school board meeting, you may find it difficult staying awake. Of course, you will have to cover the meeting anyway, because the readers will want to know about new programs in the schools, the impact of education on their property taxes and the quality of the education their children are receiving.

WHERE TO FIND YOUR FIRST REPORTING JOB

As a reporter, you will have to use many skills. You will rely on your knowledge of math to calculate the percentage the city budget is increasing. You will rely on your understanding of politics and government when you cover elections. Your familiarity with basic physical science will help you write that feature on advances in fiber optics and telecommunications.

In fact, as you rely on what you've learned in high school and college, you will find that journalism courses are not the ones you'll rely on the most. Rather, you will depend most on what you've learned in all those general courses—art, literature, biology, history, math and other areas. It is that knowledge that will help you know what questions to ask and how to interpret the answers. Of course, good journalism courses will not only teach you the basics of writing and reporting, but also expose you to government, business and the whole spectrum of institutions that you will routinely encounter in your reporting.

Many reporters get their best journalistic training on weekly newspapers, where just a few weeks covering routine meetings, fires and police calls and writing simple features will teach you more than months of journalism classes. Weeklies are also a good place to start because they involve you in areas of newspaper operation that are less accessible to reporters on daily newspapers, where jobs are more specialized—you probably will be exposed to photography, graphics, page layout, copy editing, story assignments and editorial writing. When you finally are employed by a daily newspaper, that weekly newspaper experience will help you appreciate and work with the specialists in all those areas.

But even before you get to a weekly newspaper, you will need to have a good understanding of how a news story is written, and that is where those journalism courses will be vital. You also will need a good background in grammar and spelling. And if you know how to use of all those special reference materials in the library, you will save a lot of time trying to find sources.

ARE YOU *SURE* YOU WANT TO BE A REPORTER?

As in any job, you will wake up some mornings wishing you could stay home, especially when everyone else gets the day off because it's a holiday or there is a hurricane or snowstorm.

You will have to get used to being called to cover a late-breaking news story just when you were about to go home. If there is a competing newspaper in your town, you may find that you've been beat on a story by one of its reporters, and your editors probably will want to know why.

Although the responsibility and power you carry as a journalist can be gratifying, at times it also can make you feel uneasy.

You will constantly fight to get stories done on deadline and, at the same time, get the dozens of facts and names correct. You will have to make sure you have covered and explained both sides of each issue. And you will have to try to keep your stories objective, even though you may personally feel strongly about the subject. Sometimes it will be difficult to identify the sources giving you accurate information and those who shouldn't be trusted because of some special interest they have. And there will be times, just after the newspaper goes to press, that you will feel your blood rush as you suddenly remember something important that you forgot to include or that should have been verified.

Editors will be unforgiving if you make a mistake, particularly if it gets into print; they also will be unforgiving if you miss a deadline.

Editors will criticize your story, even if *you* think it's the best piece you've ever written. You will learn how to stand back and see the validity in that criticism. And you will have to learn to recognize criticism that is invalid. Sometimes you will feel like your whole sense of reality has been shaken.

You will have to work hard to be creative under pressure. Sometimes it will be difficult to know exactly how to write a story. In some cases, you will be able to describe personalities, the way people or things look, to play up humor or irony or portray emotions, touching your reader with great happiness or sadness. Other times, you will need to stick only to the facts. There will also be stories that can be written either way.

You will have to intuitively recognize when you have collected enough information, then know what to use, what to discard, when to go back and ask more questions.

Despite all the things you have to know, despite the late hours, the tough deadlines and all the other pressures, journalism often will be just fun. For example, in 1986, another *Courant* reporter and I decided to test a new state law exempting meals under two dollars from state sales tax. What resulted was a week-long eating binge that included everything from pizza and ice cream to hamburgers and chicken. We tried to buy as many combinations of food items as we could, each combination adding up to less than two dollars. Imagine two grown men in suits standing in a diner and ordering two cheese sandwiches on white bread. Sometimes it was hard keeping a straight face.

But the ultimate result was more serious. We found that the law was so complex that fast food restaurants found it difficult to understand and follow. Our story inspired state lawmakers to change the regulations.

It is not easy to do everything and have fun, too, particularly in a busy newsroom crowded with reporters and editors all trying to meet their own deadlines. But if you *can* do it, if you can sit down after compiling and examining all the facts and write the right story, with the correct information, the proper tone and all within deadline, you will feel an incredible sense of accomplishment and satisfaction.

When you see your story in the newspaper, when you hear and see the reactions, when you think about all you have learned, you will wonder if there is anything else that can be so rewarding and self-fulfilling.

ANTHONY GIORGIANNI

Mr. Giorgianni is currently assigned to cover consumer affairs issues and public utilities. Previously, he was assigned to cover two towns outside of Hartford.

He joined the *Courant* in September, 1984, after working as a reporter and editor for two weekly newspapers in his native Long Island, New York. He is a 1978 graduate of the State University of New York at Oswego, where he studied English writing arts, including journalism.

The Hartford Courant , with a circulation of more than 221,900 daily and 309,000 Sunday, is by far the largest newspaper in Connecticut, the third largest in New England and about the 50th largest nationwide. It's also the oldest continuously published newspaper in the United States—its first edition was in 1764. It is owned by the Times Mirror Company which, in addition to numerous broadcast and cable television stations, book publishing companies and several magazines, also publishes several other major newspapers, including the *Los Angeles Times*, Long Island's *Newsday* and the *Baltimore Sun*.

CHAPTER THIRTEEN

Don't Stop the Presses!
Getting Into Editorial At A Small Paper

By

Stewart H. Benedict, Copy Editor
The Jersey Journal

How big is "small?"

There are approximately 1,700 daily newspapers, slightly more than 5,000 weeklies, in the United States right now. Of the dailies, fewer than 200 have circulations of more than 100,000; only two of the weekly papers exceed that number. So it seems fair to use 100,000 as the dividing line, which means that there are *many* small papers and, hence, many openings in their editorial departments.

It should be stressed at the outset that no stigma attaches to working for a small paper, because a newspaper's size has little to do with its influence. Of the three papers judged to be the most important in the U.S. (because they are read by the largest number of politicians, media leaders and other opinion molders), only one has a circulation of over 1,000,000. Yet one East Coast newspaper that has sold over 1,000,000 copies a day for years is not considered influential at all outside of its immediate circulation area.

But some very small papers have been very powerful, indeed. Under the editorship of William Allen White in the 1920s, '30s, and early '40s, the *Gazette* of Emporia, Kansas, was considered the "voice of enlightened Republicanism" and was widely read far beyond the borders of the Sunflower State. Similarly, the *Carolina Israelite*, edited by Harry Golden (who later achieved national prominence as a humorist), was widely appreciated outside of North Carolina.

DEAR OLD GOLDEN RULE DAYS

Where do you start on your drive to enter the hallowed halls of Editorial?

You start in the classroom.

Before World War II, newspaper editorial employees were usually high school graduates; some hadn't even gone that far. Those days are gone forever.

Unless your father or your uncle owns the newspaper, you cannot expect to get a job in the field unless you are a college graduate or on the way to becoming one. As the competition becomes more intense, many reporters are even finding it worthwhile to get graduate degrees or, at the very least, take some pertinent graduate courses. This is particularly true of reporters working in specialized areas like business, science or the arts.

The principal dilemma confronting the undergraduate heading for a career in editorial work is whether to major in journalism or select some other liberal arts field, like English, political science, or history, and minor in journalism.

The answer is: Either of the above. Some editors prefer only journalism majors, on the theory that these students will have learned the rudiments of the reporter's craft—how to write certain types of leads, how to distinguish between a news story and a feature story, how to circumvent libel laws in crime stories, etc. Other editors prefer graduates who majored in one of the humanities, on the grounds that it won't be necessary to "un-teach" anything and, consequently, will be easier to shape that beginner along whatever lines their papers favor.

Whichever path you decide to follow, you *should* make it a point to include as many writing courses as possible. If there is one criticism leveled at most current college graduates, it is that they do not write well; in some instances, they can't even write grammatically. It may sound elitist or snobbish, but that is probably the chief distinction between a graduate of, say, Columbia or Yale, and one whose A.B. comes courtesy of Western Southeast State College. And since editorial work, from the entry-level to the city editorship, involves words—either writing them or judging them—the handwriting ought to be on the campus walls.

That handwriting should also say that working on the college newspaper, the yearbook, or both is vitally important, not only because of the writing and editing experience it provides, but also because of the strong interest in the field it indicates.

...AND THE LIVIN' AIN'T EASY

One way to gain a foothold in the newspaper business before you even get your degree is to work as a summer intern. With newspapers giving their regular employees longer and longer vacations (often urging, even *requiring* them to take that time off during the summer), there are plenty of opportunities for internships; some may involve writing assignments.

Of course, the average intern will have to deal with such pedestrian tasks as collecting movie starting times for all the local theaters or assembling lists of all the local women's clubs' forthcoming meetings. Or any of a thousand other truly exciting tasks that invariably fall to the low man or woman on the proverbial totem pole.

Those *more* fortunate interns may find themselves composing obituaries. Now wait a minute. I *mean* fortunate. Writing obituaries may be formula writing, but it's excellent training: The highest degree of accuracy is demanded, since hell hath no fury like the survivor of a decedent whose name is misspelled in an obit.

The *most* fortunate may be selected to do some writing, especially feature writing, and it is here that a broad educational background is a great asset. Assume, for example, that you are an English major, minoring in biology. A Nobel Prize-winning biologist is scheduled to address a genetics seminar during the local university's summer session. Who will better understand his speech and ask more intelligent questions in an interview than you? No one. So you're elected.

How do you apply for a summer internship? Write a letter to the newspaper or, better still, news*papers* of your choice and ask about their internship programs. January or February is not too early to inquire, since selections are usually completed by April or May.

If you are an exceedingly quick study, apply *anywhere*, with the understanding that you will have to familiarize yourself with a lot of geography in a hurry. If you are more cautious and want to play it safe, apply to a local paper in the area that you know best; that way, you won't spend half your summer researching the exact locations of State Street or South Madison Lane.

STRING ALONG WITH ME

Another way to catch on with a newspaper editorial department is to get a position as a **stringer**. (For the benefit of the uninitiated, a stringer is a temporary employee hired to cover certain meetings, sports events, cultural happenings, etc. that the editor does not consider worth the time or attention of a regular staff member.) Some papers will consider using college undergraduates as stringers, some will not. Ask.

An example: Your local paper covers an area embracing 12 towns, one of which has a population of only 3,000. Meetings of that town's zoning board are customarily lackluster affairs with virtually no news value; they are not usually reported. But one day, the paper is alerted that an upcoming meeting will feature an application by the local tavern owner to add a new building—a teen dance hall and fruit juice bar—to his saloon. There may or may not be fireworks at that meeting, so it should be covered by *someone*. But if, as expected, community reaction against the addition is overwhelming, the meeting will be routine and the presence of a full-time reporter will be a waste of time. A stringer gets the assignment.

Similarly: The local college's basketball team is involved in the regional play-offs and two of the local high schools' basketball teams are engaged in a contest that climaxes their bitter rivalry. On the same night, the industrial bowling league is holding its finals. Regular sports reporters will be assigned to the first two events. There is no full-time staffer left to cover the third event; a stringer will be sent.

Since they are considered temporary employees, stringers can count on none of the benefits that permanent employees enjoy. They are not paid overtime and do not accumulate vacation or sick days or qualify for medical or dental insurance.

Some stringers are paid flat fees for the events they cover; others get what are called "space rates," an agreed-upon sum per inch of story that appears in print. In neither case can the stringer expect to become independently wealthy as a result of his or her journalistic endeavors. The aim of the stringer should be to impress an editor enough to be taken on as a full-time employee (unless, as sometimes happens, the stringer is a retired person supplementing Social Security).

A SPECIAL OCCASION

Many small papers publish special sections at certain times of the year—a spring-summer clothing guide at Easter time, a bridal section in May, a back-to-school edition in August, a Christmas gift guide in November. These sections are usually prepared under the aegis of the Advertising department, and some consist of what is called "boilerplate"—i.e., pre-written material from some syndicate or other that is published exactly as received. Yet often, local advertisers are given the opportunity to insert articles about their special offerings, sale items, and the like. Frequently a temporary employee is hired to interview these merchants and compose stories about their stores.

Even though these articles are "puff pieces," there is a challenge for the writer to make them sound as if they were *not*. As the composition of these articles is generally considered beneath the dignity of regular staff members, part-time writers may be utilized and given the chance to "strut their stuff" to whatever editors see their work.

ALL PAPERS, PLEASE COPY

If you've managed to reach your senior year in college without ever having worked as a summer intern or a stringer or a special sections reporter, then start sending out applications in January or February for a position as a **copy clerk**.

In bygone days, the chief function of the copy boy, as he was then titled (there being almost no copy *girls*), was to carry typed and proofread stories from the editorial department to the composing-room copy-cutter, who would distribute it to operators of the linotype machines to be set.

With the advent of computers, however, all that has changed. There is no longer any need to transport live copy physically from one area of the paper to another, to shepherd the wire machines (on which stories used to arrive on tape from syndicates like Associated Press and United Press International), or to carry boxes of copy paper from the supply room to the editorial department.

But there remain many menial tasks to be done, and it is the copy clerk's responsibility to do them. Files of back copies of the paper and of competing papers must be kept up to date. Supplies must be brought to the editorial room (what reporter or copy editor on a paper with a computerized operation has not found himself without a pencil at a critical juncture?). And, perhaps most important of all, orders for coffee, tea, milk, Danish, sandwiches, chow mein, etc., etc., must be taken and the food delivered—a major contribution to editorial morale.

If you're hired as a copy clerk, just try to remember your days as a college freshman. You arrived on campus as the former vice president of the student council, starter on the basketball team, and, truth be told, one heck of a smart, talented person...only to discover that you were now just a *freshman*, one of the lower forms of life.

The situation of the copy clerk is analogous, if not identical. Stepping through the front door of the editorial department, clutching a sheepskin, he is quickly asked to put down his diploma, pick up a pencil and paper, and find out who wants a pastrami on rye or tuna on white with tomato. The individual who cannot accept this new status gracefully may be in trouble!

But a copy clerk's life is not all "tote that barge, lift that bale" drudgery. Almost certainly, some of the jobs that are given to summer interns will come his way—if the reporter who compiles lists of movie starting times takes a sick day or if the obituary writer has to go to a relative's funeral, the copy clerk will almost surely be called on to fill in. And other writing opportunities will present themselves as time goes by, probably for feature stories at the start, but, eventually, for news stories.

Many newspapers set a limit as to how long a copy clerk must live in serfdom. The policy is generally stated as "12 months, then up or out" or "18 months, then up or out." Happily, most go "up" rather than "out"—someone who is a complete misfit or so lacking in skills as to be egregiously awful will have been told so long before the trial period is over.

The copy clerk who survives this ordeal will probably be promoted to **editorial assistant** or, on a very small paper, **reporter**. And from that point on, the sky's the limit.

STEWART H. BENEDICT

Mr. Benedict graduated summa cum laude from Drew University (Madison NJ) with an A.B. degree. He received his M.A. from Johns Hopkins University and did additional graduate study at New York University.

Starting in 1963, he has edited and authored books for Dell, Avon, Pinnacle and Facts on File; such titles include <u>A Teacher's Guide to Senior High School Literature</u>, <u>Contemporary Teenage Fiction</u>, and <u>Modern Drama and Poetry</u>.

In addition to his responsibilities as copy editor at the *Jersey Journal*, Mr. Benedict finds time to write plays; he's had 20 of them produced throughout the Northeast, including a recent presentation at the American Renaissance Theatre of New York.

He has received citations and awards for headline writing from the North Jersey Press Association and the New Jersey Daily Newswoman's Association. Mr. Benedict has taught journalism at Rutgers University and Jersey City State College. He resides in New York City.

CHAPTER FOURTEEN

Opportunities In Editorial At Large Papers

By

J. Randolph Jessee, Assistant to the Executive Editor
The Virginian-Pilot and *The Ledger Star*

Reporters and editors once roamed the country like itinerant tradesmen, working their way from town to town, paper to paper, trying to step a little higher on the circulation ladder at each stop. They usually had one goal in mind—reaching one of the "really big" national papers.

Today, journalists tend to stay in one place longer. They settle into their communities and their newspapers. Some find that they like community newspaper work and stay there; others still answer the siren song of the big papers.

That choice is not made without risk. At a larger paper, one person's work has a smaller impact on the overall product. The standards usually are high. But for those with talent and a desire to continue to learn and improve, the opportunities are excellent.

ENTRY-LEVEL POSITIONS IN THE NEWS DEPARTMENT

One must first understand the relationship among the departments of a metropolitan newspapers. The News department tends to be the "customer" of the others—Production,

Advertising, Circulation—that provide the pages into which the news is placed, the facilities for printing the pages, and the means of getting the papers into readers' hands.

But the News department is usually not "beholden" to these other departments—Advertising, for example, does not influence the selection or play of stories. But the efforts of all departments are needed for a successful product.

Career paths in the metropolitan newspaper traditionally have not crossed departmental lines, especially those drawn between the news and business groups. In recent years, however, there has been movement toward more cross-training. Thus, an editor with a degree in business administration may find new opportunities in departments other than news.

There are four major functions in the News department: (1) writers; (2) editors; (3) photographers; and (4) artists. The order of listing is significant. The first two are generally regarded as the "word people;" the latter are the "picture people." Collectively, they make up the staff whose job it is to provide, in words and pictures, a complete package of news, information, entertainment, and opinion for the paper's readership.

All of these jobs are entry-level positions.

Writers

Writers and editors are employed in the News, Features, Sports and Editorial departments. The job of the writer is to cover news events, gather information, interview people, and prepare complete, factual, informative and entertaining stories about a person or event. A writer in the Editorial department is expected to analyze current events and prepare informed opinions—or editorials—about them.

Writers usually begin with relatively small "beats"—the specific areas or subjects which a writer is assigned to cover. Some writers are classified "general assignment," which means they are allowed to cover a wide range of stories. In some papers, general assignment is a prized designation, signifying unusual skill or ability. In others, certain beats are prized. Some sample beats:

Police: Monitoring police activities in person and by radio; covering fast-breaking news—crimes, fire, wrecks, and major weather stories.

Medicine: Covering hospitals, medical schools, and trends in medicine; special responsibility for decoding medical jargon into terms the reader can understand. Some papers employ physicians for this beat.

Government: Covering local, state, and/or the Federal government, including meetings of governing bodies and commissions; keeping in touch with a wide variety of government agencies and departments; translating "governmentese" into everyday English.

Courts: Reporting on proceedings in criminal and civil courts, as well as trends in the legal system.

Sports: A favored beat, covering athletic events at the local and national levels; stories are both "spot news" coverage of events and features about the participants.

Some writers are assigned to features, which means they work on "people" stories that have grown out of news events or from a writer's own knowledge of the community. Such stories usually are longer than typical news stories and may occupy the front page of feature sections.

The extent to which a writer covers more than one beat usually depends on the size of the paper. The larger the paper, the more specialized the writers. On some papers, special training is required before a writer can be considered for certain beats. Some papers, for example, use writers with law degrees for cover the court beat.

When writers move up within a newspaper, they are usually transferred to more prestigious beats or those that allow them greater freedom in their handling of stories. Writers skilled in analysis may move to an editorial department.

Editors

Some writers may wish to move into editing jobs, which requires them to learn supervisory duties. A typical career path might be from **reporter** to **copy editor** to **assistant city editor** to **city editor**.

City editors and assistant city editors are the supervisors of the writers on news beats. Each editor is typically in charge of coverage of a particular area—they give assignments to writers, monitor their progress, do the first edit on the stories, and work with the writers to improve their skills. A city editor usually has at least ten years experience.

Entry-level people usually start as **copy editors** working on the copy desk. Copy editors read stories produced by staff reporters and by the wire services (e.g., Associated Press, UPI, Reuters, etc.) They try to make stories as concise and accurate as possible without damaging the style of the writer. However, they also are charged with making stories fit into prescribed amounts of space, which often requires deleting unimportant (or, at least, *less* important) material.

Copy editors also write headlines. They follow the instructions of the **layout editor**, who determines the appearance of each page and selects the particular stories and pictures that will appear. He or she also specifies the amount of space each story will occupy and the size of the headline. The copy editor edits the story and headline to meet those specifications.

The **wire editor** is a copy editor responsible for monitoring the stories that come from the wire services. He or she selects the stories according to their importance, potential impact on the local community, and informational and/or entertainment value.

Supervisors on the copy desk have such titles as **news editor** and **chief copy editor**. The news editor has overall responsibility for balancing the local and wire content of the newspaper and ensuring that the paper meets its production schedules. The chief copy editor ensures that the copy editors are editing stories carefully, that headline and size specifications are followed, and that headlines accurately reflect the content of the stories.

The news editor and chief copy editor work with their copy editors on improving their editing, headline-writing, and layout skills. Each has at least ten years experience.

Other supervisory editors include the **sports editor**, **features editor**, and **business editor**. They work with their reporters and subordinate copy editors in much the same way as the city or news editors.

Photographers

Photographers are now a vital part of the newsroom operation. Once regarded in much the same way as firemen waiting for a call, photographers today take part in the planning and execution of all major stories. Where they once carried one camera, one lens and one flash unit, they are now routinely equipped with several pieces of sophisticated equipment.

Photographers today shoot more than wrecks, fires and social events. They are called upon to produce elaborate studio shots for magazine-type feature front pages. They frequently produce the layouts that display the pictures they take.

Where photography was one an afterthought—the picture-taking *followed* the story-writing—photographers are now in on the story from the beginning, working with reporters and editors to produce a complete news and information package of words and pictures.

An entry-level photographer will usually be assigned to spot news pictures, with responsibilities growing as professional skills are developed and demonstrated.

Photographers usually work for the **picture editor** or **chief photographer**. A picture editor is frequently a photographer who has developed additional skills in layout, picture selection and picture editing. The picture editor makes photo assignments, reviews the pictures produced by staff photographers and the wire services, selects those for use in the paper, and assists with page layout. In some cases, the picture editor is responsible for the production of entire page layouts on major stories.

A photographer's career path would be from **photographer** to **picture editor** to **chief photographer** to **graphics director.**

Artists

Artists are a relatively recent addition to the newsroom staff. Yes, artists have been part of newsrooms in many places for years, but their roles were less extensive than today. Once—not so long ago—artists were primarily around to retouch pictures, draw maps, and create an occasional illustration.

Today newsroom artists play an important role in the telling of stories. One of the artist's most important tasks is the production of informational graphics. These pieces of art go beyond the usual charts, maps or diagrams. They are used to *explain* news events—*how* something happened, *where* it happened, *why* it happened—with a combination of art and a very few words.

There is a huge demand for artists skilled in international graphics. Such artists must have a knack for reading a story, understanding what happened, and knowing where to develop additional information. They cannot wait to be fed such information by the copy desk.

Artists in the newsroom play a major role in the production of feature sections. They are responsible for illustrating the feature sections with artwork that will tell the story better than a photograph. Sometimes, artists and photographers must work together on a combination of illustrations and photographs.

Newsroom artists would move from **artist** to **chief artist** to **art director** or **graphics director**.

In broad brush strokes, those are the key players in a metropolitan newsroom. To be sure, there are other jobs. But most are developed from personnel in one of these general areas. So how do you get one of these jobs?

GET INTO PRINT BY GETTING INTO PRINT

The answer is simple: Get published.

You can be published in a smaller paper.

You can be published in a school paper.

But the bottom line is: If you haven't worked on a paper *some*where, you're not likely to be hired by a metropolitan daily.

While a college degree is required, it need not be in journalism. In fact, liberal arts and business majors are just as likely to get the job if they have experience on a school or small paper.

Edward F. Rogers is assistant managing editor for recruiting for *The Virginian-Pilot* and *The Ledger Star*. Here's his point of view:

"Nothing is more frustrating to a recruiter than to interview a student who is on the wrong path toward a journalism career.

"What is the wrong path?

"Not working on the school paper.

"Not writing or editing or taking pictures or preparing artwork and being published at every possible chance.

"And waiting until their senior year to begin looking for internships."

Internships

Internships are a good foothold for a future job. Metropolitan newspapers typically hire college students for summer jobs as writers, editors and photographers. These summer jobs are reserved for students who have declared their intentions to follow journalism careers. The internships usually include some additional training programs.

An internship can be crucial, since it provides both training and experience. Says Rogers: "Although we recruit at some 20 colleges and universities and attend four minority conferences or seminars each year, we rarely hire beginning reporters. "When we *do* hire beginning reporters, they generally have had at least one internship, although some may have had as many as four."

So getting a job boils down to experience more than education?

The education is important. The four-year degree is required. But newspapers expect far more than "book learning." Experience on school papers or in internships is of major importance.

The Qualities We Look For

During an interview, Rogers looks for "...signs of aggressiveness, an ability to report and write quickly, and the dedication to get the job done, whatever it might take. Many students work up to 60 hours a week on their school papers, and that could be a consideration in determining an applicant's dedication.

"Although we do not require that an applicant's grade point average reach any certain level (ability and aggressiveness are still the key prerequisites), we do try to hire the brightest people available."

Rogers also points out that metropolitan papers often *do* hire beginners as copy editors, simply because there are fewer applicants for copy editing jobs: "At our paper, we look for people with copy editing experience, either through internships or on their school papers. They also must satisfactorily complete a battery of tests and extensive interviews with a number of editors."

Another desirable trait in any applicant is curiosity. Newspapers want people who want to know *why* and *how*. And they want people who can tell stories completely or spot the missing elements in a story.

Salaries

Salaries in the newsroom, as in most other jobs, vary widely with the size and location of the paper. But most new editors, writers, artists or photographers with experience on a school paper could expect starting salaries between $19,500 and $26,000 per year. With normal progress up the ladder, pay would be from $28,000 to $36,000 at five years, from $36,000 to $52,000 at ten years. At the very top—the managing editor or executive editor—the salary could be from $45,000 to $100,000 per year.

Newsroom personnel can (and *do!*) leave the newspaper industry for successful careers in public relations, advertising, marketing, commercial art, and commercial photography.

To sum up: You *can* get an entry-level job at a major metropolitan newspaper. But to do so, you must practice your particular skill through whatever outlets are available to you.

J. RANDOLPH JESSEE

Mr. Jessee is a graduate of Virginia Tech, where he earned a degree in sociology while working his way through school as an assistant in the university's sports information department.

He served summer internships at *The Roanoke (VA) Times and World-News*, and joined those newspapers as a general assignment writer upon graduation. He was a bureau chief and night city/state editor during his four years there.

He then spent two years as editor of *The Carroll County Times*, a then-twice-a-week paper in Westminster, Maryland, before moving to his current paper in 1976.

At *The Virginian-Pilot and The Ledger-Star*, he has been front page editor, news editor, sports editor and city editor. His current position includes responsibility for the newsroom computer system and for the training of new personnel.

CHAPTER FIFTEEN

The Changing Role Of The Financial Executive

By

John M. O'Brien, Vice President/Controller
The New York Times

I recently completed 26 years in this industry and in this profession. During that period, I've attended many seminars, conferences, cocktail parties, etc. of a non-financial nature. Invariably, the small talk that develops during the early hours of affairs like these ultimately turns to the question of where one works. When I respond *"The New York Times,"* the next question—90% of the time—is "Oh, are you a reporter?"

When I was a good deal younger, that all-too-predictable response really irked me. After all, *I* knew newspapers were and are no different than most other businesses. Many fields have their "glamour" positions (like reporters), but the vast majority of people working for America's major corporations do valuable work in far less "upfront and personal" specialties. So let's get something clear right from the start: The majority of people who work for a newspaper are *not* reporters. Or, for that matter, editors either. But don't think reporters are the only essential people around a newspaper office...or the only occupation you should consider if you want to break into newspaper publishing.

We employ salespeople to sell our advertising and our readers. The manufacturing side of our business produces and distributes our product. We offer careers in systems, personnel and industrial relations. Finally, saving the best for last, newspapers offer career opportunities in virtually all of the finance disciplines. Whether you're interested in strategic planning, internal auditing, cost accounting or the various areas of operations accounting, such as accounts payable, payroll, credit, customer service, etc., there are any number of challenging opportunities in these areas at major papers across the country.

Before we consider these opportunities in more depth, however, I should say a few words about how I arrived at the title of this article. Why the *changing* role of the financial executive? And, if you end up agreeing with my assertion that it *is* changing—somehow—*what* change am I talking about?

Prior to the early 1970s, the role of the Financial department at most newspapers was easily defined and described. The people who labored there were "the guardians of the assets." As such, they were often depicted as ominous, humorless characters who wore green eyeshades. "Bean counters" or "number crunchers" were two of the nicer nicknames. Hardly material for a Gothic romance!

Well, you won't find many novels about accountants even today, but their image *is* changing even as I write this piece. How and why did this occur? Well, Bob Newhart, an ex-accountant who became a major TV comedy star, helped dispel that "humorless" rap. Strategic planning did the rest.

STRATEGIC PLANNING, YOU SAY?

I tend to believe the rise of the "modern" financial executive in the newspaper business actually *began* with the onset of strategic (*aka* long-range) planning. Starting in the early to mid-'70s, budgets and long-range plans suddenly began to appear in the management processes at most newspapers. Newspaper CEOs and publishers, anxious to improve control over their operations, adopted these plans, whose major benefit consisted of increased analysis of all phases of the newspaper business. These budgets and plans deal with all the issues confronting newspaper management: Reader demographics, advertising and circulation pricing policy, advertising/editorial ratios, plant capacity questions, supplier pricing, ad and circulation volume, promotional campaigns, labor rates and marketing strategies, are just some of the items detailed in most newspaper's short and long-range plans. Since these plans needed to be quantified and measured in order to gauge ongoing performance, it was only natural to assign this task to the financial area.

The assignment of this task to the financial area was appropriate for two reasons. First (the obvious one), the end product of these planning exercises was usually a profit and loss or income statement covering a three to five year time frame. The income statement has long been the domain of the financial area. And second (the less obvious one) is the "filter" role the financial staff plays. What do I mean by "filter" role? Think about it for a second.

As I mentioned earlier, prior to the early 1970s, the primary financial role was as "guardian of the assets." (And, yes, I am purposefully interpreting "assets" broadly here to include a company's human assets—its people—in addition to its physical assets, such as plant and equipment.) As guardian, the financial officer needed to be aware of not only what was going on in the financial shop, but what was happening in all of the other shops, too—operations, news, sales, systems, etc.

Further, the role of the financial staff is service-oriented. They don't write the stories, sell the ads, or work at the newsstands where the copies are sold; in fact, they have nothing to do with the production or distribution of the product. What they *do* do is *support* all these essential functions. Most of this support is in the form of information and analysis —and that's where their "filter role" comes in.

Not having sales or manufacturing responsibility affords the financial staff a greater degree of independence. They are not viewing the data through a singular focus like sales, manufacturing, etc. Thus, the role of the financial executive to provide and analyze data for inclusion in the company's strategic plan also provides for their full participation in the overall management process. General management realized that properly trained financial personnel, by virtue of their unique window on overall newspaper operations, could become pivotal participants in the strategic planning process.

THE ROLE OF THE MODERN FINANCIAL NEWSPAPER EXECUTIVE

Most mid- to large-size newspapers have anywhere from six to nine independent disciplines. The six that are most often independent are advertising sales, circulation sales, manufacturing, news, personnel and financial. Systems, labor relations and marketing/promotion are sometimes independent, sometimes included under the responsibilities of the other six.

A typical Financial department might include the following functions:

- Long-range plan and budget;
- Credit, billing, collection, and customer service;
- General accounting and administration;
- Cost accounting; and
- Payroll, accounts payable, cashier's

Long-Range Plan And Budget

This area is far and away considered the most glamorous of the financial area, because it goes well beyond the strictly "debit and credit" activities of the other financial areas.

Today most newspapers have annual budgets; many have three to five year plans. The strategic planning process allows the financial analysts who inhabit this area the unique opportunity to view all the elements and disciplines that make up a newspaper. Decisions on all the strategic options—pricing, promotion, plant capacity, etc.—are embodied in the process. It is the financial analyst's role to comment and quantify their impact relative to short and long-range plans. Further, it affords the financial analyst the opportunity to discuss the critical issues affecting the newspaper with those top executives ultimately responsible for the decision-making process.

Credit/Billing/Collection/Customer Service

I have purposefully lumped all these functions together. As you might guess, this area is responsible for the granting of credit, rendering of accurate invoices, collection of same, and the courteous and efficient handling of the newspaper's customer base. This includes both advertising and circulation revenues—more and more newspapers are thinking of these separate functions as one. Why? To better serve the customer.

Again, this need to serve the customer has altered the traditional role of the financial people who work in this area. It is no longer acceptable to just "get out the bill and collect the money." The people who work here now need to appreciate the marketing aims of the newspaper they represent and understand the changes in the open market its customers are experiencing. Newspaper management has come to realize that the backroom financial operations can impact the salesman's next call—positively or negatively. Rarely does their role produce a *neutral* response. The demands of the marketplace are requiring the financial people who work in this area to be more conversant in financial statement analysis, consumer law issues and improved collection techniques, while attaining a higher level of positive customer communication and a better understanding of and working relationship with their colleagues in advertising and circulation sales.

General Accounting And Administration

In many newspapers, this is the development area, one populated by CPAs (certified public accountants). CPAs understand the theories of accounting; they must learn the "art" of business. This area maintains the books of record for the enterprise, has a liaison role to play with external and internal auditors, and, if the paper is part of a chain, is responsible for financial reporting to the home office or headquarters.

Cost Accounting

This is another traditional development area. Although not all newspapers have independent cost accounting areas, those that do generally staff them with accountants right out of college or with a minimum of job experience. As newspapers attempt to market themselves more aggressively against their competition—broadcast, magazines, other newspapers, etc.—the result has been a spate of new sections, new features, more targeted zoning, etc. All of this activity requires careful analysis to gauge whether expected goals are being achieved. Needless to say, like the budget/plan staff, this area's view of the business is broader than most and provides an excellent opportunity to develop staff.

Payroll/Accounts Payable/Cashier's

These are commonly labeled the disbursements area. Low on glamour, they are essentially the backroom operations of the financial area. Payroll is beginning to gain some notoriety as human resource systems are either added to or attempt to feed off the existing payroll data base.

SO HOW DO YOU GET ON THE BOOKS?

If I still have your interest, I suspect you want to know where to go to join and what to do to sign up.

If you've aimed your sights high and wish to pursue a financial career at a mid- to large-size daily newspaper, I'd pursue an undergraduate degree in accounting. And, while you're still in college, I'd attempt to secure an internship with a local newspaper. Unfortunately, there are very few opportunities to do this that I am aware of.

Secondly, having secured your degree, I'd seek employment at a public accounting firm. If you hope to work for one of the larger metropolitan dailies, you would improve your chances if that firm were one of the "top ten:"

1. Price Waterhouse
2. Ernst & Whinney
3. Deloitte Haskins & Sells
4. Peat Marwick Mitchell
5. Coopers & Lybrand
6. Main Hurdman
7. Arthur Andersen
8. Touche Ross
9. Arthur Young
10. Alexander Grant

Experience in a certified public accounting firm is recommended for three major reasons. First, it provides a good understanding of the basic fundamentals of accounting, converting the theory of the classroom into the practices of the boardroom. Second, with their emphasis on worksheets and documentation, they instill a sense of discipline that is usually lacking in candidates fresh out of college or those who come via a different route. Finally, they develop the analytic capabilities of their staff—a trait that will be increasingly important later on, as you ascend the newspaper management ladder.

You have your degree in accounting, have spent a couple of years with a CPA firm, and have your CPA certificate. What now? What kinds of positions should you consider?

I'd say look carefully at *any* financial analyst's position, whether in planning, profitability, general accounting or, for that matter, credit/customer service. They usually provide excellent opportunities for you to learn a great deal about the newspaper business and present you with a stage on which to demonstrate your skills.

Any entry-level management position in any of the financial areas should be considered for the same reasons noted above. Remember: You can't expect to hit a home run if you never even get to the plate.

Newspapers today, like most other businesses, don't hire people with only the skills necessary to fill the currently vacant position. That would be a short-term strategy. With labor costs at most newspapers consuming forty to fifty cents of every dollar spent, they have long since discovered the wise use of this most valuable of all assets. Today, applicants at most major newspapers are being evaluated to determine if they possess enough raw talent to advance far beyond the positions they are currently applying for. With the proper training, newspapers desire to grow them into the future CEOs and/or publishers.

As more and more newspapers emerge from the "mine shaft" philosophy that let financial people enter and exit a newspaper without ever sticking their heads out the financial area, what other skills will be necessary for budding financial executives? Clearly, they will be required to learn more about the business of newspapering. It will no longer be acceptable to merely present results in an income statement. They will be required to understand the *why* of the numbers. To do this, they will need to understand marketing philosophies, grapple with production processes and plant capacity issues, understand the needs of the readers and advertisers, and be able to communicate all of this effectively.

This brings me to my final point. If I had to pick one skill—and one skill only —to be present in the next person I hire, I would choose interpersonal skills. The newspaper executive of tomorrow, whether his or her basic training occurs in financial, sales, operations, or any other area of the paper, will need to know how to relate to and with others.

The challenges facing newspapers today, and those that are just appearing on the horizon, cannot be solved by one person laboring alone. They will require the coordinated efforts of all who toil at keeping our press free.

JOHN M. O'BRIEN

Mr. O'Brien became vice president of *The New York Times* in 1980. Previously, he served as controller, a post he assumed in 1978, after more than seven years as assistant controller in charge of budgeting and planning. In his current position, he oversees the operations of the general accounting, budget planning, advertising accounting, credit and customer service departments and the cashier's office.

He joined *The Times* in 1960 as a messenger and, by 1966, had been promoted to assistant manager of general accounting. Three years later, he became controller of the Microfilming Corporation of America, a former Times Company affiliate. In 1971, he returned to *The Times* as assistant controller.

Mr. O'Brien was elected to the board of directors of the Institute of Newspaper Financial Executives in 1984. He is chairman of its professional development committee and serves on its budget committee. In 1986, he assumed the position of secretary, becoming one of its five executive officers.

He holds a bachelor of science degree in accounting from Fairleigh-Dickinson University, Teaneck, NJ. Born on July 22, 1942, Mr. O'Brien is married, has three children, and lives in New Milford, NJ.

CHAPTER SIXTEEN

Newspaper Librarians Deliver Data On Deadline

By

Barbara P. Semonche, Library Director
Durham Morning Herald & The Durham Sun (Durham, NC)

"Information, please. Make it fast, accurate and comprehensive!"

That is the mission of today's newspaper libraries. To meet the investigative demands of today's reporters and photographers, professionally-trained information specialists and a wide array of information-age technology are available.

REACH OUT AND TEACH SOMEONE

A reporter recently called a newspaper librarian, looking for information about sightings of a monster covered with green slime. "Will you hold the line, please," the librarian asked, "while I check the monster file?"

"What! You have a file on monsters?" exclaimed the astounded inquirer.

"Well, not exactly—I have a file on Creatures and Monsters with cross references to Bigfoot, Beast of Bladen, Old Buck, Knobby, Chatham Creature, Wompus Cats, Space Monster,

Devil's Tramping Ground and Loch Ness monster...but no monster covered with green slime. Will one of those do?"

A stunned silence. Then: "What is your name, please? I've got to tell my publisher about you!"

The reporter rang off without the answer to his question, doubtless to recheck his errant tipster, but also with awakened respect for the information-retrieval expertise of a professional news librarian. And the librarian doubtless felt the exciting power of information accurately classified and promptly retrieved.

Such examples are not rare in our business. Most of us can cite instances of the library's contributions to the quality of their news organizations.

From newspaper clipping files to reference books, news librarians have more than one tool in their bag of techniques.

FOLLOW THE PAPER TRAIL

A reference librarian at a large, western, metropolitan newspaper joined her paper's management team in defending an assault on the First Amendment. Exhaustively researching precedents in law books and court records, the librarian compiled and organized a mountain of information. The battle reached the U.S. Supreme Court, which subsequently overturned lower courts' decisions and found in favor of the newspaper. The librarian and the team won a national Freedom of the Press Award.

"GOOD-BYE, GUTENBERG. HELLO, MR. CHIPS"

Today's newspaper librarians are information delivery specialists. They have discovered that in an era of great technological change in the news industry, news libraries must keep pace with both current technology and effective traditional techniques. So librarians are no longer custodians of "morgues" where clips often vanished or became nearly illegible through use or age. Most librarians have had to move beyond clip files and reference books and into the new world of computerized news data bases.

To support a series on school bus accidents and questionable bus safety records, for example, a newspaper librarian searched a dozen such data bases, discovering a number of citations and full-text articles relating to the topic. The results of that search were the foundation for further investigative reporting and analysis. The articles focused public attention on a growing problem and received widespread support and commendation.

The training new librarians receive reflect the changes in technology and the growing need of newspaper libraries for full-time professionals comfortable with that technology. Since the late 1970s, a new breed of librarian is taking over the profession. About half have degrees in library science and many can claim both computer training and journalism experience.

In addition to their field of expertise, librarians are becoming skilled managers, coordinating sophisticated electronic information cycling through all departments of their newspapers. A few library directors in recent years have been promoted to executive positions in technology management.

NEWS LIBRARIANS ARE MORE THAN PAID INFORMERS

Most newspaper librarians are involved with a variety of tasks. Generally they are responsible for:

- Establishing library policy
- Hiring, training and supervising library staffers
- Preparing budgets
- Developing library procedures
- Providing reference service to news staff
- Monitoring circulation of library materials
- Establishing staff schedules
- Serving on corporate committees
- Directing internship programs
- Conducting tours
- Keeping informed about the newest developments on the library scene.

Typically they are directly involved with reading and marking newspapers for filing. It is not unusual for librarians to also clip and file articles, select photos for retention and answer telephone requests from the public.

News staffs come to their libraries not only for information, but for ideas. Frequently, it is the individual librarian's special interests and personal experiences that shape the nature of the job and expand the range of contributions he or she can make to the entire news enterprise.

Who are these spark plugs who ignite these information searches? They are not some sort of superhuman species. They are intelligent, involved people who view themselves and their work in a special way. They are librarians with a news sense and they are proving to be invaluable contributors to their newspapers.

Therein lies the excitement---excitement generated by librarians playing an *active* role in the news gathering effort, not a passive one. They anticipate the need for information, prepare for the unexpected and recognize potential news value in seemingly ordinary, routine, clerical tasks. Librarians don't wait for exciting events to present themselves—they are alert to possibilities right under their noses. Investigative reporters need investigative librarians. It is not enough to come up with the answers on demand in today's libraries; we have to anticipate the questions.

How do news librarians acquire this expertise? From many sources. One librarian has suggested a "3M Formula." The ingredients? "Materials, methods and me!"

If all this sounds like hard work, it is. And all the twentieth-century technology is not going to make it disappear. Regardless of whether the tools of the news librarian remain scissors, file cabinets and telephones, or become computers, optical disks and satellites, the vital ingredients will always remain—the individual's intelligence and dedication.

There are other resources. The News Division of the Special Libraries Association is a mother lode of high quality professional information for inquiring students, neophyte news librarians and veteran information specialists. Likewise, the library at the American Newspaper Publishers Association maintains an impressive collection on newspaper librarianship.

TRAINING AND RECRUITMENT

Not all newspapers have staffed libraries. Weekly newspapers usually do not. In fact, few newspapers with circulations under 30,000 have designated newspaper library collections and staff. Most newspapers over 50,000 do, though the "staff" may consist of only one or two people who are nevertheless responsible for all the library tasks, e.g., reading and clipping the newspaper, collecting and filing photos, helping the news staff (and the public) find information published in the paper.

One place to start your search into the field of newspaper librarianship is your local newspaper. Call and request a visit of its library. Newspaper librarians are pleased to arrange a tour for interested students—just take care that your visit doesn't interfere with the deadline schedule.

During your tour, ask to see their clip and photo files, note the subject headings, scan their microfilm, browse their reference and map collections. Inquire about their indexes. Perhaps the librarian can demonstrate a computer search. (Computers are not ordinarily part of very small newspaper libraries.)

Big, metropolitan newspaper libraries may not be able to offer individualized visits, but they usually arrange group tours. In such large libraries the staff may be highly diversified. The director may manage several departments within the library. Separate staff may be designated for reference, serials, photo archives, indexing, microfilming, on-line data base searching, public service and more. These departmental managers are likely to be professional librarians with specialized additional training and substantial experience.

Professional advancement within smaller newspaper libraries is typically limited. Greater opportunities generally present themselves in larger organizations. However, opportunities for learning and growth are not restricted by the size of newspapers.

Some newspaper libraries have part-time job openings for night and weekend duty. This is a good way for library science and journalism students to gain newspaper experience. Occasionally these part-time jobs are coupled with college internship programs for course credit. (The News Division of the Special Libraries Association, for example, sponsors an annual Student Stipend Award of $1,000 to graduate students in library science. More about this award at the conclusion of this article.)

While there are accredited graduate schools of information and library science in most states and Canadian provinces, few offer courses in newspaper librarianship. This is where the News Division of SLA rises to meet the need.

The News Division is a close network of over 500 news librarians (newspaper, news magazine and broadcast news) in the U.S., Canada and 14 foreign countries. It offers books, newsletters, audio/visual presentations, research, seminars, workshops, conference programs, demonstrations, consultation services and more...just for the asking.

These low-cost products and services are rated very highly by neophyte and veteran news librarians alike. According to one professional librarian, "In many ways the News Division is as valuable as graduate school. It bridges the gap between theory and practice. What's new? What works? What's ahead? Someone in the Division knows...or knows who knows."

And as one Student Stipend Award winner claimed, "The conference did more than validate my library school experience; it animated it!" Job openings are frequently noted throughout this network, so you'd be wise to "hook up" as early as you can to this group of "live wire librarians."

One last reminder: News librarians are part of a larger journalistic heritage, one that is deeply embedded in our country's convictions as well as its Constitution. We are part of this country's commitment to freedom of the press and the concomitant goal of freedom of information. It is fundamental to the excitement and responsibility of our profession.

There are, however, other rewards of a more tangible sort.

A 1986 salary study of news library staff is available from the News Division. Salaries of library managers/directors are not included in this survey. Generally, salaries vary with responsibility training, experience, size and geographic location of newspaper as well as size of editorial staff. In addition, many newspapers underwrite their librarians' professional dues and support their librarians' continuing education expenses. Other fringe benefits and insurance programs are offered.

JOB FACTS

Salary Range: $15,000 to $55,000

Educational Requirements: Master of Science degree in Information and Library Science or equivalent. Journalism and data processing courses recommended.

Personal Characteristics:

- Broad interests and abilities
- Good basic liberal education
- High energy and initiative
- Intelligence
- Problem-solving orientation
- Perseverance
- Ability to work effectively with all types of people
- Able to function under deadline pressure with ease
- Highly developed organizational skills
- Comfortable in leadership role
- Effective in oral and written communication

SUMMARY

Although the job market for newspaper librarians is not large, some smaller newspapers may begin employing professional librarians for the first time in the near future. Some newspapers are expanding their library staffs to accommodate the sharply increasing demand for photo/graphic/map collection building, storage and retrieval. Technological advances may require both ends of the job skill spectrum to expand. At the higher level, more personnel with training in computers and optical disk technology may be needed. At the lower level, staff may be needed to operate such equipment, but not necessarily manage the overall high tech resources.

FOR MORE INFORMATION

News Division of the Special Libraries Association
1700 18th Street, N.W.
Washington, DC 20009

News Division Student Stipend Award
c/o Barbara Semonche
Herald-Sun Newspaper Library
115 Market Street
Durham, NC 27702

American Newspaper Publishers Association library
1160 Sunrise Valley Drive
Reston, VA 22091

BARBARA P. SEMONCHE

Mrs Semonche founded the *Herald-Sun* Newspaper Library in 1976. The library staff numbers 15 and serves the entire Durham Herald Company's 300 employees. Principal library users are the 60 news staff (reporters, editors and photographers) of the 70,000-circulation daily newspapers. Four remote news bureaus are primary users also.

The library supports a student internship program. Five out of the last nine national Student Stipend Award winners have served as library interns at the *Herald-Sun* newspaper. Further, the library publishes and markets a computerized newspaper index as well as indexing software, and produces and sells microfiche of its news clippings.

Mrs. Semonche has presented papers and written articles on newspaper library management and newspaper indexing. A graduate of the University of North Carolina-Chapel Hill School of Library Science, she is currently president of the Alumni Association. She is also a former chairman of the Newspaper Division of the Special Libraries Association and remains active on committees locally and nationally. Mrs Semonche has toured over 50 newspaper libraries in the United States, Canada and Europe and served as library consultant to newspapers with circulations from 30,000 to 300,000.

Newspaper librarianship is Mrs. Semonche's latest career. Before receiving her MS in Library Science, she was a speech therapist, a teacher of the deaf and a research assistant in children's language development.

Mrs. Semonche is married to UNC-CH professor of American legal history John Semonche, whose latest literary efforts include a play about Hanging Judge Parker. Professor and Mrs. Semonche have a daughter, Laura, who is enrolled in the UNC-CH School of Law.

CHAPTER SEVENTEEN

Production Management—
Today And Tomorrow

By

Robert L. Moyer, (Former) General Manager
The Daily Journal
(Kankakee, Illinois)

If you're interested in a career opportunity in newspaper production, you must be an adventurer possessing today's needed skills and the ability to keep pace with tomorrow's technology.

The requirements for producing a daily newspaper are varied and fascinating. They are also changing at about the same rate as the formal educational tools used by high schools, vocational schools and colleges.

No matter what newspaper Production department we talk about, today's *and* tomorrow's changes are all related to the computer. So if you're interested in any of the possible career paths in newspaper production, you would be well advised to be very proficient in the use of personal computers. Programming skills may help, but are not essential—an understanding and ability to use the computer to its full potential *is* essential.

The typical Production department of a small newspaper (15,000—50,000 circulation) normally includes a <u>composing room</u> (where stories, photos and advertisements come together to be composed into pages); the <u>pressroom</u> (where the newspaper is printed) and the <u>Building Maintenance department</u>. Depending upon the organizational structure of the individual newspaper and the special skills of the manager, other departments—e.g., the mailroom, distribution, data processing, and the camera plate department (where the press plates are made) —may also be included under the heading "production."

Newspapers with circulation above 50,000 will have additional departments (or sub-departments) because of the volume of materials and number of employees required to make the operation work properly. While a mid-sized newspaper may use 4,000 metric tons of news-print a year, for example, a metropolitan operation will use in excess of 100,000. This volume of material necessitates additional sub-departments to control it. Examples of department managers in metropolitan operations that would not normally be found in smaller operations would include: prepress operations, maintenance, general service, purchasing, delivery, electrical, machinist, quality control, newsprint, and paper handler.

NEWSPAPER PRODUCTION 1963-1988

Before I describe why you should be interested in pursuing a career in newspaper pro-duction, let's look at some of the changes that have taken place in newspaper production in the past 23 years, a period that has witnessed more changes in this area than the previous 200 years.

Until 1963, newspaper production techniques, materials, skills, etc., had changed very little from the way things were done in the early 1900s or, for that matter, the 1800s. The images that appeared in newspapers were prepared from hot metal lines of type, engravings and metal castings. Manual and tape-operated line casters, very similar to Otto Mergenthaler's original model developed in the late 1890s, were used to compose lines of type of a fixed width. There was very little standardization of the widths of newspaper columns, which varied from 10 picas (1.67 inches) to 13 picas (2.165 inches). Keyboard entry was either made directly to a slow, manual, hot metal machine or remotely, via paper tape.

The concept of speed in 1963 was a tape-driven line caster operating at 14 lines per minute. (By comparison, today's cathode ray tubes and laser photocomposition typesetters run at speeds in excess of 1,200 lines a minute and are virtually error-free.)

The composing room was the largest of all the production departments. The skills required were regarded as very high-level, especially for those assigned to producing display advertisements, both the typesetters and the ad make-up people.

Any page with a half-tone illustration (a photo on page one, for example) had an image that was produced by chemically etching away the non-printing area in the engraving department. The final locked-up, hot metal page images were transferred to a thick paper matte, which was then formed, dried and used as a mold for casting 45-pound plates, one for each standard-sized page. These plates were placed on rotary presses. The resulting reproduction was, by today's standards, mediocre at best.

In 1963, two things happened, almost simultaneously, that would change newspaper production methods forever: Photo composition devices became practical for operations and computers were added to hyphenate and justify lines of types. These two devices changed the skills required for all production professionals.

The decade from 1963 to 1973 was a revolutionary one for the newspaper industry as far as production technology was concerned. It was a period when almost everything in production changed, including the skill requirements of the managers.

By 1973, there were many newspapers across the U.S. that used photo composition for *all* news and ad images. Those 45-pound press plates now weighed only a few ounces each and were either thin relief plates only 30 *thousandths* of an inch thick or a planographic offset plate of .085" to .012" thickness.

Since 1973, the rate of change has slowed; we are now in an evolutionary period where quality is being affected by innovations more than productivity.

In the printing industry, newspapers have always been the media with the lowest quality of reproduction, the most inexpensive materials, and the most difficult labor-management problems.

That's just not so today. *USA Today* proved that you can have quality, black and white *and* color reproduction, five days a week, with the same images printed in different locations on different equipment. Materials and equipment used in today's newspaper operations now rival those used by magazines in sophistication of controls, speed and flexibility.

A byproduct of these changes has been a shift of power in the mechanical operations from labor to management. This is not a judgmental statement, merely one that should be obvious: When you reduce required skills, the number of employees, and the training period necessary to achieve proficiency, labor's position is weakened.

Today, images for the news stories, pictures and ads are composed without the old departments we knew as composing, stereo, engraving, camera, and plate. The new process called pagination and the speed and flexibility of computer equipment has made this possible, if not practical, for newspaper operations of virtually any size.

PRODUCTION CAREER PATHS

To prepare for an entry-level job in production, you should recognize the differences between independent newspapers and those that are part of a group, and the differences between small and large newspapers. (The trend is in favor of group ownership, which is beneficial from the viewpoint of career opportunities for entry-level people.)

There are 1,676 daily newspapers in the U.S. Of these, 768 are in the 10,000—50,000 circulation range. *Editor & Publisher* provides the following statistics: In the 25,000—50,000 circulation range, there are 100 morning newspapers and 167 evening papers; in the 10,000—25,000 range, there are 100 mornings and 406 evenings. That makes a grand total of 773 newspapers that are considered "small," but they're large enough to have a production manager.

Group ownership provides smaller newspaper operations with economic benefits in production management similar to those experienced by larger operations. The larger the operation or, in the case of a newspaper group, the *sum* of the operations, the greater the potential cost savings from the management of the production departments. For example, if you need to do some research that will require a significant time and financial commitment, the larger the operation (or the more sites that can benefit from the results), the greater the incentive for proceeding.

The Gannett organization has 90 daily newspaper operations, including the national daily *USA Today*. The majority of its operations are newspapers under 50,000 circulation and they are very production-oriented. This is only one of many newspaper groups, but it is the largest. Others of significant size include Knight-Ridder Newspapers Inc., Donrey Media Group, Freedom Newspapers, and Harte-Hanks Communications, Inc.

In addition to those major papers and groups listed in the *Job Opportunities Databank* of this Career Directory, you can get a complete listing of all newspaper operations at your local newspaper or library. Any daily newspaper with 15,000 circulation or more and most libraries will have an <u>Editor & Publisher International Yearbook</u>. This volume provides a brief description of the statistical size of the operation, identifies its top managers by departments, indicates whether it's an independent or part of a group, and lists the types of equipment it utilizes to compose and print its newspapers. And under the heading, "Newspaper Groups Under Common Ownership," it lists the names of each newspaper, the officers of the corporation, and the mailing address.

If you have formal training in printing from a college or trade school, contact the Production department of a newspaper group—their need for inexperienced but formally trained personnel is greater than the independents'. At this level, the job title would be something like **production assistant** or **assistant to director of production**. Both imply a staff position, not line authority and responsibility.

ENTRY-LEVEL JOB DUTIES

In an entry-level position, the job assignments will frequently involve monitoring existing operations to determine if standards are being maintained. Some examples might include:

- Checking prints from photography for proper tone values.
- Checking release of news stories and advertising copy against posted deadlines for compliance.
- Reviewing maintenance charts on equipment.
- Running test strips through film and negative processors and recording the results.
- Checking procedures, materials and equipment used in pre-press color registration.
- Running density tests on negatives or printed copies for compliance.

Candidates whose formal training or experience gained through hobbies or part-time employment satisfy minimum entrance standards for a production assistant could begin making a meaningful contribution to the Production department (in an observation and recording mode) in a very short period of time .

Next would come the evaluation phase—the identification of non-standard performance and the responsibility for explaining how performance should be changed to meet preset standards. With this background, you could then expect assignments related to research, purchasing and implementation. These skills are very valuable to either a group or the independent operation.

Finally, you would be eligible for the line responsibility of production operations.

Regardless of the extent of one's formal education, it should usually be assumed that management positions require a proven track record at the data collection level.

If you do apply for a production-oriented management position with an independent small newspaper, it is possible you would be reporting to the general manager or publisher, rather than the production manager. The Production department at newspaper of 30,000 circulation will usually consist of a manager and a secretary. Three of our newspapers are in this range and that is how they are organized. The production managers of our six mechanical operations (two produce two separate dailies) were all promoted from positions as foremen. This will happen less frequently in the future.

A TYPICAL DAY

For the next decade or so, a typical production manager's day will probably consist of:

- Beginning the day by reviewing yesterday's performance. Any messages that should be sent internally or externally would be noted.

- A visit to each department for a brief confirmation with the manager and technicians that everything is under control.

- Though the time required varies considerably, supplier and vendor communication needs will occupy about an hour of the average day.

- Labor needs—reviewing payroll changes, negotiating contracts, evaluating employees evaluations, personal employee reviews, etc., are ever present. With tomorrow's technology, the number of employees will decrease, though the potential for needing qualified replacements may increase.

- Checking the pre-press performance by the department's production services (news and advertising), the production departments, and, briefly, the mailroom and distribution departments for any possible problems that could affect production schedules.

- Handling external communications with advertisers and subscribers referred to you because the production department was identified as the responsible party. This is not necessarily bad news; compliments and requests for advice *do* occur, though, unfortunately, complaints are dominant.

HOW TO GET A JOB ON A SMALLER PAPER

If you want to get a job leading to production management on a smaller paper, you must have the skills that a newspaper or group of papers need. Formal training at R.I.T., Carnegie Tech., or other printing schools has proven beneficial in the past and remains so. Practical experience with computers, telecommunications, photography (with an emphasis on color) and/or as an offset pressman in a quality printing shop would open many doors. There isn't a school or suggested curriculum for this type of job; that's just one reason why we are such an interesting group.

THE DIFFERENCES AT A LARGER PAPER

Attempting to compare the job operations and duties of a production manager at a large newspaper operation (50,000 circulation and up) vs. a small paper is akin to comparing the lifestyles of a person in a large city to one in a small town. There are pluses and minuses in both.

For example, a metropolitan operation will be less personal, but there will be far more opportunities for employment. The large operation will be more specialized—there will be job openings for medical doctors, electrical engineers, even civil engineers. (All of them, small or large, will have openings for statisticians, mechanical engineers and printing school graduates.)

Smaller operations require generalists, who, as we've previously pointed out, will report to one of the top managers. Larger operations will have more clearly defined—but narrower—job descriptions. The person responsible for newsprint, for example, will spend the majority of his or her time dealing solely with newsprint—he or she will need to get involved with the most minute details of this single aspect of the operation. Obviously, the person in the smaller operation will have neither the training nor the time to do the same.

Another example: the production manager at a small paper, when confronted by bad weather, will be responsible for communicating with the circulation manager and the appropriate department managers (composing, press, etc.) to get an early press start. A director of operations at a metropolitan newspaper will be totally unaware that such a request has even been made, let alone be involved in making it .

There are also great similarities, especially in relation to the final product. The equipment and techniques for producing pages are similar, if not identical, at both large and small papers The equipment for producing the final products *are* identical—only the number of press units is different.

THE FUTURE OF PRODUCTION MANAGEMENT

After the next decade, I suspect the title "production manager" will be replaced by one that more accurately reflects the size and scope of the production operation—graphics department manager is one logical possibility. Technology is blurring the distinction between newsroom and composing, between advertising and composing. The pressroom seems reasonably secure for now, but it may become more aligned with the mailroom and distribution departments than it is today.

Obviously, neither of us really knows what changes are ahead; however, if you want to manage whatever entity replaces today's Production department, become as proficient as you can with computers and mathematics (regression curves, etc.), and hone your communication skills. If you do, you are going to enjoy coming to work everyday and enjoy the people you work with. You will be proud of the products you produce and as eager as today's production managers to discover what new process, material, or piece of equipment is on the horizon to help you do your job better.

ROBERT L. MOYER

Robert L. Moyer was born and educated in Iowa. He received a degree in mathematics from Parsons College and a degree in industrial engineering from Iowa State University. He has attended numerous newspaper production workshops and seminars and lectured on production systems throughout the Midwest.

Prior to *The Daily Journal*, Mr. Moyer was production manager of the *Decatur Herald & Review* and production manager and assistant general manager of the *Trenton Times*.

He was a member of the American Newspaper Publishers Association technical committee from 1978 to 1986 and president of the board of trustees of Riverside Medical Center from 1979 to 1980. He is director of the First Trust & Savings Bank of Kankakee and Midwest Financial Group and past-division chairman and general vice-chairman of the United Way of Kankakee.

CHAPTER EIGHTEEN

Ready, Set, Grow!
Promotion At Smaller Papers

By

Amy Pack, Promotion Director
Florida Today/USA Today

The newspaper industry is addictive, I give you fair warning! No two days are ever the same at a newspaper, and no two newspapers are ever the same. It's an exciting, challenging business that offers much in the way of personal and professional growth.

Because people tend to think only of reporters and editors when they consider the newspaper business, many other career opportunities are often overlooked. One of those is Promotion.

WHAT IS NEWSPAPER PROMOTION?

At a smaller newspaper, it's one or two people making maximum use of available staff and resources to produce programs and ideas that increase advertising revenue and circulation sales. Sound challenging? It is. It's also a lot of fun. Promotion activity can be as simple as having coffee cups imprinted with the newspaper's name, as complex as devising strategies for gaining 2,000 new subscribers. The activities vary, according to Publisher direction and the company's overall marketing plan.

A distinct advantage of working in Promotion at a smaller newspaper is the hands-on experience in these areas:

- Researching and applying data.
- Developing advertising sales promotion.
- Building strategies and producing materials to support circulation growth.
- Media planning and buying.
- Administering the paper's various programs, such as Newspaper in Education.
- Coordinating community events sponsored by the newspaper.
- Working directly with all newspaper departments and the general public.

Involvement in all these areas is great preparation for moving ahead into a more specialized area of Promotion at a larger paper.

CAREER SKILLS

There are five skills that I have found essential to effective newspaper promotion:

1. *Creativity:* We are constantly challenged to design innovative ways of promoting product benefits to our readers, our advertisers, and prospective customers.

2. *Communication:* The ability to write is very important, especially at the smaller newspaper. We are in the communication business. Promotion is producing a flyer, direct mail piece or ad that requires copy—DAILY. Strong written and verbal communication skills are a real asset.

3. *Public Relations:* Interaction with other employees and the general public is a vital part of the promotion function. This requires confidence, compromise, and a natural respect and understanding for people and their needs. The promotion person is an ambassador for the newspaper, so professionalism is a must!

4. *Flexibility:* Promotion work is project work—*lots* of projects going on at the same time, each with a different deadline. Deadlines that often *change*. Being flexible is a way of keeping peace with yourself and your co-workers. Changes in the market occur, oftentimes without warning. We must be ready to stop activity on a dime and respond quickly to promotion opportunities as they arise.

5. *Teamwork:* Successful promotion is a result of teamwork. The idea that's been nurtured through brainstorming with several people tends to be more exciting and successful than a single-minded notion. Teamwork also encourages good communication across departmental lines.

FINAL HINTS AND ADVICE

Research the industry. Find out which newspapers are highly regarded and why. Investigate major newspaper chains, their reputations, properties, and benefits. Talk to the people at the International Newspaper Marketing Association in Reston, Virginia. They are a terrific resource. Talk to promotion managers from small and large papers. They're friendly folks who'll gladly take a moment of their time for you.

Approach the company that best fits your career plans and goals. Be prepared for the interview—research the newspaper at which you are applying. Find out what the Promotion department's responsibilities are and to whom the promotion manager reports. (At most papers, small and large, Promotion functions as a separate department, with the manager reporting directly to the publisher or general manager.)

Remember to concentrate on the benefits of the parent company or chain first. Positions within an organization can change in a heartbeat—it's the nature of the business. So get a foot in the door with the *company* you think you'd be happy working for. You'll be well on your way to building an exciting and rewarding newspaper career!

AMY PACK

With a bachelor's degree in graphic design from San Jose State University, Amy Pack began her professional career in 1975 as an artist with a magazine in Fresno, California. In 1976, she broke into the newspaper business at the *Visalia (CA) Times-Delta,* where she moved from advertising artist into management by developing a new Promotion department. She held the position of promotion manager there until 1985, when she was named promotion director at *Florida Today* newspaper in Melbourne, Florida.

Ms. Pack's current responsibilities include coordination of promotional campaigns, research and marketing support for *Florida Today* and *USA Today,* as well as public relations and community service projects and special sales programs, including Newspaper in Education.

She's been an active member of the International Newspaper Marketing Association (INMA) since 1979, serving on both the Western and Southern Region Boards. Locally, she is active in Chamber work and serves on the boards of three organizations.

CHAPTER NINETEEN

Promotion: The Hub Of The Wheel

By

Page Haines, Promotion Manager
The Houston Chronicle

Promotion is the hub of the wheel, interfacing and acting as liaison between the newspaper marketing and editorial divisions and their publics. Newspaper promotion departments develop programs and printed materials that promote the sales of their company's two types of products—the newspapers themselves and the advertising space within them.

The word most descriptive of newspaper promotion is "diverse," because the products being promoted cover the gamut:

- Retail, general and classified advertising space;
- Newspapers, delivered to homes or sold individually;
- Editorial content; and
- Corporate image.

The products of the Promotion department are also diverse. Some examples:

- A brochure comparing the paper's circulation figures with the competition's;

• An in-newspaper ad concerning the awards recently won by one of the writers;

• A retail advertising rate book;

• A T-shirt for a newspaper-sponsored "fun run;"

• A booth at a trade show or convention;

• A booklet detailing the Research department's recent study;

• An all-media ad campaign promoting the paper's position in the community.

WHO DOES WHAT?

Job responsibilities in the Promotion department vary considerably from paper to paper, depending on a variety of factors, including whether or not an ad agency is utilized. If one is, Promotion management usually works with the agency to coordinate the paper's advertising efforts for television, radio, industry publications, etc. But even with an agency on-board, a lot of work is done in-house.

As in an ad agency, the bulk of the production is accomplished through a cooperative effort of writers and artists. Also, at least one person handles traffic—reserving advertising space and arranging printing.

Some newspapers call their promotion departments Marketing departments, in which case they usually include other functions related to promotion, such as:

• *Educational services* (or *newspaper in education*) promotes use of the newspaper in the classroom by creating lesson plans, sponsoring contests, and providing a variety of services to local schools.

• *Public relations* affects the public's image of the paper and special events.

• *In-house communication* produces employee newsletters, company-wide notices, etc.

• *The Print Shop* prints promotional materials and company forms.

• *Audio-visual* produces slide shows, client presentations, and, sometimes, broadcast commercials.

Although artists and writers must work together as a team and exchange ideas, their responsibilities are distinctly different, so we'll discuss them separately.

WRITERS

SCENARIO: The circulation manager calls a meeting to discuss a promotion that offers an incentive to new subscribers. The promotion writer can research and devise his or her own idea of an appropriate offer or work with Circulation's suggestion. The writer gets the specifics of the offer and suggests an in-paper ad, flyers for door to door sales, and a direct mail piece. A completion date is agreed on for each step of the campaign.

The writer meets with an artist to discuss the campaign, each of the projects, and a time schedule. Starting with the flyer, he writes the copy and gives it to the artist, who makes a layout. He then requests approvals (usually from the creative director and the Client department) before returning it to the artist. When the artist finishes the mechanical, the writer gets it proofed (usually by other writers) and submits it for approval and release to the printer. When it returns from the printer, the writer requests permission to release the finished materials to Circulation. He then follows a similar process with each of the other projects in the campaign.

This is an example of one of many different projects a copywriter might be working on at one time. It assumes that all approvals are given without suggested changes and that no one in Circulation changes his or her mind about the campaign details—an optimistic assumption, to say the least. Constant correction and revision are facts of life.

In promotion, the term "writer" is often a misnomer. Writers attend meetings, plan campaigns, arrange booth space at trade shows, select specialty advertising and, at times, write copy for an ad or brochure. That may be an exaggeration, but the job often involves as much account servicing as it does writing.

But promotion writers *do* write. A wordsmith will find an outlet for his or her creativity in finding new and fresh ways to promote the newspaper's products.

Entry-Level Position

COMMON JOB TITLE: Junior Copywriter

TYPICAL SALARY: $18,000

JOB DUTIES: General writer duties as described above, starting with small-scale projects. At first, the writer will be closely supervised by the creative director or a senior copywriter.

Getting Hired

Managers look at how you promote yourself in your resume as evidence of how you would promote the newspaper. Your resume can be your best writing sample. It should have the same attributes as a good sales brochure: clear, correct and convincing.

Have a portfolio of your best writing samples assembled. They can be drawn from schoolwork, internships, or previous jobs.

Copywriters do not need to *be* artists, but they do need enough knowledge of graphics to *communicate* with artists. An attractively laid-out resume or portfolio tells a manager that you are aware of graphic concepts.

A degree is usually required. Some appropriate degrees are English, journalism, advertising and communications. Courses involving writing, advertising and sales are desirable.

Desired Attributes:

Time management—Deadlines are omnipresent at newspapers. If you have planning skills and speed, you will be well ahead of the game.

Organizational skills—Because writers work on several jobs at a time, you will need to be very organized.

Typing—Although it is often not considered in hiring, typing is a skill you will use (on a typewriter or computer) daily.

Creativity—The ability to view the world from an uncommon angle and develop new solutions to old problems is a valued trait.

Writing style—Good style develops over time. Clean, clear, "invisible" style is best for an entry-level writer.

Communication skills—Several people are involved in any one promotion project. Good interpersonal communication skills will save you a great deal of time.

ARTISTS

SCENARIO: A copywriter meets with you (the artist) to discuss a circulation campaign. They are going to sell subscriptions by offering a cookbook as an incentive. They want an in-paper ad, flyers, and a direct mail piece. The two of you discuss the general requirements of the projects, possible design ideas, and a timetable with deadlines for each step of the campaign. After the writer gives you the copy, you design a "comp" to be submitted with the copy for approvals. Once it is approved, you define the type size and style and get it typeset. Then you do the mechanical and give it to the copywriter for proofing. It then goes for more approvals before release to the printer.

This scenario is as optimistic as the one for writers. With all the approvals and proofing come suggestions for changes, new ideas, and revamping. Constant correction and revision are facts of life.

As you can see, the artist uses communication skills as well as design ability and art skills.

Entry-Level Position

COMMON JOB TITLE: Junior Artist

TYPICAL SALARY: $18,000

JOB DUTIES: General artist duties as described above, starting with mostly mechanical art work. At first, the artist will be closely supervised by the art director or a senior artist.

Getting Hired

Your portfolio should include layouts, camera-ready art, and finished pieces in a variety of media. These should display all your skills. Hopefully, you will have developed these pieces in school or in previous positions. If you feel something is missing, do a piece and fill the gap.

If you do not pride yourself on your writing skills, get someone to help you write your resume.

The appearance of your resume, your portfolio, and even your attire can communicate a sense of style, design and order.

A degree is usually preferred, but not required, though lack of a degree could hinder advancement. The most important thing to get from school is the art skills listed below, but courses in advertising, photography, and business can help you grow in a job.

Desired Attributes:

Production/camera-ready art skills—Paste-up, cutting overlays, specing type, and correcting color separations.

General art skills—Illustration and design

Troubleshooting—The ability to avoid crises through knowledge of alternative methods of getting the job done.

Time management—Deadlines are omnipresent at newspapers. If you have planning skills and speed, you will be well ahead of the game.

Creativity—The ability to view the world from an uncommon angle and develop new solutions to old problems is a valued trait.

HINTS AND SUGGESTIONS FOR ALL OF YOU

If you are interested in working in a newspaper promotion department, it is a good idea to make a contact as soon as possible. Ask an appropriate manager for an informational interview: "I'm fascinated with newspapers and advertising and would like to ask you some questions about the Promotion department." You can find this person through school contacts, professional organizations or simply calling. The promotion secretary should help you find the right person. Try to set up a meeting that will give you an opportunity to leave a personal impression while gathering useful information.

Internships

Internships are a valuable way to learn about careers and make job contacts. Newspapers generally have several internships available. If there isn't one available in Promotion, try for a related one in Advertising.

Moving Up The Career Ladder

If the Promotion department feels like the home you have always looked for, you will want to move up the ladder. Artists become **senior artists** or **art directors** and can move into department management. Writers become **senior writers** or **creative directors** and can also move into management.

If you find it is time to move on, there will be opportunities outside the paper. The skills you develop as a writer or artist transfer well to other institutions. Artists can go to ad agencies, printing companies, or in-house art departments at many types of companies. Writers can go to ad agencies, other publications, or in-house communications departments.

Dos And Don'ts

Do not work in a newspaper promotion department if:

• You are a loner. Nearly all projects are team efforts.

• You have a fragile ego or superior attitude. Your work goes through an approval process that is often subjective and sometimes critical. Knowing when to take suggestions and when to back your own opinions are key skills.

• You are a one-thing-at-a-time person. Promotion workers juggle several projects at a time.

Do work in a newspaper promotion department if:

• You want to stay busy with a wide variety of projects.

• You are sales/marketing-minded, but don't want to be a salesperson.

• You want to work with a wide variety of creative people.

PAGE HAINES

In her current position, which she assumed in 1983, Ms. Haines oversees a full- and part-time staff of 36 and is responsible for all marketing communications, including promotion, public relations, advertising, newspaper in education, the in-house magazine, and marketing production. She was previously planning manager (1981-83) and creative supervisor (1978-1980). She began her career as special events manager for *The Houston Post* in 1973. She was promoted to promotion manager a year later.

Ms. Haines is a member of the board of directors of the International Newspapers Marketing Association (INMA) and is active in numerous other professional, educational and community groups and activities. She received her B.A. (Journalism) from Texas Tech, an M.B.A. from the University of Houston.

CHAPTER TWENTY

A Key To The Vault: Working In Newspaper Research In The '90s

By

James E. Smith, Research Manager
Fort Lauderdale News/Sun-Sentinel

In this age of information, the local newspaper company is very often the largest collector and purveyor of information in the community. The company's most precious resource is the information it assembles—through its reporters, salespeople and others—and disseminates in a constant flow via its products and corporate communications.

Playing a special role in this process is a small group of information specialists—the members of the Research department. Their job is to gather data of all sorts, analyze it and see that it gets to the people who need it to do their jobs better—the managers, reporters, sales and service people who shape and sell the product.

By applying research skills to the newspaper business, you turn a key to open the community's richest information vault.

WHERE TO FIND RESEARCH

Not all newspapers have a formally-constituted Research department, although even the smallest papers usually have an analyst or statistician somewhere in the company doing the job.

Almost all middle- and large-sized newspapers have full fledged Research departments, ranging in size from two to fifteen members. A few very large papers have 40 or more people working in research.

Some Research departments are headed by a company director who reports directly to the publisher, general manager or senior vice president. More commonly, Research departments are headed by managers, who report to directors of marketing or advertising. Occasionally, the research function is diffused throughout the company, with analysts operating within the Advertising, News and/or Circulation divisions and reporting to managers in those divisions.

In the larger departments, specialization is common, sometimes by the client served (e.g., **circulation analysts, advertising analysts**), sometimes by the type of data supplied (e.g., **local survey specialists, demographic** or **economic specialists**). In the smaller shops, typically, everybody does everything.

THE CLIENTELE

Newspaper researchers often operate like consultants, providing data and analysis for various clients within the company. Unlike most consultants, however, they remain within the organization, communicating and explaining the results and training the newspaper staff to make use of the data.

The Advertising division is almost always the main client of the department. Research supplies a wide variety of information on the newspaper's market and audience for use in sales materials and presentations. Many departments also provide extensive local survey data on consumer behavior as a service for advertisers and prospects.

Company management is often a major research client—for strategic research on the strengths and weaknesses of the editorial product, insight into the competitive risks and opportunities in the market, data on circulation and advertising market shares and information on economic and demographic trends.

The News division is frequently a high visibility client, seeking data processing and analysis for statistically-based stories and survey research for election and public opinion coverage. Editors are an important audience for product research as well, since they control the content of the editorial product.

The Circulation division sells and delivers the newspaper and, like any marketing organization, circulation needs good information on its customers' characteristics and attitudes in order to increase sales and minimize the loss of customers.

A lot of circulation sales support (and advertising sales support, too) goes through the Promotion department and out to the marketplace in the form of sales brochures and advertisements. You've probably seen ads for newspapers that are aimed at attracting new readers or advertisers. The Research department often plays a part in developing ideas and information for these materials.

One of the benefits of working in a full-service newspaper Research department is the broad contact that it can provide throughout the company. Very few people in the organization can build as broad a network of contacts or as wide a range of knowledge about the newspaper business as the researcher.

HOW AND WHERE TO START

College graduates seeking to develop a professional career in research usually begin as **research assistants** or **statisticians** and move up to the rank of **research analyst** or **research associate**. Someone who combines analytical skills with communication skills can develop a career writing and making research-based sales presentations. Some departments hire **data processing specialists,** although computers have become so pervasive in the field that everyone interested in newspaper research would be advised to develop computer skills.

Prior to college graduation, it is often possible to find clerical jobs in Research departments. Many departments conduct their own surveys and offer frequent opportunities for part-time work as **interviewers**. Both jobs offer a good introduction to the work of the department and a way to get a foot in the door.

But make no mistake: Research is a knowledge business, and solid, relevant academic preparation is essential for rapid advancement. Course work in the social sciences—particularly sociology, political science and economics—business courses—particularly in marketing and advertising—and journalism and communications courses are all helpful. Advanced degrees are valued, as is direct experience with research methodology, statistics and programming. Working in the news or business departments of your school paper can provide valuable insight. A broad knowledge of newspapers is more important to the researcher than to most others in the industry.

Internships are available in a few places, but because they are small, most Research departments can't afford to carry unskilled trainees who ask a lot of questions. Someone with a needed skill to trade on—interviewing or computer programming, for example—will find a better reception than a novice. Internships in other departments of the newspaper can provide valuable experience for the researcher, as well.

THE DAILY BUSINESS OF NEWSPAPER RESEARCH

Because they publish every day, newspapers tend to be very deadline-oriented places, and this leads to a "do it quick" style of operations, even in research. But accuracy and credibility are essential to a communications company, so "do it right" is also the rule.

A new employee in research can expect to spend most of the time assembling data—from the computer, the files, the library—into reports. When they are not compiling reports, researchers are usually answering questions about the data, frequently over the phone. Ad salespeople, reporters, managers and clients all call or visit fairly regularly.

Because of the breadth of territory covered by research—on the market, the media, the audience, the consumer—there is a lot to tell...and a lot to learn. Few research organizations can match the volume and variety of output a good newspaper Research department generates.

Advancement in research is directly related to the research skills and newspaper knowledge of the employee and the rate at which these qualities develop. The eclectic, inquisitive, flexible thinker can move up the ladder pretty quickly. The plodder can run in place for years. Two other criteria for advancement: a strong sense of precision (an orientation to detail and a commitment to accuracy) and an instinct for analysis (finding stories in numbers that other people don't see). Without those, the flexible thinker is just sloppy and shallow.

At the larger metropolitan newspapers, salaries start around $20,000 for recent graduates with good preparation and potential. Smaller papers in smaller cities pay less. Normal progression would mean yearly raises in the 4-6% range, depending on inflation. Promotions can result in significant jumps, with the most qualified and senior staffers earning well over twice the income of new recruits. The higher salaries usually involve the management of staff and budget and broad responsibility for research projects.

Some researchers move into advertising sales or circulation management and make good use of their accumulated knowledge in those areas. But it is more common to see them move up the ladder through marketing, becoming more involved in newspaper promotion, public relations and strategic planning.

For the person whose career commitment is to research, rather than to newspapers, the experience of working in a good newspaper research operation is among the best preparations available anywhere. With the variety and volume of work they produce, newspapers offer a crash course in applied research.

THE IDEAL CANDIDATE

Researchers who are good with numbers can open up new worlds of information to many reporters, salespeople and managers, many of whom are *not* good with numbers. That's the thing most research managers seek—candidates who see stories in numbers and are enthusiastic about sharing those stories with others.

If you can do that, you may have your own key to the vault.

JAMES E. SMITH

Jim Smith heads a ten-person department that engages in the full spectrum of newspaper research. The *News/Sun-Sentinel* is Florida's fastest-growing major daily newspaper.

Mr. Smith, 42, began his association with newspapers at McGill University, where he worked as a sports writer, columnist and news editor of the *McGill Daily*. He received his Bachelors degree in sociology from the State University of New York at Binghampton. He has a Masters degree and a Ph.D. from Cornell University, where he majored in demography and urban planning.

He taught population, urban studies and research courses at the University of Miami in the 1970s, before joining the *News/Sun Sentinel* in 1980.

He is a director of the Newspaper Research Council, chairman of its publications committee and a frequent contributor to its programs. He is a member of the newspaper industry's Future of Advertising Task Force on Marketing and Data and a contributor to the Florida Newspaper Poll and the Florida Newspaper Network.

CHAPTER TWENTY ONE

Selling Advertising In Newspapers: An Exciting Career

By

**William V. Shannon, (Former) Senior Vice President
Gannett National Newspaper Sales
Gannett Company**

The opportunity and the experience of selling national, retail, classified, and co-op advertising for newspapers is most rewarding. Each form of newspaper advertising is different, but the end result—serving the advertiser—is the same.

The next four chapters in this section cover the major areas of newspaper advertising sales—at both large and small newspapers—in great detail. So this chapter will serve as an overview of each of the specialties within the overall advertising sales function—national, retail, classified and co-op advertising sales.

Selling National Accounts

A space salesperson selling national accounts will be representing the newspaper to major advertisers (manufacturers and service companies) and their advertising agencies. This requires the personal skills that enable the salesperson to deal with a wide variety of different personality types. Experience in dealing with people is important; while few school courses can provide this experience, summer job selling would be helpful to the aspiring national accounts salesperson (or, for that matter, *any* salesperson).

It is important that the newspaper salesperson understands the advertiser's needs in terms of audience, marketing plans, and sales goals. This helps him or her present the newspaper's marketing story to the advertiser in a presentation "custom-tailored" to that advertiser's needs and wants.

Today's high cost of media has forced advertisers to target their markets and prospects. The media salesperson who can best meet these goals will get the business. National advertising is generally placed through advertising agencies. Thus, there is a need to sell both the client and the agency.

Selling Retail Accounts

Retail selling is different because advertising decisions are more often made by the local business operator, not an ad agency. National retailers (Sears, J.C. Penney, etc.), however, are beginning to control advertising decisions from the home office of the company. Advertising rates for local advertisers are lower than national rates; many local advertisers sign volume or frequency contracts to earn even lower rates. Retailers advertise a]most every week.

Retailers promote special sales with limited time price reductions on special merchandise to draw shoppers into their stores. They need the immediate sales results that newspapers can deliver. Most retailers will use "price" advertising (sales, bargains, etc.), which are specifically oriented to immediate sales, rather than longer-term "image" advertising.

As shopping malls and strip shopping centers continue to proliferate, newspaper salespeople may group together several smaller retailers into a single promotion to build traffic for the entire mall or center.

There are many types of special promotions that newspaper salespeople can use to sell retail advertising. The excitement in selling retail is when you develop an infrequent, "small space" newspaper advertiser into a frequent, "large space" one. There is satisfaction in seeing the store expand as a result of the advertiser's use of newspaper advertising.

Sales experience with a variety of sales calls is the best way to prepare for a career in retail newspaper selling.

Selling Classified Accounts

Classified newspaper selling is different than both national and retail selling. In classified, the salesperson is dealing with less sophisticated advertisers. They have a service or item they want to sell to a buyer in a very narrow audience, a buyer best reached via a specific listing on the classified page.

Much of the person-to-person classified business is telephoned in to the newspaper. The service business must be sold on a continuing basis; a good source for this type of business is the Yellow Pages or weekly newspapers. As a newspaper salesperson calling on small businesses, you will show your customer how well your newspaper reaches his potential customer and why your readers turn to the classified pages when they're looking for special items or in need of service.

In classified newspaper selling, there are inside and outside salespeople. The inside salesperson, using leads, will telephone customers and complete the sale over the telephone. The outside salesperson will have a territory and travel to the small service companies and retailers selling the advantages of a regular, small space advertising program in the newspaper. If their classified program is successful, some of these advertisers will become retail advertisers and sign a contract.

Selling Co-op Advertising

The selling of co-op advertising is different than the previous three we have discussed. Co-op advertising is a combination of national and retail advertising. The manufacturer of the product contributes advertising dollars to an advertising program; the local retailer must contribute a proportionate amount before the ads can be sold.

The newspaper co-op salesperson investigates brand name merchandise that is sold by the retailer and then checks with a co-op information company about available company co-op programs. Depending on the plan and accruals earned by the retailer, the salesperson can return to the store with a proposal for a newspaper advertising program.

Skills Required For All Selling

As is evident in our discussion of each type of advertising sales, knowing your customers' needs is a must. The more interest you demonstrate in your advertisers' success, the more encouraged they will be to buy your newspaper advertising program.

And, of course, you must know your own product—the newspaper. Understanding the news, circulation, promotion, research, production and business operations at your own newspaper is important.

Courses in marketing, psychology, and business methods are important and will help you to become a better newspaper salesperson. Simple accounting is also needed because you will be working with rate cards that have costs and various levels of inch space volume contracts. A smart salesperson will try to move each of his accounts to a higher level of activity.

Many newspapers have summer or school-year internship programs that will give you a head start on your newspaper sales career. With the proper marketing courses or a possible internship that will give you the initial experience you need, you will be on your way after graduation to a very fulfilling career in selling advertising space in newspapers.

Your Future In Advertising Sales

Opportunities today for newspaper advertising salespeople are better than ever. There are several chain or newspaper groups that offer good training, experience and opportunities for advancement—Times Mirror, Gannett, Knight-Ridder, Hearst, Newhouse and Ingersoll, among others. There are also many smaller groups that offer excellent opportunities.

Newspaper salespeople are paid on the basis of salary and commission—the total compensation percentage of commission and salary varies from newspaper to newspaper. Commission is important because it rewards the better newspaper salespeople and is the stimulant some people need to get really motivated.

Advancement to district sales manager or national, retail, classified or co-op manager are all possible at any newspaper. Today, many advertising salespeople have advanced to senior marketing vice presidents, general managers and publishers of newspapers. If the person is in a newspaper company that owns other newspapers, the opportunity to advance by moving from a smaller market to a major newspaper market exists.

Should you decide to leave the newspaper industry, you can consider moving on to broadcast time selling, outdoor media selling, direct response or magazines sales. Whatever you learn as a newspaper salesperson will be of value to you throughout your career, wherever it takes you.

WILLIAM V. SHANNON

The Gannett Company's National Newspaper Sales Division handles the advertising sales function for 90 newspapers in the company's newspaper division. In addition to his former responsibilities as senior vice president of that division, Mr. Shannon was immediate past-president of the Newspaper Advertising Sales Association (NASA) and served on the board of the International Newspaper Advertising Marketing Executives Association (INAME).

Previously, he owned his own newspaper representative firm and was a senior and executive vice president of two other major newspaper representative companies. In 1976, he joined the Gannett Company as president of their in-house newspaper sales company—today called Gannett National Newspaper Sales.

Since his graduation from Lake Forest College, where he served on the board of trustees, his entire business career was spent selling advertising for newspapers.

WE NOTE WITH SADNESS MR. SHANNON'S PASSING IN 1987

CHAPTER TWENTY TWO

A Bright Future In Classified Ad Sales

By

James T. Conner, Classified Advertising Manager
Baton Rouge (LA.) Morning Advocate and State-Times

There *is* a bright future in newspaper classified advertising sales! Classifieds are no longer just the little ads in the back of the paper. In many newspapers, classified advertising represents anywhere from one third to one half of the newspapers' total advertising revenue. This means increased job openings in telephone sales and in outside sales and more opportunities to advance into upper management.

Besides the small line ads—"want ads," as they were called for many years—most classified advertising sections now include classified display advertising, which adds a whole new dimension; much more creativity is possible with artwork, illustrations, fancy borders, etc. Also, many newspapers have their classified advertising departments selling special sections of automotive, real estate, apartment living, careers, and other ads.

Classified advertising departments are typically divided into two parts: telephone sales and outside sales. Since each is unique in its job description and requirements, I will take them separately and then tie them together before we finish, so you can see how they all fit together to make a successful classified advertising department and an opportunity for a good future for you.

GETTING STARTED IN TELEPHONE SALES

Many of the telephone salespeople at our newspaper started with us when they were seniors in high school, by participating in the Cooperative Office Education program. They went to school in the morning, taking primarily typing and office courses. In the afternoon, they worked part-time with us, learning to be telephone sales people. Then, when they graduated, we hired them full-time (in most cases). Many of them are still working with us after many years, some in other departments, some still in classified. We also have hired quite a few office administration majors from local universities; they have made particularly good employees.

For many years, the main requirement in classified advertising departments was typing —50 words per minute or better. Since telephone salespeople take ads from customers over the telephone on an electric typewriter or a video display terminal, it is fairly obvious why the ability to type rapidly and accurately has been (and continues to be) so important. Being a good speller is also very helpful. Most of the time, whatever you type is exactly what will appear in the paper, so it must be correct.

The advent of the computer has had a tremendous impact on most newspapers, and our department is no exception. Prior to the computer, most people in the phone area were called "ad-takers" or "ad-visors." Now, they are called telephone salespeople, and they are encouraged to be just that. With a video display terminal, selling is a breeze, because you can so easily add words, delete words, add white space, make words larger, or whatever.

With selling now being such a large part of job performance, selling skills have become a prerequisite for employment. A pleasant voice, good diction, and the ability to get along with the public are necessary requirements. I feel that a basic desire to help people is useful, too, because that certainly is what you do in classified—help find a lost dog, sell a car, rent an apartment, find a job, etc. If you enjoy what you are doing, it will come across to the customer and make you a much better salesperson.

Classified telephone salespeople handle both ads that are called in by individuals and regular accounts—employment agencies, real estate firms, antique dealers, used car lots, etc.— that run ads on a regular basis. Salespeople are often required to call out and solicit ads,too.

Telephone salespeople also handle classified display ads, which gives them chances to use their creativity in visualizing what an ad should look like to achieve the best possible results for the customer. Our telephone salespeople can handle anything from a three-line ad to a full page, four-color ad.

Compensation is usually a base salary plus commission. Starting pay might be around $15,000 a year; top pay could be $30,000 or more. There are chances to advance into outside sales, up to supervisory positions, and into management. Most classified telephone salespeople are female, but there are certainly occasions when males can do just as well.

GETTING STARTED IN OUTSIDE SALES

Most outside salespeople in classified are college graduates with a degree in journalism, advertising, or marketing. A college degree is not required, however, and many a fine staff member has come out of the telephone sales area or from another job. Someone just out of high school, however, would probably not have the maturity or experience to handle this type of job.

This job requires ideas—new ideas, old ideas...*any* ideas that will enable you to create an ad that will get good response for your customer. Newspaper classified outside sales is more than just selling space. Much of the time, the customer has already *bought* the space; you must show him how to use it effectively. This means writing an eye-catching headline, using a dominant illustration, and writing some dynamic body copy that will really sell. Some newspapers are even providing their outside staff with portable personal computers so that they can create a customer's ad before their very eyes.

Much of the time you *will* be selling space, though, which means convincing a prospect to use your medium instead of (or, at least, in addition to) another one. You will learn to use market research to assist you in your sales efforts. You'll learn about the mechanical operation of the newspaper so you can answer questions in a responsible manner. You'll learn the sales techniques that will enable you to answer objections and sell the most advertising possible. You'll learn and understand the rate structure of your classified advertising department, so that you can figure the correct rates and suggest to your prospect the best way for him to spend his money.

In outside sales, you are face to face with the account; it's quite different from talking to someone on the telephone. I expect my people to have a good appearance, good manners, and a good disposition. I want each customer to have complete confidence in my salespeople and feel that they are looking out for his or her best interests. If you can convince prospects that the ad you want to sell them is worth more than the money it will cost them, you are a good salesperson.

Starting pay, including commissions, would be around $25,000 per year. My top salesperson last year made over $45,000. There seems to be a trend in the industry to make commissions a larger percentage of the overall pay, with some newspapers going to straight commission.

In most newspapers, outside classified sales pay is equivalent to the retail sales side, so there is no advantage to moving to that department (except to learn more about the overall operation of the newspaper); however, opportunities for advancement into management are certainly there if a person is willing to apply himself and proves to be company-oriented.

MOVING UP TO MANAGEMENT

A classified advertising manager needs to have a good knowledge of both the telephone sales and the outside sales operation. He or she needs to have a complete knowledge of company policy, standards of acceptance, federal and state laws, and the many requirements of running a successful classified advertising department. The main requirement, though, is the ability to meld together a group of people in telephone and outside sales that can bring in sufficient revenue and enjoy doing it!

While it is true that most of the opportunities to move into top management come to the outside sales staff, many telephone salespeople have become classified advertising managers, too, and are doing fine jobs. As in every job, in the final analysis, it is up to the individual!

As the poet, James Whitcomb Riley, said:

> "If you want something, with heart dead set
> A praying for it with both eyes wet,
> And tears won't bring it,
> W'y you try sweat,
> As my uncle used to say."

JAMES T. CONNER

James T. "Jim" Conner graduated from Louisiana State University with a B.S. degree, majoring in marketing and minoring in economics. After a few years with J.C. Penney Co. and selling radio advertising, he joined the Baton Rouge newspapers as a retail advertising salesman. He later transferred to classified advertising as assistant manager, then became the manager in 1974.

He is president of the Association of Newspaper Classified Advertising Managers (ANCAM) and past-president of the Southern Classified Advertising Managers Association (SCAMA).

CHAPTER TWENTY THREE

Getting Started In Retail Ad Sales

By

Alfred Eisenpreis, Senior Vice President
Newspaper Advertising Bureau, Inc.

Newspapers are among the nation's most important and successful industries. Being part of the local newspaper organization is an affiliation of which individual salespeople can well be proud. It is a special kind of work. The salesperson can point to a product used by the overwhelming majority of the community as evidence of what he or she does for a living.

Today, there are more than 1,675 daily newspapers and nearly 800 Sunday newspapers in the U.S. Moreover, 7,711 weekly papers and 3,000 free distribution papers that include shopping news are published. Each depends, in a very important way, on advertising from local, regional and national retailers. Retailers account for more than one half of all newspaper advertising revenue, so retail selling is an important function in the newspaper business. And retail sales opportunities exist wherever there is a newspaper.

While the type and size of these thousands of newspapers vary widely, a high level of technology use is characteristic of the total industry. During the past decade, newspapers have invested billions of dollars in new presses, computerization, and color printing facilities, making the daily newspaper America's most modern advertising medium (in addition to its being the oldest). Owners of newspapers appear committed to making additional capital expendi-tures in future years. Therefore, those who consider working in the newspaper industry can look forward to being part of an essential growth industry of great national importance.

While computerization in the manufacture of the newspaper has led to personnel reductions in production areas, the number of retail selling positions is likely to increase. Also, there are many opportunities for individual growth to senior selling assignments involving the newspaper's most important customers (key accounts) and to supervisory and management levels.

WHAT DOES THE RETAIL SALESPERSON DO?

The retail salesperson works with individual retail companies in two ways: (1) by helping the advertiser select the appropriate medium and specific newspaper product in which to advertise merchandise or services; and (2) by presenting sales recommendations and ideas to individual retail accounts for the goods and services they offer.

In today's multi-media environment, retail advertising is rarely placed at the retailer's initiative alone. Advertising space must be sold. Once an advertiser has decided to use the newspaper as his only advertising medium, or as one of the ingredients in a multi-media mix, the newspaper choice must be reinforced; therefore, retail accounts must be sold and re-sold on a continuing basis.

And retail accounts must be serviced, because retail advertising involves a considerable amount of detail work. A newspaper is a complicated and highly technical product, manufactured at rapid speed and in huge quantities, to an exacting standard of perfection. Everyone involved with the production of the newspaper or its components must recognize the demand for accurate, high speed work, with great attention to detail and constant appreciation of the value of time. Nothing is as irreparable as failure to have an advertiser's instructions fulfilled on the day and in the way he wanted his ad to appear. Nothing is of as little value as yesterday's newspaper. And the retail salesperson learns quickly that yesterday's successes fade if something important was not done today.

Each retail salesperson is assigned a number of retailer accounts for whom he or she is held responsible and is given specific goals for the annual or monthly use of newspaper space that management expects each account to use. The salesperson's personal rating and compensation depend on how well these goals are met.

The salesperson will spend part of his or her time in the office preparing for sales calls and processing individual ads. However, the actual selling is done on the retailer's premises, so the salesperson must expect to spend a considerable amount of time outside the office.

Many retail salespersons start their newspaper career with a junior selling job; others are promoted from assignments in the classified or telephone sales departments or from other entry-level positions on the newspaper. It is helpful to have had a sales background or to have had experience in some area of retailing; persons who have such a background will be able to serve their retail accounts better because of their familiarity with the activities and objectives of retailing.

WHAT HAPPENS ON THE JOB

Rate of personal progress generally depends on individual performance. The opportunities for finding new accounts or for increasing the amount of newspaper usage by any one account are wide open. In every market, new retailers enter business, existing companies change their operating style, and many retailers can be convinced to change their current media pattern to include more newspaper space. Also, many newspapers intensify their competitive efforts against broadcast and other print media and require additional personnel to sell against competitive media.

Salaries vary widely depending on the size of market, the types and number of accounts, and the amount of creative effort required and put forth by individuals. Compensation for retail salespersons ranges from the low 20s to low 60s; some exceptional retail salespersons can exceed these ranges in situations involving commission compensation plans.

WHAT YOU NEED TO KNOW AND DO TO GET STARTED

Because there is so wide a range of newspapers and advertisers, and because the newspaper industry is dispersed all over the United States, there is no single profile of a newspaper salesperson. Successful salespersons include men and women; whites and Asians, blacks and Hispanics, young and old. However, successful salespeople share an interest in customer needs and are committed to high standards of professional service.

You must have a strong commitment to time management and to the value of time. You should be able to use research material and have an understanding of the principles of marketing. You will work with concepts and numbers; dealing with the latter shouldn't scare you.

Selling is communication: Effective retail sales people must be able and willing to present their newspaper's sales arguments orally and in writing to individual prospects and to groups of various sizes and composition. Skills in public speaking and in report and proposal writing must be developed; it would be helpful to have such skills when you start the job.

A salesperson needs the kind of authority and self-confidence that can be gained through leadership skills in voluntary or other organizations, so evidence of such skills is generally considered helpful.

A college degree will be required by many newspaper organizations, especially if you have no previous business experience. In individual cases—if you have a record of selling experience or other business associations which would be helpful—the requirement for a college degree may be waived.

If you are interested in entering the newspaper business by way of the retail selling route, make an effort to take courses in marketing, business planning, and advertising. You may find some general journalism courses valuable—they will give you a better understanding of the principles by which the news/editorial side of newspapers operate. You should also take courses in retail management, retail marketing and fashion marketing, and courses in general statistics, market research, and surveys.

The availability of internships is governed by local conditions and the current state of the economy. Except in those cases where a newspaper has decided to employ the candidate on a full-time basis upon graduation, assignment of interns to selling positions may be difficult; such internships may be in other areas within the newspaper. However, prospective newspaper retail salespersons might find summer or part-time employment in retail stores to be a useful asset.

Because the salesperson will be responsible for a considerable number of accounts, use of a car is necessary. In addition to the academic and technical qualifications discussed above, employers of retail salespersons look for a sense of positive energy and for evidence of interest in and aptitude for selling ideas and space to managers and owners of retail companies.

Retail selling in newspapers is a demanding occupation, requiring dedication both in terms of hours spent on the job and the follow-through necessary to ensure that advertisers' requests are filled exactly and the newspaper's requirements adhered to. Those who bring such interest to their accounts will find rewards in addition to monetary compensation—the increasing influence they have on their accounts and the deepening relationships they establish with many of their markets' important business firms. Of course, still another form of reward is found in the promotion to supervisory and management posts that frequently come to those who have established their initial record of accomplishment as retail newspaper salespeople.

ALFRED EISENPREIS

The Newspaper Advertising Bureau Inc. was founded in 1913 and serves its approximately 1,000 daily newspaper members in the areas of retail, national and classified sales by providing direction, guidance, and selling tools and by establishing a selling liaison with major national firms and the agencies that serve them. The NAB also provides support in the areas of research, creative activities, sales training, and marketing. It operates offices in New York City, Atlanta, Detroit, Chicago, Los Angeles and San Francisco.

Mr. Eisenpreis is responsible for the direction of the Bureau's services to the retail industry. He was a senior executive of the Allied Stores Corporation and served as that firm's vice president for research, planning, public relations and marketing from 1963 to 1974. From 1974 through 1976, Mr. Eisenpreis was the Economic Commissioner of the City of New York. He joined the NAB in 1976.

Mr. Eisenpreis served as chairman of the National Management Council on Marketing Education for six years, was a member of the faculty of the Graduate School for Management and Urban Professions at the New School in New York for eight years, and is the author of Retail Marketing for Newspapers. He has lectured extensively throughout the U.S., in Europe and the South Pacific on business and newspaper issues and is a regular contributor to industry magazines in the retail and advertising fields.

CHAPTER TWENTY FOUR

Moving Into National Account Sales

By

Larry Letters, General Advertising Manager
Los Angeles Times

National account sales is an interesting, rewarding and important area of newspaper publishing, one I would certainly encourage you to consider. This article is an attempt to give you a better understanding of just what such sales involve, the kind of skills you need, and my best recommendations for getting started. Since I have spent my entire, almost-30 year newspaper career with the *Times*, most of this chapter will discuss the way *we* do things. But I will also note whether a particular setup, practice or title is substantially different than at other major U.S. dailies.

The national advertising division of the *Los Angeles Times* accounts for a larger percent of revenue dollars than at most U.S. daily newspapers. In spite of newspapers' decreasing share of national advertising, the *Times* has maintained a fairly even share of national account revenue as a percent of its total revenues. I believe we have accomplished this by selecting our personnel with an eye toward their future development.

Our management team in display advertising has been developed from within our own ranks. Every manager in display started at the *Times* and has moved up to more responsible sales positions.

I believe that's how we've kept our best personnel over a span of twenty to thirty years. Nothing can be more devastating to young people entering newspaper account sales than to witness jobs in management going to persons hired from outside organizations.

The *Times* Display Advertising department is made up of the following sales divisions (the numbers underneath indicate salespeople in each area):

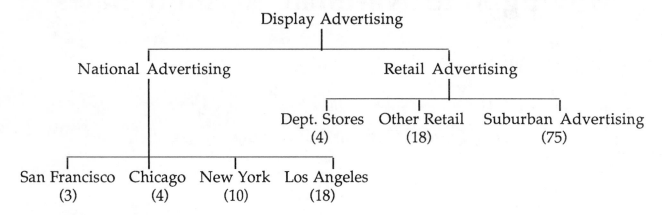

In order to manage these divisions, we have about 22 line managers, five administrative assistants, and another ten managers in staff support positions. We have about 150 sales people in account sales, 35 of whom are in national sales.

To gain a better perspective, let's take a closer look at the national division and add its national representatives to the picture painted by the previous chart:

*Million Market Newspapers/Times Mirror National Marketing offices

Unlike most daily newspapers, the *Times* does not use national representatives in the U.S. (except in Michigan and Ohio for *Los Angeles Times Magazine*, primarily for sales of the magazine to Detroit auto manufacturers).

MMN/TMN offices in Miami, Dallas, and Detroit are owned by the *Los Angeles Times* parent company, Times Mirror. Our 22 international representatives are independent agents who are paid a commission based on actual space sold (and paid for!). These include offices in Mexico, England, Japan, Germany, and other major countries throughout the world.

As I mentioned previously, we employ our own people in our U.S. offices—New York, Chicago and San Francisco. Each of these offices maintains personal and written contact with advertising agencies and clients within their assigned states. These offices cover the entire U.S. (except for the area that Los Angeles headquarters is responsible for—Southern California, Southern Nevada, Arizona, New Mexico, Utah, Colorado and Texas).

Unlike other national divisions of U.S. newspapers, we use our sales staff in category assignments—Foods & Liquor, Automotive, Travel, Financial, Computers and Hi-Tech, Appliances, Trade & Media, and Miscellaneous.

We find that a division by category permits each member of our sales staff to become an expert in a single field. This results in their ability to present more meaningful information and make more professional sales calls. In today's competitive business climate, more and more media reps are criticized for not being knowledgeable enough about an agency's or client's business. (Most radio, television, or magazine reps are assigned an agency list, then handle all business emanating from those assigned agencies. My feeling is that it's difficult, if not impossible, to be equally knowledgeable about computers, hospitals, food, automotive, financial, political and all the other types of accounts a single agency may represent.)

To the casual observer, the *Los Angeles Times* seems to have the Southern California advertising business pretty much to itself. We've led the market in total advertising linage since 1955; our classified section is the *worldwide* leader in number of advertisements sold annually. While our numbers are impressive—L.A. is the nation's No. 1 market in retail sales, automotive sales and apparel—we are also No. 1 in *media and entertainment*. No other market in the world is as fractionalized as ours. Anyone wishing to get into national account sales at the *Los Angeles Times* will be competing for advertising dollars with:

2 Metropolitan newspapers

15 Community daily newspapers

79 Radio stations

12 Commercial and 3 non-commercial television stations

28 Cable television companies

300+ Weekly & "throwaway" newspapers

100 National magazines

The nation's largest outdoor advertising systems

Almost $2 billion going into direct mail

Succeeding in this ultra-competitive environment requires creativity, a knowledge of competing media, a thorough understanding of market research and its application, good communication skills (written & verbal), a willingness to travel, making a minimum of five sales calls per day, being well organized, and spending countless hours of your own time in planning, developing presentations, and goal setting.

SKILLS NEEDED TO SUCCEED IN NATIONAL ACCOUNT SALES

Creativity

"Having the power of being creative or productive" is the way *Webster's* defines the word. In our business, "productive" is the key word. This may be an old idea that produces new business, or a brand new one. It requires a salesperson to visualize something that hasn't been seen by others. It is embodied in the expression *"nothing* happens until someone *sells* something;" that selling process today requires a creative approach. After all, there isn't much that is created today that hasn't been previously discovered.

An excellent example of this creative approach is a recent sale made by one of our national account sales reps. There are 79 radio stations in Los Angeles; their formats are constantly changing, as each continually tries to devise an approach that will give them a greater share of the market. We have wanted to publish a section on "What's New in L.A. Radio" in our Sunday Calendar section (a weekly tabloid averaging 100 or more pages a week) for some time. Since, unlike TV commentators, radio personalities are heard but not seen, what better way to enhance their image than in this section with a potential readership of over 3 million readers?.

The visualization of this rationale—the idea of one of our national sales managers—is the creative aspect of the sales strategy. Our media rep, Ken Pelton, liked the idea; in the December 14, 1986, issue he sold five pages, representing some $100,000 of new business, to a dozen local radio stations. We now believe that this feature can be sold at least quarterly in 1987.

Scotty Croll, who has been with us for 30 years, saw the need for a "New Food Products Section" in our Thursday food pages. He recognized that over 2,500 new food products enter our market each year; their successful introduction requires the promotional support newspaper advertising can offer. But the L.A. food brokers were unable to afford the tremendous investment such promotion requires. Scotty developed an "advertorial" approach: For every 1/4-page ad purchased, we would allow the broker an additional 1/4 page of "free" editorial space to talk about the product. During 1986, we published over 60 pages of "New Food Products," over $1 million in new business.

We may then say that CREATIVITY is identifying a need, coming up with the idea that meets it, and, then, selling it! I don't know whether creativity is a learned or innate skill. I *do* know, however, that it is a most important attribute for any sales field one chooses to enter.

Knowledge Of Competing Media

Advertising dollars are finite. If a national advertiser wishes to cover Los Angeles, there are numerous options...and they are all going to be very expensive. But once that advertiser decides to cover that market and chooses the media to do so, that money is no longer potential revenues for the media left out of the plan. So a national account salesperson must be familiar with how all other media are sold and bought.

Marketing Research

The *Times* Marketing Research department is probably the industry's largest. It is staffed by over 50 people and produces research on virtually every aspect of Southern California business.

A *Times* national account salesperson must be familiar with all available research, including not only demographic studies, but also psychographic lifestyles (VALS) and Prizm. Our readership measurements are based on SIMMONS-SCARBOROUGH; each account salesperson is extensively trained in its use and implementation.

Admittedly, some salespeople find it difficult to use statistics; and there are many good salespeople who are *not* statistically oriented. I would not say that it is a requirement for us—but it behooves everyone in our sales organization to hone their skills in this area.

Good Communication Skills

Our best salespeople—and those who are able to move into management the quickest—have good verbal and written communication skills. These are the skills that companies in other industries are seeking in their personnel, as well. With average U.S. TV viewing time approaching eight hours per day per household, it's no wonder that the communication skills of entry-level people are at a low ebb!

Without such skills, though, it is difficult for an entry-level salesperson to quickly move up the ladder of success in national account sales. I would have to rank this skill as the Number One attribute we seek in our people.

Travel

Two of our advertising categories—Automotive and Travel—require salespeople to be on the road up to 30 days a year. Other salespeople may be away for short stays, attending conventions or industry meetings.

Making Sales Calls

It takes a personal sales call to sell a new idea, to present our company's strategy, to meet a client's needs, and to make certain we are getting our share of an advertising expenditure. One cannot accomplish these goals with a telephone call, which is often intrusive; it has to be done by appointment. And we believe an average of four to five such sales calls should be made every day.

I believe that the Gannett Company's Media Sales Call Reminder is an excellent tool. We have not formulated a printed version of ours, so I am, therefore, reproducing Gannett's plan (with which we agree in principle):

- *Specific Personalized Proposals:* Make it look custom. Use the advertiser's name throughout printed material. Show how important his business is to you.

- *Spec Layouts:* Keep them loose. Involve the advertiser.

- *Maps:* Match your coverage with their distribution or trading areas.

- *Market Research:* Simmons, Scarborough, etc., or a local study.

- *Product Sample:* <u>Always</u> have your paper with you.

- *Cost Estimates or Proposal:* Not just a rate card.

- *Media Efficiency:* Talk the language; use CPMs, reach and frequency comparisons to other media or competition when appropriate. (CAREFUL! Sell <u>your</u> product. Don't fall into the "bang the other guy" trap. You could shoot yourself in the foot!)

- *Demo Matching:* Know your strengths and play them. Index audiences and show how the advertiser's product fits.

An individual who operates on an 8:30 to 5:30 work schedule in national sales at the *Times* will most likely not be able to progress very far. It is difficult to imagine a salesperson moving up the ladder without spending a good deal of his or her own time keeping abreast of the local advertising business via the advertising trade press and reading books on advertising, sales and management. It requires a continuous program of self improvement—a lifelong process.

Over the years, each of our salespeople has attended (1) Investment in Excellence (3-day seminar); 2) the Dale Carnegie course (3 days); and 3) numerous "motivational" films.

Each month our Marketing Research department has a one-day refresher update that any salesperson may attend.

The *Times* is a goal-oriented sales organization. It starts each summer in our department budgeting process for the following calendar year. Each division—retail, department stores, suburban and national—projects their advertising volume, based on individual input from each salesperson. Out-of-business accounts, mergers, economic forecasts on inflation, and the state of the economy are evaluated to determine their impact on projections. During the course of the year, each salesperson is asked to submit projections of his or her territory each month. It is incumbent upon each salesperson to know his or her advertisers and their advertising plans for the month and quarter ahead.

Our best salespeople are also our most accurate budgeters.

SO HOW DO YOU BREAK IN?

Where do we obtain people who are so creative, self-starting, motivated, etc.? We select sales candidates based not only on good communication skills, but also on past advertising experience. Sales personnel who move to national accounts from another sales division are evaluated on the basis of their achievements in that division.

We would like to see all of our national salespeople begin in suburban sales. A three-year stint there is ideal. The achievers are then promoted to our retail division for another two years of experience. After five years, they should be ready for national account sales.

We have a sales trainee program in which we select promising college graduates to work in clerical positions. They may be assigned to our suburban, retail or national divisions. Current assignments, for example, are in travel, entertainment, retail restaurants, telemarketing, and in our Orange County edition and Westside zone. In all, we have about a dozen sales trainees. They will serve an apprenticeship of approximately a year, after which they will be assigned minor sales positions in one of our seven suburban zones.

Starting pay for a sales trainee is $437 per week. After he or she has been assigned a sales position, a salesperson can expect to make about $475 per week in salary, with the possibility of making up to 35% of that salary in additional bonuses that are paid monthly. After a year in a territory, a salesperson could be making $524.50 per week. Salespeople can also qualify for a new company automobile if their weekly business mileage exceeds 200 miles. (The salesperson pays a minimum of $15 per week for personal use of the auto; the company pays for all fuel, maintenance, insurance, etc.)

With five years of work experience, a sales trainee can be expected to make up to $35,000 a year in base salary and another $6,000 - $8,000 in bonuses.

Some major newspaper companies in the U.S. have slightly different programs for account salespeople. The *Chicago Tribune* has qualified sales candidates spend a year in their Marketing Research department. *The New York Times* starts its candidates in telephone classified sales. Each of these programs, and other like them, has a great deal of merit and provides the necessary learning process for entry-level salespeople.

Two of the 17 salespeople on our national staff in Los Angeles started as sales trainees. We operate in the belief that the salespeople in our New York, Chicago and San Francisco offices should also have Los Angeles sales experience. Therefore, anyone selected for these offices is paid a higher base salary—a minimum of $700 per week. Account sales people in our outside offices are expected to travel and it is extensive—often as much as 60 days annually. This experience may lead to relocation back to Los Angeles in a managerial position or to a supervisory position in these offices.

For a college graduate looking for an entry-level sales position in the advertising business, a most important attribute is work experience—selling Yellow Page Directories, small shopper newspapers, Pennysaver-type media, etc. This experience will better your chances for acceptance by larger media companies such as the *Los Angeles Times*.

To be selected for our sales trainee program, a college degree is necessary. We have no requirement as to its type—some of our most successful salespeople have teaching certificates.

Courses that are most helpful are: English and business writing, psychology and philosophy, mathematics and statistics, marketing research, economics and finance, public speaking, communications of print, advertising and marketing.

What do we look for in our selection process of sales candidates? In order of importance, I would list:

• Communication skills—verbal and written.

• Grooming—in sync with accepted business practice. One does not call on a vice president of a $100 million company in casual wear. We expect suits and ties for men, business suits or dresses for women.

• Ability to quickly assimilate complex technical knowledge about:

— *Los Angeles Times* policy;
— Marketing research on media and the Southern California market and it's proper implementation
— Customer contact

• Their "on-the-job" training experience will reveal to us other important attributes. Is he or she:

— Creative?
— A self starter?
— Easily motivated?
— Curious?

— Outgoing or introverted?

— Ready (and able) to accept responsibility?

— A "team" player?

— Punctual?

— Organized?

— Able to close a sale?

A career in advertising sales will prove to be a most rewarding lifelong endeavor. It is a business that is challenging, interesting, and ever-changing. Those who are the most successful —if we measure success in terms of earning power—will find that they must be on a continual program of self improvement, steadily increasing their knowledge of the advertising profession and their ability to communicate this experience to others. Those of you who succeed will find yourselves in the top 10% of the nation's income earners!

GOOD LUCK AND GOOD SELLING!

LARRY LETTERS

Mr. Letters started at the *Los Angeles Times* as a trainee in national classified ad sales in 1959. In 1968, he moved to the San Francisco office as an account executive; he later held the same title in the New York and Chicago offices. He became Eastern sales manager in 1978, national sales manager in 1984, and general advertising manager in 1985.

In his current position, he is responsible for all areas of national and international advertising, supervising all U.S. offices and representatives and 27 international reps.

Mr. Letters attended New York University, Fairfield University, and the Columbia Sales Management Program in their Graduate School of Business.

CHAPTER TWENTY FIVE

Advertising Sales For A Smaller Paper

By

John M. Greklek,, Marketing Manager
The Daily Freeman (Kingston, NY)

Newspapers are the nation's number one information medium. In greater detail than radio or television can deliver, newspapers provide readers with news of the events that shape their daily lives. This is particularly true of small newspapers—those serving small towns across the country.

A good local newspaper's news staff has a strong feeling for those things that most concern its community; the staff does its best to reflect those concerns through the news stories it reports. In each community it serves, the local newspaper has developed a flavor or character that stimulates reader interest, urging them to buy the newspaper each publication day.

The Advertising department is an essential ingredient in any newspaper's company structure. Along with the Circulation department, which physically distributes and "sells" the paper, it is the key revenue producer financing the operation of the whole company. From circulation and advertising sales come the dollars that pay for salaries, supplies and all those other necessities that keep the paper going.

Each department in a newspaper has a staff manager who's responsible for both the quality of work produced and the completion of that work within an established time frame. If one department fails to meet its time objective, it could cause delays in other areas; serious enough delays may cause the printing of the paper to be late. This is a serious consequence to small town newspaper readers, who expect "their" newspaper to be at the newsstands or delivered to their homes at the customary time. They accept no excuses.

WHAT YOU'LL BE DOING IN AD SALES FOR A SMALL PAPER

A newspaper advertising sales representative usually is responsible for servicing a specified group of accounts, categorized either by area —Uptown, Shopping Mall, etc.—or by type of business—Automotive, Theatre, Real Estate, etc. The paper's representative will sell advertising space in both the regular pages of the paper and in special feature sections that relate directly to the advertiser's business.

At small newspapers, most of the advertising selling is directed to local merchants, so long distance traveling is not required. Each ad sales representative typically visits a fixed number of accounts each day, depending on what part of the week the accounts are accustomed to advertising. All ads must be submitted by each day's deadline in order to make a particular issue. A lot of small papers don't have a separate Layout or Graphics department, so you may be required to do some of your own layout work.

It's not as difficult as it may sound, even if you're not artistic. You'll most likely have at your disposal some clip art service books from which you can cut out appropriate artwork or even fully completed ads for a particular category. All you'll have to do is specify to the typesetter and composing department where the customer's logo should be placed and submit new body copy with item prices to be typeset. If you have an opportunity either at school or through some work experience to learn a little about ad layout, it will obviously help you a lot later.

When a customer gives you the body copy for an ad, you must at least be able to figure out how much space that copy and the specified pictures or illustrations might occupy. If the allotted space is too small, you need to either recommend a change in the ad content or an increase in ad size. Your account, after all, will expect results—more customers—from his ad. An ad that's too crowded is difficult to read and may be overlooked. Showing that merchant how to bring in more customers is what your job is really all about. So you need to know enough about advertising and its many facets—copywriting, design, layout, etc.—to counsel your accounts.

If you can't get any experience in ad layout in school or at another job, try this: Go through a newspaper and pick out some ads you like. Start with the smaller ads first. Lay a piece of tracing paper over the ad. Trace around the artwork and headline, plus any other bold face copy within the ad. Draw a straight line through each line of the body copy. Lift off the tracing and behold: your first ad layout.

Now, refer back to the newspaper page. What first attracted your eye to that ad? Was it the headline, a price, the artwork? How does it appear on your tracing? If you practice enough, you're on your way to understanding the relationship between well-written copy, clean layout, and good design and gaining a good feel for spatial relationships in ads.

Organizing your sales activities is essential to do an efficient job. You need to plan ahead for each day's sales calls. With proper organization, you can expand your call list, adding new accounts each week. You'll need to increase not only the *quantity* of calls, but their quality, too, by continually coming up with new ideas, concepts, layouts, etc., and by learning more about your product—the newspaper—so you can more effectively sell the benefits of advertising in it. A school course in marketing and advertising would help you attain some of these basic skills.

Since most newspapers pay a commission on sales or a combination of salary plus commission, your pay is directly proportional to how well you do the job of "needs satisfaction selling." Beginning sales incomes range from $15,000 to $20,000 and can ultimately reach $40,000 to $60,000 or more in a very short time.

HOW TO PREPARE FOR A CAREER IN AD SALES

If you're not already a regular newspaper reader, become one. Read your own local paper and others so you can make some comparisons.

Write or, even better, visit your local newspaper. Meet the sales representatives and the advertising sales manager. You'll find most newspaper salespeople *like* to talk about what they do. To become more familiar with their particular operation, ask for a copy of the advertising rate schedule. Have them show you what a typical newspaper ad size is and what it would cost to place that particular ad in the paper. Ask for some of the marketing materials that describe the number of households the paper reaches and the demographics of those households. Learn what's special about that newspaper.

Ask for a tour of the newspaper plant. You'll be able to follow the process of coordinating the sale and design of advertising, the development and production of news copy, the composition of set pages, platemaking, and the ultimate distribution of the printed end product. You'll come away with an appreciation for newspaper publishing far greater than you'd receive from the best written description. Learning about what's special about newspapers will help you understand what's special about working for one.

While you're still in school, get a summer job in sales. Learn basic sales skills—when you land that entry-level newspaper position, you'll be five steps ahead of everyone else.

Although the situation is changing of late, most small newspapers don't have either a high powered or systematic sales training program for their staffs, so coming to a newspaper with *any* kind of sales experience or training under your belt will certainly help.

You certainly don't need to get that training at another newspaper. Many industries, such as insurance and industrial supplies, have extensive sales training programs. Even over-the-counter retail sales can be a good training ground for ad sales careers.

Have you ever gone to a clothing store to buy a single item and left with all the accessories that go with it? A good salesperson probably made sure you bought those extras and made sure you left the store feeling good about buying them!

That salesperson accomplished a number of things through the sale. As the result of his or her sales experience, the salesperson made more money for the store, increased his own earnings through added commission, and made you a satisfied customer who will most likely return to the store over and over again. He expertly got you to buy what you really needed, and maybe eventually bought anyway—but he got you to buy everything at *his* store. That's what advertising sales is all about—satisfying the needs of a customer who's attempting to bring more customers to his place of business. The service you sell satisfies that need.

A college degree is not absolutely necessary to be successful in the newspaper business, but it will increase your chances for advancement into upper management positions. While you're in school, getting a position on the staff of the school newspaper will give you a taste of what newspapers are about and you'll find out in short order whether or not you're interested in a newspaper career.

Summer or internship jobs are difficult to find at small newspaper ad departments. Most of your education and training will have to be derived from other sources, as I suggested before. But there are other areas of study that would help you as an ad salesperson that I *haven't* mentioned yet—like acting and public speaking. If you're the kind of person who lacks self-confidence, or one unaccustomed to speaking in front of a group or to persons not in your own age bracket, acting and speaking courses will help you turn yourself around. There's an old adage that 90% of "selling" an idea is in its presentation. Think about the times you've been unable to put across an idea you've had, simply because you didn't present it well. Then learn presentation skills—they're essential in any kind of sales position.

WHAT AD MANAGERS ARE LOOKING FOR

Newspaper advertising departments are always looking for talent. Here's what ad department managers look for:

• Sales experience at any other type of job (summer or part-time employment in a retail store, selling door to door, etc.).

• Neat appearance—you have to look good to properly represent the newspaper to customers.

• An extroverted, sociable, confident person—a good salesperson must be in control when making a presentation to his customer.

• A degree in advertising or marketing helps, but may be considered secondary to sales experience and the impression the ad manager gets of your personality.

• Good references.

• Knowledge—which is why I stressed earlier the importance of learning all you can about the newspaper. Refer to what you already know about the company you're applying to during the interview. Ask questions about the newspaper's operation, not just about the pay and the working hours. Intelligent questions will create a positive impression in the mind of the ad manager. Remember: You're not the only person he'll be interviewing for a job. Make sure he remembers you.

• Interest in advancing to a management position—if you're sure you understand what working in the newspaper advertising field is all about and are ready to make a firm commitment, express that commitment to the person interviewing you.

MOVING UP OR OUT

Once you're employed at a newspaper, continue learning about all phases of the operation, not just the Advertising department. It will bring you that much closer to promotions, job titles, and more income. People who have learned all the skills and demonstrated their ability to lead others may receive promotions in one to four years or so following their initial employment.

You could expect to move up to positions like **sales manager**, **advertising director** (heads all advertising functions), **marketing manager** or **director**, **general manager**, even **publisher**. If your newspaper is part of a group of papers owned by a parent company, you may even be offered a position at the corporate level, perhaps as **corporate advertising director**, **advertising sales trainer**, etc.

As previously mentioned, the successful operation of a small newspaper relies heavily on the close cooperation of all departments. Rarely does a day pass when you would not have a business-related conversation with some staff member of a department other than your own. It is because of this special relationship that it's entirely possible for an employee of one department to switch from his or her present position to a job in another department. You may, for example, have been able to get a part-time job in the Composing Room, pasting up ads and news copy, though your true ambition may be a full-time position in graphic arts, ad layout or advertising sales. By learning all you can about these other departments and demonstrating your ability, you can more effectively capture the interest of the appropriate department manager.

If you are able to obtain an entry-level position in telephone sales, either in the circulation or classified departments, it may take six months to a year (or more) to develop your selling skills to a level that will qualify you for that travelling sales rep's job you find more appealing. But once you've achieved that skill level, your chances of moving over to that new position are much greater. You have the advantage over someone from the "outside"—you're already familiar with the paper's day-to-day operations and will, therefore, probably require less training for the new job. That's a big plus in the view of most department managers.

If you were first employed as a clerk at the dispatch desk (which records and organizes the list of all advertising in each publication), you would become familiar with just about all the advertisers, have an understanding of their businesses, and, most likely, even have had phone or personal contact with them. Again, you'd be a strong candidate for a sales rep position.

A career in newspaper advertising offers you an opportunity to express your creativity in ways you never thought possible and earn a substantial income while you do so. If that's your goal, be sure to stop in and speak with us at the *Daily Freeman*. You'll be glad you did.

JOHN M. GREKLEK

A graduate of Pratt Institute (Brooklyn New York) with a Bachelors degree in industrial design, Mr. Greklek began his employment at the *Daily Freeman* in 1976 as a retail advertising sales representative. In 1978, he was named advertising coordinator, as which he assisted in managing the *Freeman's* classified ad department. Two years later, he was named marketing director, supervising both the retail and classified ad departments. Recently, he was named marketing manager; he is responsible for advanced planning, research and development of marketing/sales aids for the staff and shares some of the development time with other newspapers within the corporate structure of the company.

Previously, Mr. Greklek was employed as a corporate aircraft interior designer and toy designer at New York City companies, and sold insurance for Metropolitan Life.

He is a board member of the N.Y. State Advertising & Marketing Executives Association and active in a number of professional and community organizations.

SECTION III

The Job Search Process

CHAPTER TWENTY SIX

Getting Started: Self Evaluation And Career Objectives

Getting a job may be a one-step, couple of weeks or months-long operation.

Starting, nurturing and developing a career (or even a series of careers) is a lifelong process.

What we'll be talking about in the four chapters that together form our Job Search Process are those basic steps to take, assumptions to make, things to think about if you want a job—especially a first job in newspaper publishing. But when these steps—this process—are applied and expanded over a lifetime, most if not all of them are the same procedures, carried out over and over again, that are necessary to develop a successful, lifelong, professional career.

What does all this have to do with putting together a resume, writing a cover letter, heading off for interviews and the other "traditional" steps necessary to get a job? Whether your college graduation is just around the corner or a far-distant memory, you will continuously need to focus, evaluate and re-evaluate your response to the ever-changing challenge of your future: Just what do you want to do with the rest of your life? Whether you like it or not, you're all looking for that "entry-level opportunity."

You're already one or two steps ahead of the competition—you're sure (pretty sure?) you want to pursue a career in newspapers. By heeding the advice of the many professionals who have written chapters for this <u>Career Directory</u>—and utilizing the extensive industry and newspaper information we've included—you're well on your way to fulfilling that dream. But there are some key decisions and time-consuming preparations to make if you want to transform that hopeful dream into a real, live publishing job.

The actual process of finding the right publishing company, right newspaper, right career path and, most importantly, the right first job, begins long before you start mailing out resumes to potential employers. The choices and decisions you make now are not irrevocable, but this first job will have a definite impact on the career options you leave yourself. To help you make some of the right decisions and choices along the way (and avoid some of the most notable traps and pitfalls), the following chapters will lead you through a series of organized steps. If the entire job search process we are recommending here is properly executed, it will undoubtedly help you land exactly the job you want.

If you're currently in high school and hope, after college, to land a job on a newspaper,, then attending the right college, choosing the right major and getting the summer work experience many publishers look for are all important steps. Read the section of this <u>Career Directory</u> that covers your job specialty—many of the contributors have recommended colleges or vocational schools they favor.

If you're hoping to jump right into the newspaper industry with*out* a college degree or other professional training, our best and only advice is—don't do it. As you'll soon see in the detailed information included in the *Job Opportunities Databank* in Section IV, there are not *that* many job openings for students without a college degree. Those that do exist are generally clerical and will only rarely lead to promising careers.

THE CONCEPT OF A JOB SEARCH PROCESS

These are the key steps in the detailed job search process we will cover in this and the following three chapters:

1. *Evaluating yourself*: Know thyself. What skills and abilities can you offer a prospective employer? What do you enjoy doing? What are your strengths and weaknesses? What do you *want* to do?

2. *Establishing your career objectives*: Where do you want to be next year, three years, five years from now? What do you ultimately want to accomplish in your career and your life?

3. *Creating a publisher target list*: How to prepare a "Hit List" of potential employers—researching them, matching their needs with your skills and starting your job search assault. Preparing publisher/newspaper information sheets and evaluating your chances.

4. *Networking for success:* Learning how to utilize every contact, every friend, every relative and anyone else you can think of to break down the barriers facing any would-be publishing professional. How to organize your home office to keep track of your communications and stay on top of your job campaign.

5. *Preparing your resume:* How to encapsulate years of school and little actual work experience into a professional, selling resume. Learning when and how to use it.

6. *Preparing cover letters:* The many ordinary and the all-too-few extraordinary cover letters, the kind that land interviews and jobs.

7. *Interviewing:* How to make the interview process work for you—from the first "hello" to the first day on the job.

We won't try to kid you—it *is* a lot of work. To do it right, you have to get started early, probably quite a bit earlier than you'd planned. Frankly, we recommend beginning this process one full year prior to the day you plan to start work.

So if you're in college, the end of your junior year is the right time to begin your research and preparations. That should give you enough time during summer vacation to set up your files and begin your library research.

Whether you're in college or graduate school, one item may need to be planned even earlier—allowing enough free time in your schedule of classes for interview preparations and appointments. Waiting until your senior year to "make some time" is already too late. Searching for a full-time job is itself a full-time job! Though you're naturally restricted by your schedule, it's not difficult to plan ahead and prepare for your upcoming job search. Try to leave at least a couple of free mornings or afternoons a week. A day or even two without classes is even better.

Otherwise, you'll find yourself, crazed and distracted, trying to prepare for an interview in the ten-minute period between your Politics and the Press lecture and your Creative Writing seminar. Not the best way to make a first impression and certainly not the way you want to approach an important meeting.

THE SELF-EVALUATION PROCESS

Plato had it right: "Know thyself." Learning about who you are, what you want to be, what you *can* be, are critical first steps in the job search process and, unfortunately, the ones most often ignored by job seekers everywhere, especially students eager to leave the ivy behind and plunge into the "real world." But avoiding this crucial self evaluation can hinder your progress and even damage some decent prospects.

Why? Because in order to land a job with a newspaper at which you'll actually be happy, you need to be able to identify those publishers and/or job descriptions that best match your own skills, likes and strengths. The more you know about yourself, the more you'll bring to this process and the more accurate the "match-ups." You'll be able to structure your presentation (resume, cover letter, interviews) to stress your most marketable skills and talents (and, dare we say it, conveniently avoid your weaknesses?). Later, you'll be able to evaluate potential employers and job offers on the basis of your own needs and desires. This spells the difference between waking up in the morning ready to enthusiastically tackle a new day of challenges and shutting off the alarm in the hopes the day (and your job) will just disappear.

Creating Your Self-Evaluation Form

Take a sheet of lined notebook paper. Set up eight columns across the top—Strengths, Weaknesses, Skills, Hobbies, Courses, Experience, Likes, Dislikes.

Now, fill in each of these columns according to these guidelines:

Strengths: Describe personality traits you consider your strengths (and try to look at them as an employer would)—e.g., persistence, organization, ambition, intelligence, logic, assertiveness, aggression, leadership, etc.

Weaknesses: The traits you consider glaring weaknesses—e.g., impatience, conceit, etc. (And remember: Look at these as a potential employer would. Don't assume that the personal traits you consider weaknesses will necessarily be considered negatives in the business world. You may be "easily bored," a trait that led to lousy grades early on because teachers couldn't keep you interested in the subjects they were teaching. Well, many entrepreneurs need ever-changing challenges. Strength or weakness?)

Skills: Any skill you have, whether you think it's marketable or not. Everything from basic business skills—like typing, word processing and stenography—to computer, accounting or teaching experience and foreign language literacy. Don't forget possibly obscure but marketable skills like "good telephone voice."

Hobbies: The things you enjoy doing that, more than likely, have no overt connection to career objectives. These should be distinct from the skills listed above, and may include activities such as reading, games, travel, sports and the like. While these may not be marketable in any general sense, they may well be useful in specific circumstances. (If you love travel, you may be perfect for that assistant editorial spot with the Travel section of your local paper. And your "hobbies" may just get it for you!)

Courses: All the general subject areas (history, literature, etc.) and/or specific courses you've taken which may be marketable (computer, business, marketing, economics, etc.), you really enjoyed, or both.

Experience: Just the specific functions you performed at any part-time (school year) or full-time (summer) jobs. Entries may include "General Office" (typing, filing, answering phones, etc.), "Sales," "Writing," "Research," etc.

Likes: List all your "likes," those important considerations that you haven't listed anywhere else yet. These might include the types of people you like to be with, the kind of environment you prefer (city, country, large places, small places, quiet, loud, fast-paced, slow-paced) and anything else which hasn't shown up somewhere on this form. However, try not to include entries which refer to specific jobs or companies. We'll list those on another form.

Dislikes: All the people, places and things you can easily live without.

Now assess the "marketability" of each item you've listed. (In other words, are some of your likes, skills or courses easier to match to a publishing job description, or do they have little to do with a specific job or publisher?) Mark highly marketable skills with an "H." Use "M" to characterize those skills which may be marketable in a particular set of circumstances, "L" for those with minimal potential application to any job. Some obvious examples: Typing, word processing and stenography are always marketable, so you'd mark them with an "H". Teaching, computer and accounting skills would also qualify as highly marketable. Similarly, if you listed high energy or perseverance as a strength, any advertising sales manager will find it a highly desirable trait. Speaking French, however, gets an "M." While not marketable in all job situations, it might well be a requirement for certain industries (e.g., importing and exporting) or jobs (working for the *International Herald Tribune*...in Paris).

Referring back to the same list, decide if you'd enjoy using your marketable skills or talents as part of your everyday job—"Y" for yes, "N" for no. You may type 80 words a minute but truly despise typing (or worry that stressing it too much will land you on the permanent clerical staff). If so, mark typing with an "N." (Keep one thing in mind—just because you dislike typing shouldn't mean you absolutely won't accept a job that requires it. Most do.)

Now, go over the entire form carefully. Look for inconsistencies. After you are satisfied that the form is as accurate as you can make it—and gotten over the shock of some of your honest answers—pass it along to a close friend or two. Ask *them* to check it for accuracy—you'll not only uncover areas you may have fudged a bit, but learn a great deal about what the rest of the world thinks of you. After they've completed their assessment of the person you've committed to paper, put the form aside for the time being.

ESTABLISHING YOUR CAREER OBJECTIVE(S)

For better or worse, you now know something more of who and what you are. But we've yet to establish and evaluate another important area—your overall needs, desires and goals. Where are you going? What do you want to accomplish?

If you're getting ready to graduate from college or graduate school, the next five years are the most critical period of your whole career. You need to make the initial transition from college to the workplace, establish yourself in a new and completely unfamiliar company environment and begin to build the professional credentials necessary to achieve your career goals.

If that strikes you as a pretty tall order, well, it *is*. Unless you've narrowly prepared yourself for a specific profession, you're probably most *ill*-prepared for any real job. Instead, you've (hopefully) learned some basic principles—research and analytical skills that are necessary for success at almost any level—and, more or less, how to think. But that's all. You probably don't have the faintest clue about how the newspaper business (let alone a specific publisher or department) functions or any of the specific information necessary to perform even the lowliest task.

It's tough to face, but face it you must: No matter what your college, major or degree, all you represent right now is potential. How you package that potential and what you eventually make of it is completely up to you. And it's an unfortunate fact that many newspapers will take a professional with barely a year or two experience over *any* newcomer, no matter how promising. Smaller papers, especially, can rarely afford to hire someone who can't begin contributing immediately.

So you have to be prepared to take your comparatively modest skills and experience and package them in a way that will get you interviewed and hired. Quite a challenge.

There are a number of different ways to approach such a task. If you find yourself confused or unable to list such goals, you might want to check a few books in your local library that have more time to spend on the topic of "goal-oriented planning." Four that may help: 1) Your First Resume by Ronald W. Fry, our own attempt to simplify the entire job search process for first timers, available via the mail order coupon in the back of this volume; 2) The ubiquitous What Color is Your Parachute, still the Bible of the job search field (though if you find it absurdly complicated, you're not alone): 3) After College: The Business of Getting Jobs by Jack Falvey, a far more readable (though somewhat controversial) overview of the job search process; and 4) (by the same author) What's Next? Career Strategies After 35, for you post-35ers out there. The latter two books are also available from The Career Press.

YES, BUT IS NEWSPAPER PUBLISHING RIGHT FOR *YOU*?

Presuming you now have a much better idea of yourself and where you'd like to be—job-career- and life-wise in the foreseeable future—let's make sure some of your basic assumptions are right. We presume you purchased this Career Directory because you're considering a career in newspaper publishing. Are you sure? Do you know enough about the industry to decide whether it's right for you? Probably not. Do you know enough about the two other major areas of publishing—magazines and books—let alone the possibilities of getting involved in one of the peripheral areas, such as working for an independent rep or starting to freelance your own articles? Doubtful. So start your research *now*—learn as much about the newspaper business as you now know about yourself.

Start with Section I. These six articles will give you an excellent overview of the business, some very specialized (and growing) areas of the industry and some things to consider about yourself and publishing. This will give you a relatively simplified, though very necessary, understanding of just what people who work in newspaper publishing actually do.

Other sources you should consider consulting to learn more about this business are listed in the various Appendices.

In Appendix A, we've listed all the trade organizations associated with the newspaper publishing industry. While educational information available from these associations is often limited (and, for the most part, already a part of this Career Directory), you should certainly consider writing each of the pertinent associations, letting them know you're interested in a career in publishing and would appreciate whatever help and advice they're willing to impart. You'll find many sponsor seminars and conferences throughout the country, some of which you may be able to attend.

In Appendix B, we've listed the trade newspapers dedicated to the highly specific interests of the publishing community. These magazines are generally not available at newsstands (unless you live in or near New York City), but you may be able to obtain back issues at your local library (most major libraries have extensive collections of such journals) or by writing to the magazines' circulation/subscription departments.

You may also try writing to the publishers and/or editors of these business publications. State in your cover letter what area of the business you're considering and ask them for whatever help and advice they can offer. But be specific. These are busy professionals and they do not have the time or the inclination to simply "tell me everything you can about newspaper publishing."

If you can afford it now, we strongly suggest subscribing to *Editor & Publisher*, the major trade newspaper for the newspaper business—plus whichever of the other trade magazines are applicable to the specialty you're considering. If you can't subscribe to all of them, make it a point to regularly read the copies that arrive at your local public or college library.

These publications may well provide the most imaginative and far-reaching information for your job search. Even a quick perusal of an issue or two will give you an excellent "feel" for the industry. After reading only a few articles, you'll already get a handle on what's happening in the field and some of publishing's peculiar and particular jargon. Later, more detailed study will aid you in your search for a specific job.

Authors of the articles themselves may well turn out to be important resources. If an article is directly related to your chosen specialty, why not call the author and ask some questions? You'd be amazed how willing many of these professionals will be to talk to you and answer your questions. They may even tell you about job openings at their companies! (But *do* use common sense—authors will not *always* respond graciously to your invitation to "chat about the business." And don't be *too* aggressive here.)

You'll find such research to be a double-edged sword. In addition to helping you get a handle on whether the newspaper business is really right for you, you'll slowly learn enough about particular specialties, publishers, the industry, etc., to actually sound like you know what you're talking about when you hit the pavement looking for your first job. And nothing is better than sounding like a pro...except being one.

NEWSPAPERS ARE IT. NOW WHAT?

After all this research, we're going to assume you've reached that final decision—you really *do* want a career in newspaper publishing. It is with this vague certainty that all too many of you will race off, hunting for any paper willing to give you a job. You'll manage to get interviews at a couple and, smiling brightly, tell everyone you meet, "I want a career in newspaper publishing." The interviewers, unfortunately, will all ask the same awkward question—"What *exactly* do you want to do at our newspaper?"—and that will be the end of that.

It is simply not enough to narrow your job search to a specific industry. And so far, that's all you've done. You must now establish a specific career objective—the job you want to start, the career you want to pursue. Just knowing that you "want to get into newspaper publishing" doesn't mean anything to anybody. If that's all you can tell an interviewer, it demonstrates a lack of research into the industry itself and your failure to think ahead. Do you want to start as an reporter, hoping to work your way up the ladder to editor-in-chief, or catch on as a sales rep, with VP-sales your eventual goal? The two entry-level positions are completely different. They require different skills and educational backgrounds.

Interviewers will *not* welcome you with open arms if you're still vague about your career goals. If you've managed to get an "informative interview" with an executive whose company currently has no job openings, what is he supposed to do with your resume after you leave? Who should he send it to for future consideration? Since *you* don't seem to know exactly what you want to do, how's *he* going to figure it out? Worse, he'll probably resent your asking him to function as your personal career counselor.

Remember, the more specific your career objective, the better your chances of finding a job. It's that simple and that important. Naturally, before you declare your objective to the world, check once again to make sure your specific job target matches the skills and interests you defined in your self evaluation. Eventually, you may want to state such an objective on your resume and "To obtain an entry-level position as an editorial assistant editor at a major daily newspaper" is quite a bit better than "I want a career in newspaper publishing." Do not consider this step final until you can summarize your job/career objective in a single, short, accurate sentence.

CHAPTER TWENTY SEVEN

Targeting Newspapers And Networking For Success

If you've spent the time and effort going through the self-evaluation process in the previous chapter, you're now sure—you *know* what you want to do. The next question: Where are you going to get a job doing it? There are thousands of newspaper publishers, ranging in size from the biggest (Gannett, Knight Ridder, Newhouse) to the smallest (a plethora of publishers with a single paper). Small or large? New York, Dallas or Oshkosh? Just which of the publishers is the right one for you?

YOUR IDEAL NEWSPAPER PROFILE

Let's establish some criteria to evaluate potential employers. This will enable you to identify your target newspapers, the places you'd really like to work. (This process, as we've pointed out, is not newspaper-specific; the same steps, with perhaps some research resource variations, are applicable to any job, any company, any industry. But for this volume, we are now specifically concerned with jobs in the newspaper business. If you are primarily interested in working for a magazine publisher, see the brand-new third edition of our <u>Magazines Career</u>

<u>Directory</u>. And for you aspiring book editors, designers and advertising salespeople—the third edition of our <u>Book Publishing Career Directory</u> is also available.)

Take another sheet of blank paper and divide it into three vertical columns. Title it "Newspaper Publisher—Ideal Profile." Call the left-hand column "Musts," the middle column "Preferences," and the right-hand column "Nevers."

We've listed a series of questions below. After considering each question, decide whether a particular criteria *must* be met, whether you would simply *prefer* it or *never* would consider it at all. If there are other criteria you consider important, feel free to add them to the list below and mark them accordingly on your Profile.

1. What are your geographical preferences? (Possible answers: U.S., Canada, International, Anywhere). If you only want to work in the U.S., then "Work in United States" would be the entry in the "Must" column. "Work in Canada or Foreign Country" might be the first entry in your "Never" column. There would be no applicable entry for this question in the "Preference" column. If, however, you will consider working in two of the three, then your "Must" column entry might read "Work in U.S. or Canada," your "Preference" entry—if you preferred one over the other—could read "Work in U.S.," and the "Never" column , "Work Overseas."

2. If you prefer to work in the U.S. or Canada, what area, state(s) or province(s)? If Overseas, what area or countries?

3. Do you prefer a large city, small city, town, or somewhere as far away from civilization as possible?

4. In regard to question 3, any specific preferences?

5. Do you prefer a warm or cold climate?

6. Do you prefer a large or small newspaper? Define your terms (by circulation, income, employees, offices, etc.).

7. Do you mind relocating right now? Do you want to work for a publisher of many papers with a reputation for *frequently* relocating top people?

8. Do you mind travelling frequently? What percent do you consider reasonable? (Make sure this matches the normal requirements of the job specialization you're considering.)

9. What salary would you *like* to receive (put in the "Preference" column)? What's the *lowest* salary you'll accept (in the "Must" column)?

10. Are there any benefits (such as an expense account, medical and/or dental insurance, company car, etc.) you must or would like to have?

11. Are you planning to attend graduate school at some point in the future and, if so, is a tuition reimbursement plan important to you?

12. Do you feel a formal training program necessary?

13. What kind of newsp;aper (large metropolitan daily, mid-sized daily, small weekly, etc.) would you prefer to work on?

14. Do you want to work only for a particular publisher or newspaper?

It's important to keep revising this new form, just as you should continue to update your Self-Evaluation Form. After all, it contains the criteria by which you will judge every potential employer. It may even lead you to avoid interviewing at a specific newspaper (if, for example, they're located in a state on your "never" list!). So be sure your "nevers" aren't frivolous. Likewise, make your "musts" and "preferences" at least semi-realistic. If your "must" salary for a position as an assistant editor is $30,000, you will wind up eliminating every newspaper out there!

Armed with a complete list of such criteria, you're now ready to find all the publishers that match them.

TARGETING INDIVIDUAL NEWSPAPERS & PUBLISHERS

To begin creating your initial list of targeted newspapers, start with the *Job Opportunities Databank* (Section IV). We've listed virtually every major publisher, most of which completed questionnaires we supplied, providing us (and you!) with a plethora of data concerning their overall operations, hiring practices and other important information on entry-level job opportunities. This latter information includes key contacts (names), the average number of entry-level people they hire each year, along with complete job descriptions and requirements.

This section also includes lists of newspapers offering salaried and non-salaried internships or some of each, and those with formal training programs for "new hires." All of the detailed information in these two chapters was provided by the publishers themselves. To our knowledge, it is available only in this Career Directory.

We have attempted to include information on those major newspapers /publishers that represent most of the entry-level jobs out there. But there are, of course, many other papers of all sizes and shapes that you may also wish to research. In the next section, we will discuss some other reference books you can use to obtain more information on the publishers we've listed, as well as those we haven't.

OTHER REFERENCE TOOLS

In order to obtain some of the detailed information you need, you will probably need to do further research, either in the library or by meeting and chatting with people familiar with the newspapers you're interested in.

A key reference resource is the Editor & Publisher International Yearbook, an annual publication that lists U.S. and Canadian dailies and weeklies, foreign newspaers, news services, major newspaper groups and pertinent organizations (city state and regional press associations, schools and departments of journalism, etc.). It should be considered a required companion to this Career Directory and should be available in virtually any public or school library.

Less complete information on most U.S. papers is included in the various editions of Standard Rate and Data Service *(SRDS)*, the bible of ad agency media buyers. Much of the information, however, isn't directly pertinent to *your* areas of concern—you'll find, for example, virtually no information on the publishing *companies*.

For more general research (pertinent to all publishers,), you might want to start with How To Find Information About Companies (Washington Researchers, 1985); the Encyclopedia of Business Information Sources (Gale Research, Book Tower, Detroit, MI 48226); and/or the

Guide to American Directories (B. Klein Publications, P.O. Box 8503, Coral Springs, FL 33065), which lists directories for over 3,000 fields.

If you want to work for one of the associations which serves the newspaper publishing industry (or the fields with which it's most closely allied), we've listed all those in Appendix A. Other associations may be researched in the Encyclopedia of Associations (Gale Research Co.) or National Trade and Professional Associations of the United States (Columbia Books, Inc., 777 14th St., NW, Suite 236, Washington, DC 20005).

There are, in addition, some general corporate directories which may give you additional information on major publishers. (But do remember: Many newspapers are not publicly-owned companies, and, therefore, not particularly forthcoming with information or listed in such all-inclusive reference books.) These volumes should all be available in the reference (and/or business) section of your local library:

*Dun and Bradstreet's family of corporate reference resources: the Million Dollar Directory (160,000 companies with a net worth of more than $500,000), Top 50,000 Companies (those with a minimum net worth of just under $2 million), and Business Rankings (details on the top 7,500 firms). A new volume from Dun's —Reference Book of Corporate Managements/America's Corporate Leaders— provides detailed biographical data on the principal officers and directors of some 12,000-odd corporations. Who says you can't find out about the quirks and hobbies of the guy you're interviewing with? All of these volumes are available in most libraries or from Dun's Marketing Services (3 Century Drive, Parsippany, NJ 07054).

*Standard & Poor's Register of Corporations, Directors and Executives includes corporate listings for over 45,000 firms and 72,000 biographical listings. (Available from Standard and Poor's, 25 Broadway, New York, NY 10004.)

*Moody's Industrial Manual (Available from Moody's Investors Ser-vice, Inc., 99 Church St., New York, NY 10007.)

*Thomas's Register of American Manufacturing (Thomas Publishing Company, 1 Penn Plaza, New York, NY 10001.)

*Ward's Business Directory, a three-volume reference work that includes listings of nearly 100,000 companies, the majority of them privately-held, and details that are usually most difficult to acquire about such firms (number of employees, annual sales, etc.). Published by Information Access Company.

Primary sources which should be utilized from now on to complete your research are The *Wall Street Journal*, *Barron's*, *Dun's Business Month*, *Business Week*, *Forbes*, *Fortune* and *Inc.* Naturally, the trade magazines which you've been studying (and to which you've already subscribed) like *Editor & Publisher*, offer a steady stream of information. Become as familiar as possible with the publishing companies, papers, issues, jargon, topics covered and the industry.

One last note on potential sources of leads. The Oxbridge Directory of Newsletters (available from Oxbridge Communications, 183 Madison Ave., Suite 1108, New York, NY 10016) lists thousands of newsletters in a plethora of industries and might well give you some ideas and names. And the Professional Exhibits Directory (Gale Research Co.) lists more than 2,000 trade shows and conventions. Such shows are excellent places to "run into" sales reps, editors, etc. and offer unexpected opportunities to learn about the business "from the horse's mouth."

NETWORKING FOR SUCCESS

You're now as prepared as any Boy or Girl Scout in history. You know not only the field you want to enter, but an exact job title, summarized in a concise career objective. You know whether you're heading for a major metropolitan daily, a smaller daily or the weekly in your home town. And you have a complete preliminary list of newspapers, with detailed data on each, that reflects your own needs, wants and goals.

It's time to start *networking*, telling everybody you know and everybody *they* know exactly the kind of job you're looking for. Faster than you expect, you will begin to develop a network of friends, relatives, acquaintances and contacts. It is most likely that the skillful use of this network and *not* the more traditional approach to job hunting—studying the want ads and sending out resumes to PO Box Numbers—is going to be the key factor in landing a first job.

Why? Because on any day of the week, the vast majority of available jobs, perhaps as high as 85% of all the jobs out there waiting to be filled, are not advertised anywhere. Many of those jobs that are advertised only remain in the classifieds for a day or two. After that, they're pulled and, for the next few weeks, various company personnel sift through resumes while the job is still sitting there, unfilled, just waiting for the right applicant to grab it!

There are some things to keep in mind while you prepare to crack what others have labeled "the hidden job market." First and foremost, remember that there are *always* jobs out there. Nearly 20% of all the jobs in the United States (and probably many more in publishing, a notoriously fluid field) change hands every year, good years and bad. People retire, move on to another job or industry, get promoted. Companies expand. The result is near-constant movement in the job market, if only you know where to look.

Second, people in a company will generally know about a job opening weeks before the outside world gets a clue, certainly before (if) it shows up in a newspaper ad.

Third, just knowing that this hidden market exists is an asset a lot of your colleagues (hereafter, let's just consider them competitors) don't have.

Last, but by no means least, your industry and company research has already made you a most knowledgeable graduate. This will undoubtedly work to your advantage.

CREATING THE IDEAL NETWORK

As in most endeavors, there's a wrong way and a right way to network. The following tips will help you construct a wide-ranging, information-gathering, interview-generating group —your very own network.

Diversify

Unlike the Harvard or Princeton Universities networks—confined to former graduates of each school—*your* network should be as diversified and wide-ranging as possible. You never know who might be in a position to help, so don't limit your group of friends. The more diverse they are, the greater the variety of information they may supply you with.

Don't Forget...

...to include everyone you know in your initial networking list: friends, relatives, social acquaintances, classmates, college alumni, professors, teachers; your dentist, doctor, family lawyer, insurance agent, banker, travel agent; elected officials in your community; ministers; fellow church members; local tradesmen; local business or social club officers. And everybody *they* know!

Be Specific

Make a list of the kinds of assistance you will require from those in your network, then make specific requests of each. Do they know of jobs at their company? Can they introduce you to the proper executives? Have they heard something about or know someone at the company you're planning to inter-view with next week?

The more organized you are, the easier it will be to target the information you need and figure out who might have it. Calling everyone and simply asking for "whatever help you can give me" is unfair to the people you're calling and a less-effective way to garner the information you need.

Know The Difference...

...between an **informational** interview and a **job** interview. The former requires you to cast yourself in the role of information-gatherer; *you* are the interviewer and knowledge is your goal—about an industry, company, job function, key executive, etc. Such a meeting with someone already doing what you soon *hope* to be doing is by far the best way to find out everything you need to know...before you walk through the door and sit down for a formal job interview, at which time your purpose is more sharply-defined: to get the job you're interviewing for.

If you learn of a specific job opening during an informational interview, you are in a position to find out details about the job, identify the interviewer and, possibly, even learn some things about him or her. In addition, presuming you get your contact's permission, you may be able to use his or her name as a referral. Calling up the interviewer and saying, "Joan Smith in your News department suggested I contact you regarding openings for reporters" is far superior to "Hello. Do you have any job openings on your newspaper?"

(In such a case, be careful about referring to a specific job opening, even if your contact told you about it. It may not be something you're supposed to know about. By presenting your query as an open-ended question, you give your prospective employer the option of exploring your background without further commitment. If there is a job there and you're qualified for it, you'll find out soon enough.)

Don't Waste A Contact

Not everyone you call on your highly-diversified networking list will know about a job opening. It would be surprising if each one did. But what about *their* friends and colleagues? It's amazing how everyone knows someone who knows someone. Ask—you'll find that someone.

Value Your Contacts

If you've taken our admonitions about record keeping to heart, this is where you'll begin to appreciate the dividends. If someone has provided you with helpful information or an introduction to a friend or colleague, keep him or her informed about how it all turns out. A referral that's panned out should be reported to the person who opened the door for you in the first place. Such courtesy will be appreciated...and may lead to more contacts. If someone has nothing to offer today, a call back in the future is still appropriate and may yet pay off.

The lesson is clear: Keep your options open and your contact list alive. Keeping detailed records of your network—who you spoke with, when, what transpired, etc.—will certainly help you keep track of your overall progress and organize what can be a complicated and involved process.

Organizing Your Home Office

With so many other people working for you, you must carefully and completely organize your own personal employment office. If you've already started filing detailed company data in separate folders, you're already a step ahead.

We suggest preparing a separate folder for each person you're working with, along with a centralized phone list. Throughout your job search, be prepared to keep accurate and organized records every step of the way. Keep copies of your research notes, photocopy every letter you mail, and keep detailed notes of telephone conversations. Always send off a timely and polite thank-you note to those helping out. That simple gesture will demonstrate a degree of professionalism and good manners often overlooked by students.

If you can afford one, consider purchasing a telephone answering machine. An employer who may have seen and liked your resume—one who's even willing to interview you—will rarely call more than once to set up an appointment.

IF THE PROCESS SCARES YOU

Some of you will undoubtedly be hesitant about, even fear, the networking process. It is not an unusual response—it is very human to want to accomplish things "on your own," without anyone's help. Understandable and commendable as such independence might seem, it is, in reality, an impediment if it limits your involvement in this important process. Networking has such universal application because *there is no other effective way to bridge the gap between job applicant and job.* Employers are grateful for its existence. You should be, too.

Whether you are a first-time applicant or reentering the work force now that the children are grown, the networking process will more than likely be your point of entry. Sending out mass mailings of your resume and answering the help-wanted ads may well be less personal (and, therefore, "easier") approaches, but they will also be far less effective. The natural selection process of the networking phenomenon is your assurance that water does indeed seek its own level—you will be matched up with publishers and job opportunities in which there is a mutual fit.

CHAPTER TWENTY EIGHT

Preparing Resumes And Cover Letters

Your resume is a one- or two-page summary of you—your education, skills, employment experience and career objective(s). It is not a biography, but a "quick and dirty" way to identify and describe you to potential employers. Most importantly, its real purpose is to sell you to the publisher you want to work for. It must set you apart from all the other applicants (those competitors) out there. So, when you sit down to formulate your resume, remember you're trying to present the pertinent information in a format and manner that will convince an executive to grant you an interview, the prelude to any job offer. (If you feel you need more help in resume preparation, or even in the entire job search area, we recommend <u>Your First Resume</u> by Ronald W. Fry,. a brand-new publication now available from The Career Press. See the coupon in back of this book to order.)

AN OVERVIEW OF RESUME PREPARATION

• **Know what you're doing**—your resume is a personal billboard of accomplishments. It must communicate your worth to a prospective employer in specific terms.

- **Your language should be action-oriented,** full of "doing"-type words. And less is better than more—be concise and direct. Don't worry about using complete sentences.

- **Be persuasive.** In those sections that allow you the freedom to do so, don't hesitate to communicate your worth in the strongest language. This does not mean a numbing list of self-congratulatory superlatives; it does mean truthful claims about your abilities and the evidence (educational, experiential) that supports them.

- **Don't be cheap or gaudy.** Don't hesitate to spend the few extra dollars necessary to present a professional-looking resume. Do avoid outlandish (and generally ineffective) gimmicks like over-sized or brightly-colored paper.

- **Find an editor.** Every good writer needs one, and you are writing your resume. At the very least, it will offer you a second set of eyes proofreading for embarrassing typos. But if you are fortunate enough to have a professional in the field—a recruiter or personnel executive—critique a draft, grab the opportunity and be immensely grateful.

- **If you're the next Michaelangelo,** so multi-talented that you can easily qualify for jobs in different career areas, don't hesitate to prepare two or more completely different resumes. This will enable you to change the emphasis on your education and skills according to the specific career objective on each resume, a necessary alteration that will correctly target each one.

- **Choose the proper format.** There are only three we recommend— chronological, functional and combination—and it's important you use the one that's right for you.

THE RECORDS YOU NEED

The reason for organizing records is to be more efficient and accurate when you sit down to prepare the ingredients for your resume. Records do NOT belong scattered throughout the household or dumped into the family "record file" in a kitchen drawer. Organizing your records in a single location, filed by topic, will save you time, energy and stress.

So start by deciding upon a single location in which to store your personal records. Develop a good filing system and, if you don't own a file cabinet, consider buying one of two products available at most stationery or office supply stores: an expandable pocket portfolio or a solid plastic file box (sturdier, but less compact). In either container, designate a separate folder for each of the following categories of important documents:

REPORT CARDS—Along with actual report cards, you might save samples of your work— especially in courses pertinent to your career objective. The actual work easily records interests, talents, difficulties and accomplishments.

TRANSCRIPTS/GPA/CLASS RANK—Transcripts are your school's official record of your academic history. They are generally kept in the guidance office (high school) or registrar's office (college). Make sure honors courses are noted in the transcript.

The GPA (Grade Point Average) is usually found on the transcript. Many schools generally calculate this by computing credits times a numerical grade equivalent (often "A" = 4.0, "B" = 3.0, etc.). Class rank is simply a listing of GPAs, from highest to lowest. Example: 75/306 (75th out of a class of 306 students).

ACTIVITY RECORDS—This should be a comprehensive list of sports, clubs, honor societies and other extracurricular or special activities in which you've participated, either inside or outside school. Make sure you list any leadership positions held

AWARDS/HONORS—List award name, date received and significance of the award. Example: Peabody Scholar, 1987, awarded to Jefferson High School senior who demonstrates musical prowess and an interest in pursuing a musical career.

WORK/VOLUNTEER RECORDS—List each job title, dates of employment, business name, address and phone number, name of immediate supervisor, responsibilities. Any work experience, from babysitting to lawn mowing, should be listed. Also list any volunteer work, even if it was only for one day. You may wish to keep a separate folder for Letters of Recommendation from any of these employers.

MILITARY RECORDS—Include complete military history, if pertinent.

TRAVEL RECORDS—Keep a list of your travel experiences and, perhaps, some personal reactions to each trip. Travel experience helps demonstrate that you are well-rounded, and the written reactions might prompt responses to interview questions.

THIS IS NOT THE TIME OR PLACE TO BE MODEST! Keep track of all your accomplishments, no matter how trivial they may seem to you. Brainstorm about what you've gained from your experiences and be sure you are able to talk about what you've accomplished. You probably have more to offer than you think!

From this growing collection of records and achievements, you will begin to get a clearer picture of what you really have to offer the world.

Once you have this information in hand, you have a lot of options about what to include or leave out. In general, we suggest you always include the following data:

1. Your name, address and telephone number.
2. Pertinent work history
3. Pertinent educational history
4. Academic honors
5. Memberships in professional organizations.
6. Contributions to professional publications.

You have the option of including the following:

1. Your career objective
2. Personal data (marital status, etc.)
3. Hobbies
4. Feelings about travel and/or relocation
5. Military service history

And you should *never* include the following:

1. Why you left past jobs
2. Photographs or illustrations (of yourself or anything else!)
3. References
4. Past salaries or present salary objectives/requirements

CHRONOLOGICAL AND FUNCTIONAL RESUMES

The two standard resume formats are chronological, arranged by date (last job first), and functional, which emphasizes skills rather than the sequential history of your experiences. Generally, since students have yet to develop specific, highly employable skills or the experience to indicate proficiency in specific job functions, they should use the chronological format. A bit of sales, a touch of writing, and a smidgen of research will not impress anyone on a functional resume. The latter is useful, however, if you have a great deal of pertinent job expertise, since it emphasizes qualifications and abilities in terms of job titles and responsibilities. Dates are usually omitted (though we personally feel that leaving dates out altogether lessens the effectiveness of any resume. We'd find a way to include dates—perhaps in a brief, chronological, job history section.) At the end of this chapter are examples of both.

(There are other kinds of resumes—analytical, synoptic, "creative" approaches that defy easy classification. None of these are as efficient or easily understood and accepted as the two basic formats. And none of them are at all adaptable to an entry-level candidate. So stick with the chronological or, in exceptional cases, the functional.)

GUIDELINES FOR RESUME PREPARATION

Your resume should be limited to a single page if possible, two at most. It should be printed, not xeroxed, on 8 1/2" x 11" white, cream or ivory stock. The ink should be black or, at most, a royal blue. Don't scrimp on the paper quality—use the best bond you can afford. And since printing 100 or even 200 copies will cost little more than 50, tend to overestimate your needs and opt for the highest quantity you think you may need.

When you're laying out the resume, try to leave a reasonable amount of "white space"—generous margins all around and spacing between entries. A resume is not a complete biography and anything that is not, in some way, a qualification for the type of position you're seeking should be omitted.

Be brief. Use phraseology rather than complete sentences. Your resume is a summary of your talents, not an English Lit paper. Choose your words carefully and use "power words" whenever possible. "Organized" is more powerful than "put together;" "supervised" better than "oversaw;" "formulated" better than "thought up." Strong words like these can make the most mundane clerical work sound like a series of responsible, professional positions. And, of course, they will tend to make your resume stand out. Here's a "starter list" of words which you may want to use in your resume:

achieved	administered	advised	analyzed
applied	arranged	budgeted	calculated
classified	communicated	completed	computed
conceptualized	coordinated	critiqued	delegated
determined	developed	devised	directed
established	evaluated	executed	formulated
gathered	generated	guided	implemented
improved	initiated	instituted	instructed
introduced	invented	issued	launched

lectured	litigated	lobbied	managed
negotiated	operated	organized	overhauled
planned	prepared	presented	presided
programmed	promoted	recommended	researched
reviewed	revised	reorganized	regulated
selected	solved	scheduled	supervised
systematized	taught	tested	traced
trained	updated	utilized	wrote

An important suggestion: When you've completed writing and designing your resume, have a couple of close friends or family members proofread it for typographical errors *before* you send it to the printer. For some reason, the more you check it yourself, the less likely you'll catch the errors you missed the first time around. A fresh look from someone not as familiar with it will catch these glaring (and potentially embarrassing) errors before they're duplicated a couple of hundred times.

PREPARING COVER LETTERS

A cover letter should be included with each resume you send out. It may be addressed to a particular individual your networking has identified (or with whom you've already met or spoken) or sent in response to a newspaper ad (even those that refer you solely to post office boxes). Whatever the case, each cover letter should be personalized—targeted to the individual company, executive and position. To our mind—and most executives with whom we've talked seem to agree—the cover letter tells them more about a candidate, and is, therefore, more important from your standpoint, than the resume.

Each cover letter should be error-free, neatly typed, and correctly formatted. Such a letter should probably never be handwritten. A handwritten note screams of informality, so don't use one unless that's the precise impression you're trying to convey. Students, in particular, sometimes send out cover letters reminiscent of letters home from camp, complete with the requisite stains from lunch. That is both unprofessional (you *are* trying to impress them with your professionalism) and downright offensive to any potential employer. These letters should be business letters. If you are unfamiliar with the correct way to format such a letter—and, sadly, far too many of you *are*—study the examples we've included (and, if necessary, go to your local library and study the appropriate books in the business section).

Address each letter to the proper person at the publishing company (i.e., don't write to the editor-in-chief to find a job in retail ad sales). The *Job Opportunities Databank* in Section IV, which details the extensive data we received from publishers, including the name and title of the specific individual each paper recommended you initially contact.

Some newspaper or trade magazine ads will not include a contact name, but will instruct you to send your resume to a post office box. In this case (and this case only), "Dear Sir:" is an appropriate salutation. And if the ad lists a series of instructions ("write, don't call;" "send letter including salary requirements; send unreturnable copy sample;" etc.), follow them exactly. Don't call; don't ask for your sample back. Failing to follow precise instructions (they are there for a *reason*) could mean you already failed their "pre-screening interview." You'll have lost the job before you even started chasing it!

The Correct Format

First paragraph: State the reason for the letter, the specific job or type of work for which you're applying, and where (or from whom) you learned of the opening.

Second paragraph: Indicate why you're interested in their company and that particular position and, more important, what you have to offer them. Without repeating information from your resume verbatim, explain the appropriate academic or work experiences that specifically qualify you for the position.

Third paragraph: Refer him to the resume you've enclosed and add anything else you feel it's important he know about you.

Final paragraph: Indicate your desire to meet for a personal interview and your flexibility as to the place and time. Try to close the letter with a statement or question that will encourage him to take some action. Instead of "looking forward to hearing" from him, tell him when he should expect to hear from you. Otherwise, be prepared to *not* hear from him. Newspaper executives get streams of letters, and can't *(don't)* answer most of them.

Try to personalize each letter you write—mention the newspaper's name whenever and wherever you have the chance. Refer to some of their specific sections, trade advertisements, awards, scoops, features, or anything else your research has uncovered. Executives at the top newspaper companies receive hundreds of applications, letters and unsolicited resumes from students and others looking for jobs...*weekly*. They can spot a "form letter" a mile away. Take this opportunity to show them that you are, in fact, serious about working at their company and that you've taken the time to learn something about them. And don't hesitate to demonstrate the fruits of your research in your letters.

Don't make a common mistake and simply recopy half your resume into the body of the cover letter. The letter offers you the opportunity to be a little creative, compensate for some glaring weakness or omission in your resume, and make a good, professional first impression. If the cover letter doesn't "sell" them, they may never even bother looking at the resume.

Two sample cover letters are reproduced at the end of this chapter (after some sample resumes). Cover Letter 1 might have been written in response to a small "want ad" in *Editor & Publisher*, one that didn't identify the paper and directed all inquiries to a PO Box number. Letter 2 is one we'd write to the advertising director at a paper one of our contacts told us might be hiring two or three new people for their Advertising Sales Training Program.

SAMPLE RESUME #1: CHRONOLOGICAL

GILDA H. RADNER

HOME ADDRESS:
80 Stemmons Freeway,
Dallas, TX 87540
(214)788-0000

SCHOOL ADDRESS:
4240 Hill St.,
Los Angeles, CA 90410
(213)001-0100

JOB OBJECTIVE

A position offering challenge and responsibility in newspaper publishing marketing research, advertising or promotion

EDUCATION

U.C.L.A.

1984-1988 Graduating in June, 1988, with a B.A. degree in Marketing. Deans List four years; Summa cum laude.

Fields of study include: marketing and advertising theory, research, business law, economics, mass communications, statistical analysis and research methodology.

Graduate courses in advertising theory and policies, consumer behavioral theory, sales management.

1979-1983 Greg Wright High School, Los Angeles, Calif. National Honor Society. Senior Class President. United Way Club Head Fund Raiser.

WORK EXPERIENCE (SUMMERS)

1987: JIM CANNON , INC., Los Angeles, Ca. Administrative assistant in Research Department. Trained in behavioral research techniques. Responsible for record keeping, expense reports, public relations, lab report dissemination, correspondence.

1984 - 1986: KISCHTRONICS, San Diego, Ca. Basic sales and management training at this major research and development facility. Duties included billing, inventory control, shipping and distribution, lab maintenance and delivery schedules.

SAMPLE RESUME #2: FUNCTIONAL

JIM BEAM
76 Cortlandt St.,
New York, NY 10017
(212)555-1111

Career Objective: A position as a sales representative
at a major metropolitan daily

SUMMARY

I am completing my degree in journalism, specializing in marketing, at University State. Last summer, I interned as an assistant account executive (with copywriting responsibilities) for a local advertising agency. I also have one year's experience selling advertising space (and supervising a staff of three salespeople) on my college newspaper. Both jobs have convinced me I will be successful in newspaper advertising sales.

EXPERIENCE

Summer, 1985 & 86: Intern, Kay Silver & Associates, Inc.
Summer, 1984 : Intern, Committee to Re-elect Kim Kerr

1985/86 school year:Ad Director, *The Daily Planet*
1986/87 school year:Salesman, Joe's University Book Store.

EDUCATION

B.A. Journalism (Marketing) University State - June, 1987
(summa cum laude).

PROFESSIONAL MEMBERSHIPS AND BUSINESS SKILLS

Member of the young Professionals Division of the Advertising Club of New York. Skills: Sales, media placement, typing (50 wpm), word processing, computer literate.

PERSONAL

Age: 21. Health: Excellent. Language Skills: Fluent (read/write/speak) in German and French.

References Available Upon Request

COVER LETTER 1

May 6, 1988

Bill Killpatrick
422 W. 22nd St.,
New York, NY 10000
(212)888-1111

Post Office Box 1000
Editor & Publisher
11 West 19th St.
New York, New York 10011

Dear Sir:

The entry-level advertising sales position briefly outlined in your May 5th advertisement is very appealing to me. Please accept this letter and the attached resume as my application for this position.

While majoring in journalism (with a marketing emphasis) at Stein University, I worked on a number of projects which required the communication skills you specified in your ad. In addition, as advertising director for the Daily Planet, and a summer intern for a local advertising agency, I demonstrated the sales and interpersonal skills such a position requires.

I am especially excited about the possibility of working in the Midwest, as your ad indicates this new employee would. As I was born and raised in Indiana, I am already familiar with and enjoy Chicago, St. Louis, Minneapolis, and the other major cities this territory encompasses.

I would like to meet with you at your convenience to discuss this position and my qualifications for it in more detail. I will be in Chicago for other interviews the week of May 27th. I will call you the week of May 14th, to see if we can set up an appointment for that week.

Thank you for your time. I look forward to meeting with you.

Sincerely yours,

Bill Killpatrick

COVER LETTER 2

May 6, 1988

Tim Carhart
44 Overview Circle,
Fargo, North Dakota
(718)888-0101

Ms. Pamela Cummings
Advertising Director
All The News That Fits, We Print Co.
2435 Dyer Street,
Kokomo, IN 46254

Dear Ms. Cummings:

I recently met your colleague, Arthur Hyman, at a seminar sponsored by Editor & Publisher magazine. He mentioned you were considering hiring two or three entry-level people for your Advertising Sales Training Program and suggested I contact you.

Ms. Cummings, it has been my dream to work at a major metropolitan daily like the Kokomo Times-Herald-Gazette-Leader. If at all possible, I had hoped to be accepted in a well-respected, formal advertising sales training program. Your training program is the best in the industry.

And I'm the right person for you to hire. A journalism major (with a marketing emphasis) at University State, I earned a 3.8 GPA in all my courses, a 3.95 in my journalism and marketing major. In addition, as ad director for the Centennial and, this past summer, working as an account services intern for a local agency, I clearly demonstrated my sales, communication and interpersonal skills.

Ms. Cummings, I will be returning home to Indiana in one week and would like to meet with you soon thereafter to discuss this opportunity in more detail. I will call you on May 14th to schedule an appointment. I look forward to talking with you then.

Sincerely yours,

Tim Carhart

CHAPTER TWENTY NINE

Questions For You, Questions For Them

Well, the days of research, preparation, chart-making, form-filling and resume-printing worked. They're lining up to meet you! So it's time to prepare once again—for the interviewing process that will inevitably determine the job offers you actually get.

Interviews shouldn't scare you. After all, the very concept of two (or more) persons meeting to determine if they are right for each other is a good one. As important as research, resumes, letters and phone calls are, they are inherently impersonal. The interview is your chance to really see and feel the company firsthand—"up close and personal;" so think of it as a positive opportunity—your chance to succeed.

This chapter will focus on the kinds of questions you are likely to be asked, how to answer them and the questions you should be ready to ask yourself. By removing the workings of the interview process from the "unknown" category, you will reduce the fear it engenders. (If you feel you need more help with interviewing, we suggest Interview For Success by Drs. Caryl & Ron Krannich, a brand-new edition of which is now available through The Career Press.)

GETTING ORGANIZED, GETTING STARTED

Start by setting up a calendar on which you can enter and track all your scheduled appointments. When you schedule an interview with a publisher, ask them how much time you should allow for the appointment. Some companies require all new applicants to fill out numerous forms and/or complete a battery of intelligence or psychological tests—all before the first interview. If you've only allowed an hour for the interview—and scheduled another at a nearby paper ten minutes later—the first time you confront a three-hour test series will effectively destroy any schedule.

Some companies, especially if the first interview is very positive, like to keep applicants around to talk to other executives. This process may be planned or, in a lot of cases, a spontaneous decision by an interviewer who likes you and wants you to meet some other key decision makers. Other companies will tend to schedule such a series of second interviews on a separate day. Find out, if you can, how the publisher you're planning to visit generally operates. Other-wise, especially if you've traveled to New York or another city to interview with a number of companies in a short period of time, a schedule that's too tight will fall apart in no time at all.

If you need to travel out-of-state to interview with a publisher, be sure to ask if they will be paying some or all of your travel expenses. (It's generally expected that you'll be paying your own way to companies within your home state.) If the publisher doesn't offer—and you don't ask—presume you're paying the freight.

Even if the paper agrees to reimburse you, make sure you have enough money to pay all the expenses yourself. While some companies may reimburse you immediately, handing you a check as you leave the building, the majority may take from a week to a month to forward you an expense check.

PRE-INTERVIEW RESEARCH

The research you did to find these publishing companies is nothing compared to the research you need to do now that you're beginning to narrow your search. If you followed our detailed suggestions when you started targeting these publishers in the first place, you've already amassed a lot of information about them. If you didn't bother to do the research *then*, you sure better decide to do it *now*. Study each publishing company as if you were going to be tested on your detailed knowledge of their organization and operations. Here's a complete checklist of the facts you should try to know about each company you plan to visit for a job interview:

The Basics

1. The address of (and directions to) the office you're visiting.
2. Headquarters location (if different).
3. Some idea of domestic and international branches.
4. Relative size (compared to other papers).
5. Annual sales and income (last two years).
6. Subsidiary companies; specialized divisions.
7. Departments (overall company structure).
8. Number of papers published; circulation of each

The Extras

1. The history of the company (including specialties, honors and awards, famous names, etc.).
2. Names, titles and backgrounds of top management.

3. Major columnists, reporters, etc. associated with the paper.

4. Existence (and type) of training program.

5. Relocation policy.

6. Relative salaries (compared to other publishers).

7. Recent developments concerning the company or its papers (from your trade magazine and newspaper reading).

8. Everything you can learn about the career, likes and dislikes of the person(s) interviewing you.

The amount of time and work necessary to be *this* well-prepared for an interview is considerable. It will not be accomplished the day before the interview. You may even find some of the information you need to be unavailable on short notice. (Is it really so important to do all this? Well, *some*body out there is going to. And if you happen to be interviewing for the same job as that other, well-prepared, knowledgeable candidate, who do *you* think will impress the interview more?)

If you give yourself enough time, most of this information is surprisingly easy to obtain. In addition to the detailed information in the *Job Opportunities Databank* (Section IV) of this Career Directory and the other reference sources we covered in the earlier chapters of this job search section, the publishing company itself can supply you with a great deal of data. A company's Annual Report—which all publicly-owned companies must publish yearly for their stockholders—is a virtual treasure trove of information. Write each paper and request copies of their last two Annual Reports. A comparison of circulation, sales, income and other data over this period may enable you to infer some interesting things about the company's overall financial health and growth potential. Many libraries also have collections of annual reports from major corporations. Also, each paper has a media file that it prepares (primarily) for its advertisers. This will help you be current on circulation and ad rate data, new sections, special issues, etc.

Attempting to learn about your interviewer is a chore, the importance of which is underestimated by most applicants (who then, of course, don't bother to do it). Being one of the exceptions may get you a job. Use the biographical references mentioned earlier in this section. If he is listed in any of these sources, you'll be able to learn an awful lot about his background. In addition, find out if he's written any articles that have appeared in the trade press or, even better, books on his area(s) of expertise. Referring to his own writings during the course of an interview, without making it *too* obvious a compliment, can be very effective. We all have egos and we all like people to talk about us. The interviewer is no different from the rest of us. You might also check to see if any of your networking contacts worked with him at his current (or a previous) paper and can help "fill you in."

THE DAY OF THE INTERVIEW

On the day of the interview, wear a conservative business suit (not a sports coat, not a "nice" blouse and skirt).

It's not unusual for resumes and cover letters to head in different directions when a company starts passing them around to a number of executives. If you sent them, both may even be long gone. So bring along extra copies of your resume and your own copy of the cover letter that originally accompanied it. Whether or not you make them available, we suggest you prepare a neatly-typed list of references (including the name, title, company, address and phone number of each person). You may want to bring along a copy of your college transcript, especially if it's something to brag about. (Once you get your first job, you'll probably never use it—or be asked for it—again, so enjoy it while you can!) And, if appropriate or required, make sure you bring samples of your work (e.g., your art portfolio or "clippings file").

Plan to arrive fifteen minutes before your scheduled appointment. If you're in an unfamiliar city, or have a long drive to the company, allow extra time for the unexpected delays that seem to occur with mind-numbing regularity on days like this. Arriving early will give you some time to check your appearance, catch your breath, check in with the receptionist, learn how to correctly pronounce the interviewer's name, and get yourself organized and battle-ready.

Arriving late does not make a sterling first impression. If you are only a few minutes late, it's probably best not to mention it or even excuse yourself. With a little luck, everybody else is behind schedule and no one will notice. However, if you're more than fifteen minutes late, have an honest (or serviceable) explanation ready and offer it at your first opportunity. Then drop the subject as quickly as possible and move on to the interview.

When you meet the interviewer, shake hands firmly. People pay attention to handshakes. Ask for a business card. This will make sure you get the name and title right when you write your follow-up letter. You can staple it to the company file for easy reference as you continue your networking.

Try to maintain eye contact with the interviewer as you talk. This will indicate you're interested in what he has to say. Sit straight. Keep your voice at a comfortable level, and try to sound enthusiastic (without imitating a high school cheerleader). Be confident and poised, and provide direct, accurate and honest answers to his trickiest questions. And, as you try to remember all this, just be yourself and try to act like you're comfortable and enjoying yourself!

Interviews are sometimes conducted over lunch, though this is not usually the case with entry-level people. If it does happen to you, though, try to order something in the middle price range, neither filet mignon nor a cheeseburger. Do not order alcohol. If your interviewer orders a carafe of wine, you may share it. Otherwise, alcohol should be considered *verboten*, under any and all circumstances. Then hope your mother taught you the correct way to eat and talk at the same time. If not, just do your best to maintain your poise.

There are some things interviewers will always view with displeasure—street language, complete lack of eye contact, insufficient or vague explanations or answers, a noticeable lack of energy, poor interpersonal skills (i.e., not listening or the basic inability to carry on an intelligent conversation) and a demonstrable lack of motivation.

Before you allow an interview to end, summarize why you want the job, why you are qualified and what, in particular, you can offer their company. Then, take some action. If the interviewer hasn't told you about the rest of the interview process and/or where you stand, ask him. Will you be seeing other people that day? If so, ask him for some background on the other people with whom you'll be interviewing. If there are no other meetings that day, what's the next step? When can you expect to hear from them about coming back?

When you return home, file all the business cards, copies of correspondence, and notes from the interview(s) with each company in the appropriate files. Finally, but most importantly, ask yourself which publishers you really want to work for and which you are no longer interested in. This will quickly determine how far you want the process at each paper to develop before you politely tell them to stop considering you for the job.

Immediately send a thank-you letter to each executive you met. These should, of course, be neatly-typed business letters, not handwritten notes (unless you are most friendly, indeed, with the interviewer and want to *stress* the "informal" nature of your note). If you are still interested in pursuing a position at their paper, tell them in no uncertain terms. Reiterate why you feel you're the best candidate and tell each of the executives when you hope (expect?) to hear from them.

QUESTIONS EVERY INTERVIEWER KNOWS...AND MOST USE

Preparing for your interviews by learning about the publishing company is a key first step. Preparing to deal with the questions the interviewer will throw at you is a necessary second one. Don't go in "cold," oblivious to what's going to occur when you walk into his office. There are certain questions we can almost guarantee will be asked during any first interview. Study the list of questions (and hints) that follow, and prepare at least one solid, concise answer that you can trot out on cue. Practice with a friend until your answers to these most-asked questions sound intelligent, professional and, most important, unmemorized and unrehearsed.

"Why do you want to be in newspaper publishing?" Using your knowledge and understanding of the newspaper industry, explain why you find the business exciting, and where and how you see yourself fitting in.

"Why do you think you'll be successful in this business?" Using the information from your self evaluation and the research you did on that particular paper, formulate an answer which marries your strengths to theirs and to the characteristics of the position for which you're applying.

"Why did you choose our paper?" This is an excellent opportunity to explain the extensive process of research and education you've undertaken. Tell them about your strengths and how you match up with their paper. Emphasize specific things about their paper that led you to seek an interview. Be a salesperson—be convincing.

"What can you do for us?" Construct an answer that essentially lists your strengths, the experience you have which will contribute to your job performance and any other unique qualifications that will place you at the head of the applicant pack. Be careful: This is a question specifically designed to <u>eliminate</u> some of that pack. Sell yourself. Be one of the few called back for a second interview.

"What position here interests you?" If you're interviewing for a specific position, answer accordingly. If you want to make sure you don't close the door on other opportunities of which you might be unaware, you can follow up with your own question: "I'm here to apply for your Reporter Training Program. Is there another position open for which you feel I'm qualified?"

If you've arranged an interview with a paper without knowing of any specific openings, use the answer to this question to describe the kind of work you'd like to do and why you're qualified to do it. Avoid a specific job title, since they will tend to vary from paper to paper. If you're on a first interview with the personnel department, just answer the question. They only want to figure out where to send you.

"What are your strengths and weaknesses?" and **"What are your hobbies (or outside interests)?"** Both questions can be easily answered using the data you gathered to complete the self-evaluation process. Be wary of being too forthcoming about your glaring faults (nobody expects you to volunteer every weakness and mistake), but do *not* reply, "I don't have any." They won't believe you and, what's worse, *you* won't believe you. After all, you did the evaluation—you know it's a lie!

"What are your career goals?"...Which is why we suggested you think about such things in the first place. Tell them what you want to do.

"What jobs have you held and why did you leave them?" Or the direct approach, "Have you ever been fired?" Take the opportunity to expand on your resume, rather than precisely answering the question by merely recapping your job experiences. In discussing each job, point out what you liked about it, what factors led to your leaving, and how the next job added to your continuing professional education. If you have been fired, say so. It's very easy to check.

"What are your salary requirements?" If they are at all interested in you, this question will probably come up. The danger, of course, is that you may price yourself too low or, even worse, right out of a job you want. Since you will have a general idea of industry figures for that position (and may even have an idea of what that paper tends to pay new people for the position), why not refer to a *range* of salaries, such as "$16,000 - $19,000?"

If the interviewer doesn't bring up salary at all, it's doubtful you're being seriously considered, so you probably don't need to even bring the subject up. (If you know you aren't getting the job or aren't interested in it if offered, you may try to nail down a salary figure in order to be better prepared for the next publisher interview).

"Tell me about yourself." Watch out for this one! It's often one of the first questions asked. If you falter here, the rest of the interview could quickly become a downward slide to nowhere. Be prepared, and consider it an opportunity to combine your answers to many of the previous questions into one concise description of who you are, what you want to be and why that publisher should take a chance on you. Summarize your resume—briefly—and expand on particular courses or experiences relevant to the company, paper or position. Do not go on about your hobbies or personal life, your dog, where you spent your summer vacation, etc. None of that is particularly relevant to securing that job. You may explain how that particular job fits in with your long-range career goals and talk specifically about what attracted you to their paper.

The Not-So-Obvious Questions

Every interviewer is different and, unfortunately, there are no rules saying he has to use all or any of the "basic" questions. But we think the odds are against his avoiding *all* of them. Whichever of these he includes, be assured most interviewers do like to come up with questions that are "uniquely theirs." It may be just one or a whole series—questions he's developed over the years that he feels help separate the wheat from the chaff.

You can't exactly prepare yourself for questions like, "What would you do if...(fill in the blank with some obscure occurrence)?," "Tell me about your father," or "What's your favorite ice cream flavor?" Every interviewer we know has his or her favorites and all of these questions seem to come out of left field. Just stay relaxed, grit your teeth (quietly) and take a few seconds to frame a reasonably intelligent reply.

Some questions may be downright inappropriate. Young women, for example, may be asked about their plans for marriage and children. Don't call the interviewer a chauvinist (or worse). And don't point out that the question may be a little outside the law. (The nonprofessional interviewer may not realize such questions are illegal, and a huffy response may confuse —and anger—him.) Whenever any questions are raised about your personal life—and this question surely qualifies—it is much more effective to respond that you are very interested in the position and have no reason to believe that your personal life will preclude you from doing an excellent job.

"Do you have any questions?" It's the fatal twelfth question on our list—often the last one an interviewer throws at you—after an hour or two of grilling. Unless the interview has been very long and unusually thorough, you probably *should* have questions about the job, the company, even the industry.

Preparing yourself for an interview means more than having answers for some of the questions an interviewer may ask. It means having your *own* set of questions—at least five or six—for the interviewer. The interviewer is trying to find the right person for the job. *You're* trying to find the right job. So you should be just as curious about him and his company as he is about you. Here's a short list of questions you may consider asking on any interview:

1. What will my typical day be like?

2. What happened to the last person who had this job?

3. Given my attitude and qualifications, how would you estimate my chances for career advancement at your paper?

4. Why did you come to work here? What keeps you here?

5. If you were I, would you start here again?

6. How would you characterize the management philosophy of your paper?

7. What characteristics do the successful_____ at your company have in common (fill in the blank with an appropriate title, such as "editors," "sales reps," "reporters," "designers," etc.)?

8. What's the best (and worst) thing about working here?

9. On a scale of 1 to 10, how would you rate your paper in terms of salaries, benefits and employee satisfaction, in comparison to others your size?

Other questions about the newspaper or position will be obvious—they're the areas your research hasn't been able to fill in. Ask the interviewer. But be careful and use common sense. No one is going to answer highly personal, rude or indiscreet questions. Even innocent questions might be misconstrued if you don't think about the best way to pose them—*before* they come trippingly off your tongue.

Unless you're interviewing with the Personnel (or Human Resources) department, remember that most, if not all, of the executives you'll be meeting will *not* be professional interviewers. Which means they might well spend more time talking about themselves than the company, the position or you. If that happens, use it as an opportunity to create an informal dialogue. Such a "conversational approach" is often a more productive way of finding out important information, and selling yourself, than a straightforward question and answer session anyway.

No job search is an easy one. They all require time, energy, research and more than a modicum of luck. And jobs at "big name" publishing companies are never easy to get. The detailed job search process we've outlined in these chapters is complicated, time-consuming and, we expect, far more involved than most of you will like. None of you will precisely follow each recommended step. But, hopefully, you will come to understand why we've made each recommendations and find them helpful in your own search.

Because the extra work you do now *will* pay off in the long run. The more time and effort you put into your career *now*—as you're just starting out—the more likely you'll end up at the right publisher, in the right department, heading in the right direction, and well on your way to achieving the personal goals you set. ***Good luck!***

SECTION IV

Job Opportunties
Databank

CHAPTER THIRTY

Entry-Level
Job Listings

There are two chapters in this section. This one includes information on the newspaper publishers we surveyed regarding entry-level job opportunities; We are happy to note that the vast majority of the top papers in the U.S. responded to our survey; information on all of them is included here. (Chapter 31 includes internship and training program information.) This information was compiled by our staff through direct mail questionnaires and telephone calls and represents data that is completely unavailable anywhere else. (We have, however, recently published the first two volumes of our brand-new **Internship Series**. Those of you interested in journalism internships should, therefore, also consult **Internships, Volume 2: Newspaper, Magazine and Book Publishing,** which includes more information on the papers and publishers listed in these two chapters, as well as those magazine and book publishers listed in the *Job Opportunities Databanks* of our other two publishing Career Directories.

It isn't hard to see that the majority of entry-level opportunities are at the biggest publishers—those with more than a single paper, or a paper with a circulation of significant size. But there are also a surprising number of smaller publishers—with just that one, small-circulation paper and a few employees—that are ready to hire a surprising number of recent college graduates.

As should be obvious, this is not a complete listing of U. S. newspaper publishers. However, it is a nearly complete list of those major publishers offering entry-level opportunities and/or internships and, as a matter of fact, includes listings for virtually every major newspaper publisher in the country. With these listings as a guide, you should be able to get a better feel for the possibilities out there. You can then use a reference book like SRDS or the Editor & Publisher International Yearbook to find other papers/publishers that match those listed here in size or location. But even if you just stick with this list, you will be working with the publishers and papers that will probably end up hiring the majority of entry-level candidates.

Most of the information should be self-explanatory. If a newspaper indicated different employment contacts on a department basis, we have listed them all. And if a publisher has more than one newspaper, we listed the detailed information under one of the papers, noted the names of the others under "Other Newspapers Published," and then listed *these* alphabetically as well, with cross-references to the main listing for that publisher.

"Average Entry-level Hiring" is that publisher's best estimate of anticipated need for new people each year. *"Total employees"* lists all full-time employees. Part-time employees, if any, are noted in parentheses.

Two important points: 1) A "?" following the "average entry-level hiring" entry means *they tend to hire entry-level people;* they were just unable to come up with any specific number. 2) If the publisher indicates they do not plan to hire any entry-level people, they may still have listed "Opportunities." In this case, these should not be considered actual jobs, merely the positions they consider entry-level...whether or not they currently have openings.

If the publishers themselves had any specific suggestions, we've included them. These will help you get a head start on other applicants—you'll know what the companies want you to do!

Whenever we couldn't confirm the accuracy of an entry, we merely entered "NA"— Not Available.

Oh, and don't forget the second chapter of this section—it lists all of the newspaper publishers we've identified that offer internships and/or training programs.

ABILENE REPORTER-NEWS
PO Box 30
Abilene, TX 79604
915-673-4271
Employment Contact: Betty Walden, Personnel Director
Total Employees: 250
Average Entry-Level Hiring: 3-4
Opportunities: Clerk, Pressmen, Production—High school graduates. Reporter—College degree. No other requirements specified.

AKRON BEACON JOURNAL
44 Exchange Street
Akron OH 44328
216-375-8571
Employment Contact: Barbara Dean, Head of Personnel
Total Employees: 725 (plus 80 part-time)
Average Entry-Level Hiring: 10-20
Opportunities: Newsroom, Circulation Sales, Advertising Sales—College degree. Production Dept.—High school graduate (at least). No other requirements specified.

ALBUQUERQUE JOURNAL
ALBUQUERQUE TRIBUNE
Listings deleted at Publisher's request

ANCHORAGE DAILY NEWS
PO Box 149001
Anchorage, AK 99514-9001
907-786-4200

Employment Contact: Lou Ann Henning, Personnel Manager
Total Employees: 320
Average Entry-Level Hiring: 3-4
Opportunities: Mailroom Inserter, Loading Dock Assistant, Clerks—High school graduates. Sales Rep—College degree (BA or BS). No other requirements specified.

ANN ARBOR NEWS
340 E Huron Street
Ann Arbor, MI 48104
313-994-6989

Employment Contact: David Busak, Head of Personnel
Total Employees: 350
Average Entry-Level Hiring: 20
Opportunities: Reporters, Sales Reps, Production Personnel, Clerical—no requirements specified.

ARIZONA DAILY STAR
Box 26807
Tucson, AZ 85726
602-573-4400

Employment Contact: John Peck, Managing Editor
Total Employees: 150
Average Entry-Level Hiring: 3
Opportunities: Reporter, Photographer, Account Executive——College degree required, two years experience preferrred.

ARIZONA DAILY SUN
PO Box 1849
Flagstaff, AZ 86002
602-774-4545

Employment Contact: Cheryle Dawn, Head of Personnel
Total Employees: 420 (plus 40 part-time)
Average Entry-Level Hiring: 3
Opportunities: Clerk, Sales Rep, Circulation—High school graduates. Reporter—College degree (BA or BS) required; 2 years experience preferred.

ARIZONA REPUBLIC
See listings for Central Newspapers, Inc. and Phoenix Newspapers, Inc.

ASHEVILLE CITIZEN-TIMES
PO Box 2090
Asheville, NC 28802
704-252-5611

Employment Contact: Personnel Department
Total Employees: 221 (plus 56 part-time)
Average Entry-Level Hiring: 10-15
Opportunities: Reporters—College degree (in English preferred). Clerical, Sales Dept.—High school graduates. No other requirements specified.

ATLANTA JOURNAL
See listing for Atlanta Morning Constitution

ATLANTA MORNING CONSTITUTION
PO Box 4689, 72 Marietta Street
Atlanta, GA 30303
404-526-5151

Other Newspapers Published: Atlanta Journal
Employment Contact: Cheryl Bingham, Employment Manager
Total Employees: 2,400 (plus 3,400 part-time)
Average Entry-Level Hiring: 70-80
Opportunities: Telephone Sales, Clerical (Secretary), Mailroom, Programmers—High school graduates. No other requirements specified.

AUGUSTA CHRONICLE
Box 1928
Augusta, GA 30913
404-724-0851

Other Newspapers Published: Augusta Herald
Employment Contact: Howard Eanes, Executive Editor
Total Employees: 3,600
Average Entry-Level Hiring: 7
Opportunities: Reporter—College degree (BA or BS). No other requirements specified.

AUGUSTA HERALD
See listing for the Augusta Chronicle

BALTIMORE SUN
501 N Calvert Street
Baltimore, MD 21278
301-332-6000
Employment Contact: Barbara Scott Jones,
Personnel Manager
Total Employees: 2,100
Average Entry-Level Hiring: 6-8
Opportunities: Clerks—High school graduates.
Advertising, Word Processing—College degree.
No other requirements specified.

THE BATESVILLE GUARD
PO box 2036
Batesville, AR 72503
501-793-2383
Employment Contact: Jo Cargill, Vice President
Total Employees: 35
Average Entry-Level Hiring: 4
Opportunities: Editor, Advertising—College
degree (BA preferred). No other requirements
specified.

THE BAY TIMES
See listing for The Kent Group

BEE PUBLICATIONS
5564 Main St.
Williamsville, NY 14221
716-632-4700
Newspapers Published: Nine suburban papers in
the Buffalo area.
Employment Contact: Donald J. Goreham,
Executive Editor
Total Employees: 85
Average Entry-Level Hiring: 1
Opportunities: Account Executive, Journalist—
College degree (BA or BS). No other requirements
specified.

BOCA RATON NEWS
PO Box 580, 34 SE 2nd Street
Boca Raton, FL 33482
305-395-8300
Employment Contact: Wendy Graffel, Personnel
Manager
Total Employees: 180
Average Entry-Level Hiring: 2-3
Opportunities: Newsroom. Advertising,
Composing, Sales—High school graduates. No
other requirements specified.

BOSTON GLOBE
Listing deleted at Publisher's request.

THE BOSTON TAB
See listing for The Tab Newspaper

THE BRADENTON HERALD
102 Manatee Avenue W, PO Box 921
Bradenton, FL 33506
813-748-0411
Employment Contact: Barbara Cashian,
Personnel Director
Total Employees: 220
Average Entry-Level Hiring: 3-6
Opportunities: Clerk, Reporter, Sales, Press-
men—No particular educational or skill
requirements specified.

THE BROOKLINE TAB
See listing for The Tab Newspapers

BUCKS COUNTY COURIER TIMES
8400 Route 13
Levittown, PA 19057
215-752-6701
Employment Contact: Joe Halberstein, Associate
Editor
Total Employees: 500
Average Entry-Level Hiring: 3-5
Opportunities: Reporter, Account Executive—
College degree (BA or BS) required; 2 years
experience preferred.

BUFFALO NEWS
1 News Plaza, PO Box 100
Buffalo, NY 14240
716-849-3434
Employment Contact: Richard Feather, Sr. VP-
Human Resources
Total Employees: 1,200
Average Entry-Level Hiring: 3-7
Opportunities: Clerical. Advertising Sales—
High school graduates. Reporters—College
degree (BA or BS) required, 2-3 years experience.

CALIFORNIA VOICE
See listing for Reporter Publications

CALLER TIMES
PO Box 9136
Corpus Christi, TX 78469
512-884-2011
Employment Contact: Becky Gonzales, Personnel Department
Total Employees: 400
Average Entry-Level Hiring: 3-5
Opportunities: "Experience is required in all departments. No completely inexperienced people, please."

THE CAMBRIDGE TAB
See listing for The Tab Newspapers

CAMDEN CHRONICLE-INDEPENDENT
1115 Broad Street
Camden, SC 29020
803-432-6157
Employment Contact: Glenn Tucker, Co-Publisher
Total Employees: 26 (20 Part-time)
Average Entry-Level Hiring: 1-2
Opportunities: Clerks, Sales—High school graduates. Reporters—College degree (in journalism preferred).

THE CANTON ENTERPRISE
See listing for The News and Observer Publishing Company

CAPITOL NEWS SERVICE
1113 H Street
Sacramento, CA 95814
916-445-6336
Employment Contact: Verna Kline, Bureau Chief
Total Employees: 6
Average Entry-Level Hiring: 0
Opportunities: Journalism, Account Executive—College degree (BA or BS); 2 years experience preferred.
Comments: Company specializes in political reporting; covers Sacramento for 100+ papers throughout the state.

CARY NEWS
See listing for the News and Observer Publishing Co.

CEDAR RAPIDS-MARION GAZETTE
500 Third Avenue SE
Cedar Rapids-Marion, IA 52401
319-398-8211

Employment Contact: Mary Collins, Director of Personnel
Total Employees: 430
Average Entry-Level Hiring: ?
Opportunities: Clerks, Sales, Pressmen, Promotion—High school graduates. Reporters—College degree (in journalism preferred).

CENTER FOR INVESTIGATIVE REPORTING, INC.
54 Mint St., 4th Floor
San Francisco, CA 94103
415-543-1200
Employment Contact: Dan Noyes, Managing Editor
Total Employees: 15
Average Entry-Level Hiring: 0
Opportunities: Account Executive—College degree (BA or BS); 1-2 years experience preferred.
Comments: Non-profit corporation that produces articles and stories for magazines, newspapers and television on a variety of international issues, including the environment, nuclear arms, civil and human rights, etc.

CENTRAL NEWSPAPERS, INC.
307 N. Penn
Indianapolis, IN 46204
317-633-9208
Newspapers Published: The Indianapolis News, Indianapolis Star (see separate listing for two prior) Arizona Republic, Phoenix Gazette (see listing for Phoenix Newspapers)
Employment Contact: Harvey C. Jacobs, Editor
Total Employees: 1,600
Average Entry-Level Hiring: 10-15
Opportunities: Reporter—College degree (BA or BS). No other requirements specified.
Note: See individual listings for newspapers.

CENTRE DAILY TIMES
3400 E College Avenue
State College, PA 16801
814-238-5000
Employment Contact: Karen Lobeck, Managing Editor
Total Employees: 135
Average Entry-Level Hiring: 3-5
Opportunities: Clerks—High school graduates. Sports-News Dept., Advertising, Sales—College degree in specific field. No other requirements specified.

CENTURY PUBLICATIONS, INC.
3 Church St.
Winchester, MA 01890
617-729-8100
Newspapers Published: A number of suburban weekly papers in Boston area.
Employment Contact: William Finucane, Executive Editor
Total Employees: 15
Average Entry-Level Hiring: 3-5
Opportunities: Journalism—College degree (BA or BS). No other requirements specified.

CHARLESTON DAILY MAIL
See listing for Charleston Gazette

CHARLESTON GAZETTE
1001 Virginia Street E
Charleston, WV 25301
304-348-5105
Other Newspapers Published: Charleston Daily Mail
Employment Contact: John Bowyer, Head of Personnel
Total Employees: 400
Average Entry-Level Hiring: 8-10
Opportunities: Clerks, Sales—High school graduates. Reporter—College degree (BS in journalism preferred).

CHARLOTTE OBSERVER
PO Box 32188, 600 S Tryon Street
Charlotte, NC 28202
704-379-6660
Employment Contact: Paul Connelly, Personnel Services Manager
Total Employees: 1,400
Average Entry-Level Hiring: 1-2
Opportunities: Marketing Sales, Reporters—College degree (BA or BS) and/or previous experience (prefer 2-3 years experience in appropriate area). Clerks, Sales—High school graduates.

CHATTANOOGA NEWS-FREE PRESS
400 E 11th Street
Chattanooga, TN 37401
615-756-6900
Employment Contact: Ray Marler, Director of Personnel
Total Employees: 550
Average Entry-Level Hiring: 3-4
Opportunities: Clerks, Sales—High school graduates. Reporters—College degree. 2-3 years journalism experience preferred.

CHICAGO SUN-TIMES
401 N Wabash Avenue
Chicago, IL 60611
312-321-3000
Employment Contact: Jack Nettis, Director of Personnel and Labor Relations
Total Employees: 465
Average Entry-Level Hiring: 3-4
Opportunities: Clerks, Sales—High school graduates. Reporters—College degree (BS in journalism preferred). 2-3 years experience.

CHICAGO TRIBUNE
435 North Michigan Avenue
Chicago, IL 60611
312-222-4571
Employment Contact: Ronald Williams, Employment Manager
Total Employees: 4,000
Average Entry-Level Hiring: ?
Opportunities: Advertising Sales - College degree (Liberal Arts), communications and business skills. Circulation Department - College degree (Liberal arts preferred), business skills.

CINCINNATI ENQUIRER
617 Vine Street
Cincinnati, OH 45201
513-721-2700
Employment Contact: Maureen, Donohue, Personnel Manager
Total Employees: 1,000
Average Entry-Level Hiring: 7-8
Opportunities: Clerks, Sales, Reporters—No educational or skill requirements specified.

CINCINNATI POST
125 East Court St.
Cincinnati, OH 45202
513-352-2000
Employment Contact: Carole Philipps, Assistant Managing Editor Administration
Total Employees: 114
Average Entry-Level Hiring: 4-5
Opportunities: Clerk—High school graduates. Reporters, Copy Desk, Advertising Sales—College degree; 1-2 years experience preferred.

CLEVELAND PLAIN DEALER
1801 Superior Avenue NE
Cleveland, OH 44114
216-344-4970
Employment Contact: Russ Pinzone, Managing
Editor-Personnel
Total Employees: 1,800
Average Entry-Level Hiring: 7-10
Opportunities: Clerks—High school graduates,
no experience. Reporter, Advertising, Marketing,
Sales—College degree (BA or BS), 2-3 years
experience preferred.

THE CLOVER HERALD
See listing for the News and Observer Publishing
Company

COLUMBUS LEDGER
PO Box 711, 17 W 12th Street
Columbus, GA 31994
404-324-5526
Employment Contact: Henry Wood, Personnel
Director
Total Employees: 600
Average Entry-Level Hiring: 4-6
Opportunities: Clerks, Sales—High school
graduates. Marketing, Newsroom, Reporters—
College degree. No experience for any of these
positions.

COURIER JOURNAL
525 W Broadway
Louisville, KY 40202
502-582-4011
Employment Contact: Larry Vonderhaar, VP
Human Resources (Job Line—(502) 582-7000
Total Employees: 1,060
Average Entry-Level Hiring: 8
Opportunities: Clerks, Sales—High school
graduate. Reporter, Marketing—College degree
(BA or BS), prefer 3-4 years experience.

THE DAILY DISPATCH
1720 Fifth Ave.
Moline, IL 61265
309-764-4344
Other Newspapers Published: Rock Island Argus
Employment Contact: Russell H. Scott, Managing
Editor
Total Employees: 250
Average Entry-Level Hiring: 2-4

THE DAILY JOURNAL
8 Dearborn Square
Kankakee, IL 60901
815-937 3300
Employment Contact: Mark Gibson, Managing
Editor
Total Employees: 130
Average Entry-Level Hiring: 4-6
Opportunities: Clerks, Sales—High school grad-
uates. Reporters, Art Dept., Printing Technician
—College degree. No experience for any of these
positions. No other requirements specified.

THE DAILY REVIEW
116 Main St.
Towanda, PA 18848
717-265-2151
Employment Contact: Dennis Irvine, Editor
Total Employees: 75
Average Entry-Level Hiring: 3
Opportunities: Editorial (News) Dept.—College
degree (journalism major); prefer 1-2 years
experience.

DALLAS MORNING NEWS
Communications Center
Dallas, TX 75265
214-977-8222
Employment Contact: Paula La Rocque, Assistant
Managing Editor - Personnel
Total Employees: 300
Average Entry-Level Hiring: 6-8
Opportunities: Clerks, Sales—High school grad-
uates. Reporter, Marketing—College degree (BA
only); prefer 2-3 years experience.

DALLAS OBSERVER
2330 Butler #115
Dallas, TX 75235
214-637-2072
Employment Contact: Ken Kirk, Personnel
Director
Total Employees: 25
Average Entry-Level Hiring: 2-3
Opportunities: Sales–High school graduates, no
experience. Reporters, News Room, Marketing—
College degree, prefer 2-3 years experience.

DALLAS TIMES HERALD
1101 Pacific Avenue
Dallas, TX 75202
214-720-6111

Employment Contact: Tom Rice, Sr. VP Human Resources
Total Employees: 1,400
Average Entry-Level Hiring: 7-8
Opportunities: Clerks—High school graduates. Editorial, Production, Sales—College degree. No experience for any of these areas; no other requirements specified.

DAYTONA BEACH JOURNAL
901 Sixth Street
Daytona Beach, FL 32015
904-252-1511

Employment Contact: Richard Kearley, Personnel Director
Total Employees: 600
Average Entry-Level Hiring: 6
Opportunities: Clerks—High school graduates. Reporters, Marketing, Sales—College degree; 2-3 years experience preferred.

DECATUR HERALD AND REVIEW
601 E. William St., Box 311
Decatur, IL 62525
217-429-5151

Employment Contact: Terri Kuhle, Personnel Manager
Total Employees: NA
Average Entry-Level Hiring: 1-2
Opportunities: Entry-level people are expected to be experienced reporters, on the order of 2-3 years, although returning interns have a very good chance of being hired.

DELAWARE COUNTY DAILY TIMES
500 Mildred Ave.
Primos, PA
215-284-7200

Employment Contact: Linda DeMeglio, Managing Editor
Total Employees: 140
Average Entry-Level Hiring: 0
Opportunities: Editorial Dept.—College degree, good writing and spelling skills.

THE DESERET NEWS PUBLISHING CO.
30 East First South St., PO Box 1257
Salt Lake City, UT 84110
801-237-2800

Other Newspapers Published: The Tribune
Employment Contact: Jay Livingood, Personnel Director
Total Employees: 150
Average Entry-Level Hiring: 0
Comments: Hiring freeze in effect (2/15/88)

DES MOINES REGISTER
PO Box 957
Des Moines, IA 50304
515-284-8000

Other Newspapers Published: Indinola Register, Independence Newspaper
Employment Contact: Martha Gelhaus, Personnel Manager
Total Employees: 1,150
Average Entry-Level Hiring: 3-5
Opportunities: Classified Advertising, Advertising, Customer Service—High school diploma or equivalent. No experience. Marketing Services, Advertising Sales—College degree BA or BS); 2 years experience preferred.

DENVER POST
650 15th Street, PO Box 1709
Denver, CO 80202
303-820-1746

Employment Contact: Mary Bender, Employment Manager-Editorial (Job-Line 303-820-1820)
Total Employees: 1,700
Average Entry-Level Hiring: 1-2
Opportunities: Clerical/Typist - prefer previous clerical or secretarial experience. Business, Editorial, Reporters, Sales—College degree.

DETROIT FREE PRESS
321 W Lafayette Boulevard
Detroit, MI 48231
313-222-6490

Employment Contact: Kathy Warbelow
Total Employees: 2,200
Average Entry-Level Hiring: ?

DETROIT NEWS
615 Lafayette Boulevard
Detroit, MI 48231
313-222-2095

Employment Contact: Gordon Sakstrup, Personnel Manager

Total Employees: 2,300
Average Entry-Level Hiring: 6-10
Opportunities: Clerical—High school graduates. Reporters, Advertising Sales—College degree; prefer 2-3 years experience.

DURHAM HERALD COMPANY, INC.
115 Market St.
Durham, NC 27702
919-682-8181
Newspapers Published: Durham Morning Herald, The Durham Sun
Employment Contact: Sandra Gainey, Personnel Director
Total Employees: 400
Average Entry-Level Hiring: 15
Opportunities: All of the following require no experience; college degree (4-year) is preferred: Reporter, Copy Editor, District Sales Manager, Advertising Sales Representative, Artist, Photographer.

EMPIRE STATE WEEKLIES
2010 Empire Blvd.
Webster, NY 14580
716-671-1533
Newspapers Published: Webster Herald, Penfield Press, Pair Port-Punton Herald Mail, Wayne County Mail, Victor Herald, Soduf Record
Employment Contact: James J. Gertner, Managing Editor
Total Employees: 40
Average Entry-Level Hiring: 13
Opportunities: Assistant in Mailroom—No experiencerequired; no educational or skill requirements specified.

THE EVENING POST PUBLISHING CO.
134 Columbus Street
Charleston, SC 29402
803-577-7111
Other Newspapers Published: The News & Courier
Employment Contact: Mr. Evan Buffy, Executive Editor
Total Employees: 500+
Average Entry-Level Hiring: ?
Opportunities: Publishing, Reporters, Sales—College degree. No other requirements specified.

FAIR PORT-PUNTON HERALD MAIL
See Listing for Empire State Weeklies

FAYETTEVILLE OBSERVER
458 Whitfield Street, PO Box 849
Fayetteville, NC 28302
919-323-4848
Other Newspapers Published: Fayetteville Times
Employment Contact: John Holmes, Personnel Director
Total Employees: 450
Average Entry-Level Hiring: 2-4
Opportunities: Reporters, News Room—College degree (BA or BS), 2-3 years experience required. Clerical—High school graduates.

FAYETTEVILLE TIMES
See listing for Fayetteville Observer

FLORIDA TIMES-UNION
1 Riverside Avenue, PO Box 1949F
Jacksonville, FL 32231
904-359-4111
Employment Contact: Mildred Young, Employment Manager
Total Employees: 950
Average Entry-Level Hiring: 10-15
Opportunities: Clerical, Publishing, Sales—No specific educational or skill requirements.

FORT WAYNE NEWSPAPERS
600 W Main Street
Fort Wayne, IN 46801
219-461-8444
Other Newspapers Published: The Journal Gazette, The News-Sentinel
Employment Contact: Tim Harmon, Managing Editor
Total Employees: 550
Average Entry-Level Hiring: 10-12
Opportunities: Clerical—High school graduates. Reporters, Advertising Sales—College degree (BA or BS only); prefer 2-3 years experience.

FORT WORTH STAR TELEGRAM
PO Box 1870
Fort Worth, TX 76101
817-390-7400
Employment Contact: Jim Mason, Personnel Department
Total Employees: 1,200
Average Entry-Level Hiring: 4-6
Opportunities: Reporters, Advertising Sales—College degree (BA or BS), 3-5 years pertinent experience required.

THE FRAMINGHAM TAB
See listing for The Tab Newspapers

GAINESVILLE SUN
2700 SW 13th Street, Drawer A
Gainesville, FL 32608
904-378-1411
Employment Contact: Virginia Rhoes, Office
Manager
Total Employees: 220
Average Entry-Level Hiring: 5-7
Opportunities: Clerks—High school graduates.
Reporter, Photographer—College degree. No
experience for previous three positions. Adver-
tising Sales—College degree (BA or BS), 2 years
experience required.

GANNETT CO., INC.
1100 Wilson Boulevard
Arlington, VA 22209
703-284-6000
Newspapers Published: 90 daily (including *USA
Today*), 39 non-daily (many are listed separately
in this chapter; consult <u>Editor & Publisher Year-
book</u> for up-to-date listings of newspaper group
ownership).
Employment Contact: Sheila J. Gibbons, Manager
of Public Affairs (Contact each newspaper for
specific opportunities.)
Total Employees: 3,600
Average Entry-Level Hiring: 10-12
Opportunities: News Assistant/Researcher—
College degree (BA or BS), 2 years experience,
fact-finding skills. Reporter—College degree, 2
years experience, research and writing ability

GARY POST-TRIBUNE
1065 Broadway
Gary, IN 46402
219-881-3000
Employment Contact: Al Johnson, Executive
Managing Editor
Total Employees: 320
Average Entry-Level Hiring: 3-4
Opportunities: Clerks—High school graduates,
no experience necessary. Reporters, Copywriters,
Advertising Sales—College degree (BA or BS), 2-
3 years experience required.

GOLD LEAF FARMER
See listing for The News and Observer Publishing
Company

GRAND FORKS HERALD
120 N 4th Street
Grand Forks, ND 58201
701-780-1100
Employment Contact: Anne J. Van Camp,
Personnel Manager
Total Employees: 250
Average Entry-Level Hiring: 7-10
Opportunities: Reporters—College degree (BA or
BS), 2-3 years experience required. Data Proces-
sing—2-3 years experience in data processing
preferred. Advertising Sales—College degree
(BS preferred), 2-3 years experience required.

GREENSBORO NEWS AND RECORD
200 East Market St.
Greensboro, NC 27420
919-373-7000
Employment Contact: Ned Cline, Managing
Editor
Total Employees: 112
Average Entry-Level Hiring: 2
Opportunities: Assistant Reporters, Asst. in
Advertising Dept., General Help—High school
graduates, no experience.

HARRISBURG EVENING NEWS
812 Market Street, PO Box 2265
Harrisburg, PA 17105
717-255-8100
Employment Contact: Mary Runkle, Personnel
Manager
Total Employees: 490
Average Entry-Level Hiring: 4-6

HOUSTON CHRONICLE
801 Texas Avenue
Houston, TX 77002
713-220-7171
Employment Contact: Ann Turnbach, Director of
Personnel
Total Employees: 2,000
Average Entry-Level Hiring: 7-8
Opportunities: Reporters, Advertising Sales—
College degree (BA or BS), 2-3 years experience
required. Clerks—High school graduates, no
experience required.

HOUSTON POST
4747 Southwest Freeway
Houston, TX 77027
713-840-5600

Employment Contact: Ernie Williamson, Managing Editor
Total Employees: 1,200
Average Entry-Level Hiring: 7-12
Opportunities: General Assignment Clerks—High school graduates. Reporters, Advertising Sales—College degree; 2 years experience required.

THE INDEPENDENCE
See listing for Des Moines Register

INDIANAPOLIS STAR AND NEWS
307 N Pennsylvania Street
Indianapolis, IN 46206
317-633-9051

Employment Contact: Larry Roberts, Personnel Director
Total Employees: 1,700
Average Entry-Level Hiring: 7-10
Opportunities: Clerk—High school graduates. Reporter, Advertising Sales, Editorial Assistant—College degree (BA or BS), 2-3 years experience.
See also listing for Central Newspapers Inc.

THE INDINOLA REGISTER
See listing for Des Moines Register

THE INTERNATIONAL HERALD TRIBUNE
850 Third Ave.
New York, NY 10022
212-752-3890

Employment Contact: Christine Dempster, Account Manager
Total Employees: 20
Average Entry-Level Hiring: 1
Opportunities: Clerks—High school graduates. Reporters, Editorial, Marketing, Advertising Sales—College degree (BA or BS only), 2-3 years experience required

THE JERSEY JOURNAL
30 Journal Square
Jersey City, NJ 07306
201-653-1000

Employment Contact: Steven Newhouse, Editor
Total Employees: 300

Average Entry-Level Hiring: 7-12
Opportunities: Reporter, Editorial Assistant, Advertising Sales—College degree (BA preferred) and 2-3 years news writing experience

THE JOURNAL GAZETTE
See listing for Fort Wayne Newspapers

THE JOURNAL OF COMMERCE
110 Wall Street
New York, NY 10005
212-425-1616

Employment Contact: Stan Erickson, Managaing Editor
Total Employees: 118
Average Entry-Level Hiring: 6
Opportunities: Reporters, Clerks, Advertising Sales—No educational or skill requirements specified.

THE JOURNAL OF COMMERCE
445 Marshall Street
Phillipsburg, NJ 08865
201-859-1300

Employment Contact: Lucille Zinno, Personnel Director
Total Employees: 260
Average Entry-Level Hiring: ?
Opportunities: Input Clerks - College degree and some experience.

KALAMAZOO GAZETTE
401 S Burdick Street
Kalamazoo, MI 49003
616-345-3511

Employment Contact: Ron Carpenter, Controller
Total Employees: 208 (98 part-time)
Average Entry-Level Hiring: 10-14
Opportunities: Clerks—High school graduates. Reporter, Advertising Sales—College degree (BA or BS), 2-3 years experience preferred.

KENT COUNTY NEWS
See listing for the Kent Group

THE KENT GROUP
A Subsidiary of Chesapeake Publishing Corporation
PO Box 30
Chestertown, MD 21620
301-778-2011

Newspapers Published: Kent County News (Chestertown); Queen Anne's Record-Observer

(Centreville); The Bay Times (Stevensville)
Employment Contact: H. Hurtt Deringer, Publisher & Editor
Total Employees: 12
Average Entry-Level Hiring: 1-2
Opportunities: All of the following require a college degree: Advertising Sales, Reporter, Marketing, Editorial.

LA CROSSE TRIBUNE
401 N 3rd Street
La Crosse, WI 54601
608-782-9710

Employment Contact: Meribeth Catania, Human Resource Manager
Total Employees: 126 (75 Part-time)
Average Entry-Level Hiring: 8-10
Opportunities: Editorial—College degree (journalism) some experience (part-time or college newspaper). Advertising Sales—College degree, some retail sales experience. Circulation—College degree, some newspaper and sales experience. Clerks—High school graduates, no experience.

LAS VEGAS REVIEW-JOURNAL
Box 70
Las Vegas, NV 89125
702-383-0289

Employment Contact: Charles Zobell
Total Employees: NA
Average Entry-Level Hiring: 0-1
Comments: Do not hire recent graduates without participation in a solid internship program.

THE LEADER-TELEGRAM
701 S Farwell
Eau Claire, WI 54701
715-834-3471

Employment Contact: John Grasskap, Personnel Manager
Total Employees: 250
Average Entry-Level Hiring: 15-20
Opportunities: No specific educational or skill requirements specified, but no experience necessary for entry-level positions in all departments.

THE LEDGER
Box 408
Lakeland, FL 33802
813-687-7820

Employment Contact: Bruce Giles, Managing Editor

Total Employees: 300
Average Entry-Level Hiring: 5
Opportunities: Clerical, Beginning Reporter—two positions requiring no experience. The following two positions require a college degree and 1-2 years experience: Reporter, Copy Editor.

THE LEDGER STAR
See listing for The Virginian-Pilot

LONG BEACH INDEPENDENT VOICE
320 East Park Ave.
Long Beach, NY 11561
516-432-0065

Employment Contact: Terry Kohn, Managing Editor
Total Employees: 3
Average Entry-Level Hiring: 2
Opportunities: Paste-up and layout work—High school graduate, no experience. Writers—College degree, 1-2 years experience preferred.

LONG ISLAND JOURNAL
Box 697
Long Beach, NY 11561
516-889-1822

Employment Contact: John Gold

LOS ANGELES HERALD-EXAMINER
1111 S Broadway, PO Box 2416
Los Angeles, CA 90015
213-744-8000

Employment Contact: Grace Gonzalez, Personnel Manager
Total Employees: 800
Average Entry-Level Hiring: 4-5
Opportunities: Clerical, Secretarial—High school graduates. Sales—College degree (BS preferred). No experience for any of these positions.

LOS ANGELES TIMES
A Division of Times Mirror
Times Mirror Square
Los Angeles, CA 90053
213-237-3700

Employment Contact: Herman Fields, Asst. Human Resources Director
Total Employees: 8,000
Average Entry-Level Hiring: ?

Opportunities: Clerks—High school graduates. Advertising Sales, Marketing, Reporters—College degree (BS preferred); 1-2 years years experience preferred.

MACON TELEGRAPH AND NEWS

120 Broadway, PO Box 4167
Macon, GA 31213
912-744-4200

Employment Contact: Ed Campbell, Personnel Director
Total Employees: 380
Average Entry-Level Hiring: 5-6
Opportunities: Secretarial. Data-Entry Clerk. Receptionist—High school graduates, no experience. Advertising Sales—College degree (BS preferred), 1-2 years experience.

MANCHESTER UNION LEADER

35 Amherst Street
Manchester, NH 03105
603-668-4321

Employment Contact: William Hip, Personnel Manager
Total Employees: 350
Average Entry-Level Hiring: 5-10
Opportunities: Clerical, Secretarial—High school graduates, no experience.

THE MARSHALL RECORD

See listing for The News and Observer Publishding Companyt

MEMPHIS JOURNAL

88 Union Avenue Ste 102
Memphis, TN 38103
901-523-0437

Employment Contact: Barney Du Bois, Publisher
Total Employees: 38
Average Entry-Level Hiring: 3-5
Opportunities: Publishing Dept., Reporters—College degree (BS preferred), 2 years experience Clerk—High school graduates, no experience.

METRO REPORTER

See listing for Reporter Publications

MIAMI HERALD

One Herald Plaza
Miami, FL 33132-1693
305-350-2111

Employment Contact: Bevin Spence, Employment Manager

Total Employees: 4,000
Average Entry-Level Hiring: 12-14
Opportunities: Reporters, Advertising Sales—College degree (BS preferred), 2 years experience. Clerks—High school graduates, no experience.

MICHIGAN CHRONICLE

479 Ledyard
Detroit, MI 48201
313-963-5522

Employment Contact: Sylvia Sherer, Personnel Manager
Total Employees: 120
Average Entry-Level Hiring: 4-6
Opportunities: Reporters, Ad Sales—College degree (BS preferred). Clerks—High school graduates.

MILWAUKEE JOURNAL

Box 661
Milwaukee, WI 53201
414-224-2355

Employment Contact: Paul Salsini, Staff Editor
Total Employees: 3,000
Average Entry-Level Hiring: 5
Opportunities: Clerical, Messenger—High school graduates, no experience. Reporters, Copy Editors—College degree (BS preferred), 2-5 years experience.

MOBILE BEACON

2311 Costaries Street
Mobile, AL 36617
205-479-0629

Employment Contact: Ms. Blackman or Ms. Thomas, Personnel Department
Total Employees: 8
Average Entry-Level Hiring: 1
Opportunities: Publishing, Reporter—College degree (BS preferred), 2 years experience.

THE MORNING ADVOCATE

See listing for The State-Times

MT. OLIVE TRIBUNE

See listing for News and Observer Publishing Co.

NASHVILLE BANNER

1100 Broadway
Nashville, TN 37202
615-259-8800

Employment Contact: Cathy Cheatham, Director of Personnel

Total Employees: 2,200
Average Entry-Level Hiring: 6-10
Opportunities: Reporters, Publishing Room, Advertising Sales—College degree (BS preferred), 2 years experience Clerks—High school graduates. No experience.

NATCHEZ DEMOCRAT
503 N Canal Street, PO Box 1447
Natchez, MS 39120
601-442-9101
Employment Contact: Jim Elsberry, Personnel Manager; John Matthew, Asst. Editor
Total Employees: 55
Average Entry-Level Hiring: 2
Opportunities: Editorial Department—College degree (journalism preferred). Advertising, Business Departments—College degree (prefer marketing, journalism, business)

THE NATICK TAB
See listing for The Tab Newspapers

N.E. SENIOR CITIZEN
See listing for Prime National Publishing Corporation

NEWARK STAR LEDGER
Star Ledger Plaza
Newark, NJ 07101
201-877-4141
Employment Contact: Mark Herrick, Personnel Department
Total Employees: 1,200
Average Entry-Level Hiring: 7-10
Opportunities: Clerks—HIgh school graduates, no experience. Reporters, Sales, Advertising Dept.—College degree (BS preferred), no experience.

THE NEWPORT NEWS DAILY PRESS AND TIMES HERALD
7505 Warwick Boulevard, PO Box 746
Newport News, VA 23607
804-244-8424
Employment Contact: Margaret Simonson, Human Resources Director
Total Employees: 600
Average Entry-Level Hiring: 7-8
Opportunities: Clerks—High school graduates, no experience. Reporters, Marketing, Sales—College degree (BS preferred), 1-2 years experience

THE NEWS AND COURIER
See listing for the Evening Post Publishing Co.

THE NEWS AND OBSERVER PUBLISHING COMPANY
2155 Mc Dowell Street, PO Box 191
Raleigh, NC 27602
919-829-4500
Newspapers Published: The News and Observer, The Raleigh Times, Smithfield Herald, Cary News, Yorkville Inquirer, The Clover Herald, The Canton Enterprise, The Marshall Record, The Mt. Olive Tribune, The Gold Leaf Farmer, The Zebulon Record.
Employment Contact: Hunter George, Asst. Managing Editor
Total Employees: 165
Average Entry-Level Hiring: 5-6
Opportunities: Clerks—High school graduates. Reporters, Advertising Sales—College degree. No experience or skill requirements specified.

NEWSDAY
235 Pinelawn Avenue
Melville, NY 11747
516-454-2020
Employment Contact: Barbara Sanchaz, Personnel Manager
Total Employees: 3,500
Average Entry-Level Hiring: 15-20
Opportunities: Reporter, Advertising Sales—College degree. Clerk, Mail Room—High school graduates. No experience necessary for these positions.

NEWSPAPER PRINTING CORPORATION
315 S Boulder, PO Box 1770
Tulsa, OK 74102
918-581-8000
Newspapers Published: The World, The Tribune
Employment Contact: Edward Knighten, Director of Personnel
Total Employees: 800
Average Entry-Level Hiring: 6-8
Opportunities: Reporters, Editorial, Sales—College degree. No other requirements specified.

NEWS PRESS
2442 Anderson Ave.
Fort Myers, FL 33902
813-335-0280
Employment Contact: Lou Brancaccia, Managing Editor

Total Employees: 700
Average Entry-Level Hiring: 6
Opportunities: Reporters, Photographers—College degree (BA or bS), prefer 1-2 years experience. Beginning Reporters—No experience.

THE NEWS-SENTINEL
See listing for Fort Wayne Newspaper

THE NEWS-TRIBUNE
1 Hoover Way
Woodbridge, NJ 07095
201-442-0400
Employment Contact: Tom Kerrigan, Director of Personnel
Total Employees: 250
Average Entry-Level Hiring: 2-4
Opportunities: Reporters, Advertising Sales—College degree (BA or BS). Clerks—High school graduates. No experience specified for these positions.

THE NEWTON TAB
See listing for The Tab Newspapers

THE NEW YORK DAILY NEWS
220 E 42nd Street
New York, NY 10017
212-210-2100
Employment Contact: Jay Klinek, Director of Personnel
Total Employees: 400
Average Entry-Level Hiring: 12-15
Opportunities: Reporters, Advertising Sales—College degree (BA or BS). Clerks—High school graduates. No experience specified for these positions.

THE NEW YORK POST
210 South Street
New York, NY 10002
212-815-8000
Employment Contact: Personnel Department
Total Employees: 1,300
Average Entry-Level Hiring: 7-12
Opportunities: Reporters, Advertising Sales—College degree (BA or BS). Clerks—High school graduates. No experience specified for these positions.

THE NEW YORK TIMES
229 W 43rd Street
New York, NY 10036
212-556-1234
Employment Contact: Personnel Department
Total Employees: 5,000
Average Entry-Level Hiring: 12-15
Opportunities: Very few entry-level positions, primarily "go-fers," copy boys and girls, mainly through employee recommendations. Writing samples required

NURSINGWORLD JOURNAL
See listing for Prime National Publishing Corporation

THE OAKLAND PRESS
48 W Huron Street
Pontiac, MI 48056
313-332-8181
Employment Contact: Jan Allan, Head of Personnel
Total Employees: 300
Average Entry-Level Hiring: 4-6
Opportunities: Reporters, Advertising Sales—College degree (BA or BS). Clerks—High school graduates. No experience specified for these positions.

THE OMAHA WORLD-HERALD
World Herald Square
Omaha, NE 68102
402-444-1000
Employment Contact: PGene Overman, Personnel Manager
Total Employees: 960
Average Entry-Level Hiring: 6-7
Opportunities: Reporter—College degree. Clerk—High school graduate. Junior Assistant Account Representatives—2 years of college.

OREGONIAN
1320 SW Broadway
Portland, OR 97201
503-221-8280
Employment Contact: Frank Lesage, Personnel Director
Total Employees: 1,121
Average Entry-Level Hiring: 10-15
Opportunities: Production Assistant, Asst. Salespeople—High school graduates. Reporters—College degree. No experience specified for these positions.

THE ORLANDO SENTINEL

633 North Orange Ave.
Orlando, FL 32801
305-420-5000

Employment Contact: James C. Clark, Deputy Managing Editor
Total Employees: 1,200
Average Entry-Level Hiring: 2
Opportunities: Reporting—no experience. Following positions require college degree (BA or BS) plus 1-2 years experience: Photography, Business Dept., Reporters.

PENFIELD PRESS

See listing for Empire State Weeklies

THE PENINSULA DAILY NEWS

Box 1330
Port Angeles, WA 98362
206-452-2345

Employment Contact: Steve Boyer, Managing Editor
Total Employees: 80
Average Entry-Level Hiring: 3
Opportunities: Editorial Dept.—College degree (BA or BS), good with people, good spelling and writing skills.

PENSACOLA NEWS JOURNAL

1 News Journal Plaza
Pensacola, FL 32501
904-435-8591

Employment Contact: James Barnett, Director of Human Resources
Total Employees: 425
Average Entry-Level Hiring: 7-10
Opportunities: Reporters—College degree (prefer BA or BS in Journalism). Account Executives—College degree (prefer BA or BS Masrketing). District Sales Managers—College degree (prefer BA or BS Marketing).

THE PHILADELPHIA DAILY NEWS

North Broad St.
Philadelphia, PA 19101
215-854-5851

Employment Contact: Don Haskin, Associate Editor
Total Employees: 175
Average Entry-Level Hiring: 0
Opportunities: College degree plus 2-3 years experience required for: Reporters, Photographers

THE PHILADELPHIA INQUIRER

400 N Broad Street
Philadelphia, PA 19101
215-854-2000

Employment Contact: Personnel Department
Total Employees: 5,000
Average Entry-Level Hiring: 3-5
Opportunities: Marketing—College degree (preferred)Accountants—College degree (preferred) Advertising Sales—College degree (preferred); prefer experience in marketing.

PHOENIX NEWSPAPERS, INC.

A subsidiary of Central Newspapers, Inc.
120 E Van Buren Avenue
Phoenix, AZ 85004
602-271-8000

Newspapers Published: The Phoenix Gazette, The Arizona Republic
Employment Contact: Sam Perkins, Personnel Analyst
Total Employees: 2,500 (500 part-time)
Average Entry-Level Hiring: 7-10
Opportunities: Newsroom - College degree (journalism minimum). Business - College degree (business); experience. Data Processing - experience. Advertising - experience. Circulation Department - Clerical. Production Mailers (part-time)

PITTSBURGH POST GAZETTE

566 Boulevard of Allies
Pittsburgh, PA 15222
412-263-1524

Employment Contact: John B. Craig, Jr., Editor
Total Employees: 1,200
Average Entry-Level Hiring: 0
Opportunities: Experience personnel only.

THE POST BULLETIN

18 First St SE
Rochester, MN 55904
507-285-7640

Employment Contact: Lynne Miller, Personnel Manager
Total Employees: 260
Average Entry-Level Hiring: 5-6
Opportunities: Classified Sales Representatives. Customer Services Representatives. Proofreaders. Clerks—College degree preferred, not required.

THE PRESS-TELEGRAM
604 Pine Avenue
Long Beach, CA 90844
213-435-1161
Employment Contact: Jim Nolan, Assistant
Managing Editor; John Risler, Assistant Editor
Total Employees: 700
Average Entry-Level Hiring: 7-10
Opportunities: Commission Sales Positions. Staff
Accounting. Reporters—College degree preferred
for all such positions.

**PRIME NATIONAL PUBLISHING
CORPORATION**
470 Boston Post Road
Weston, MA 02193
617-899-2702
Newspapers Published: N.E. Senior Citizen,
Senior American News, Nursingworld Journal, PT
Job News
Employment Contact: William Haslam, General
Manager
Total Employees: 30
Average Entry-Level Hiring: 1-3
Opportunities: Advertising Sales, Reporters—
College degree (preferred), ability to communi-
cate and be trained.

THE PROVIDENCE JOURNAL-BULLETIN
75 Fountain Street
Providence, RI 02902
401-277-7200
Employment Contact: Donald W. Zimmerman
Total Employees: 2,000
Average Entry-Level Hiring: 2-4
Opportunities: Inside Display Sales, Inside
Telephone Sales. No specific requirements
forthcoming from company.

PT JOB NEWS
See listing for Prime National Publishing
Corporation

QUEEN ANNE'S RECORD-OBSERVER
See listing for The Kent Group

THE RALEIGH TIMES
See listing for The News and Observer Publishing
Company

REPORTER PUBLICATIONS
1366 Turk Street
San Francisco, CA 94115
415-931-5778
Newspapers Published: California Voice, Sun
Reporter, Metro Reporter Group (San Francisco,
Peninsula/San Jose, San Joaquin, Oakland,
Berkeley, Richmond, Vallejo)
Employment Contact: Orville Luster and
Circulation Manager (Press), Amelia Ashley-
Ward, Managing Editor (Editorial). Clarence
Gatson, Manager Production Department
(Production).
Total Employees: 37
Average Entry-Level Hiring: 4-5
Opportunities: Apprentice Pressman - High
school (at least 16 years of age). Reporter -
College degree + Masters in Journalism or
Political Science. Cub Reporter - Minimum 2 years
college (major Journalism or Political Science).
Production Department (layout) - Minimum 2
years college in graphics work. Marketing and
sales - Minimum 2 years college.
Comments: They like returning interns—they are
always given first consideration.

RICHMOND NEWS LEADER
333 E Grace Street, PO Box C-32333
Richmond, VA 23293
804-649-6000
Other Newspapers Published: The Richmond
Times Dispatch
Employment Contact: Personnel Department
Total Employees: 1,500
Average Entry-Level Hiring: 7-15
Opportunities: Circulation District Assistants,
Advertising Dept., Clerks, Reporters, Sales—All
college degree preferred.

RICHMOND TIMES DISPATCH
See listing for the Richmond News Leader

ROANOKE TIMES AND WORLD-NEWS
201-09 W Campbell Avenue
Roanoke, VA 24010
703-981-3100
Employment Contact: William K. Warren,
Managing Editor
Total Employees: 645
Average Entry-Level Hiring: 10-12
Opportunities: Sales Assistants. Clerks,
Reporters—College degree preferred.

ROCHESTER DEMOCRAT AND CHRONICLE

55 Exchange Street
Rochester, NY 14614
716-232-7100

Employment Contact: Personnel Department
Total Employees: 1,400
Average Entry-Level Hiring: 7-10
Opportunities: Sales Department. Circulation Department, Clerical—College degree preferred.

ROCK ISLAND ARGUS

See listing for the Daily Dispatch

ROCKY MOUNTAIN NEWS

400 W Colfax Avenue, PO Box 719
Denver, CO 80204
303-892-5000

Employment Contact: Andy Martelon, Managing Editor
Total Employees: 1,500
Average Entry-Level Hiring: 7-10
Opportunities: Production Department, Circulation Department, Clerks, Sales—High school graduates.

ST. LOUIS GLOBE-DEMOCRAT

No longer published

ST. LOUIS POST-DISPATCH

9090 N Tucker Boulevard
St. Louis, MO 63101
314-622-7000

Employment Contact: Personnel Department
Total Employees: 1,600
Average Entry-Level Hiring: 7-10
Opportunities: Clerks. Mechanical Maintenance Interns, Sales—High school graduates, no experience.

ST. PAUL PIONEER PRESS DISPATCH

345 Cedar Street
St. Paul, MN 55101
612-222-5011

Employment Contact: Mary Ann Thomas, Manager Human Resources (Circulation and Advertising); Wayne Hassell, Asst. to the Executive Editor (Editorial)
Total Employees: 900
Average Entry-Level Hiring: 6-15
Opportunities: Clerks, Accountants, Telephone Sales—College degree preferred for all these positions.

ST. PETERSBURG TIMES INDEPENDENCE

PO Box 1121
St. Petersburg, FL 33701
813-893-8111

Employment Contact: Emmett Kilpatrick, Employment Manager
Total Employees: 3,000
Average Entry-Level Hiring: 15-20
Opportunities: Clerks, Reporters, Sales—High school graduates; college a plus.

SAN ANTONIO EXPRESS NEWS

PO Box 2171
San Antonio, TX 78297
512-225-7411

Employment Contact: Personnel Department
Total Employees: 800
Average Entry-Level Hiring: 7-10
Opportunities: Editorial Assistant, Advertising Sales—College degree required for both positions.

SAN ANTONIO LIGHT

420 Broadway
San Antonio, TX 78205
512-271-2971

Employment Contact: Personnel Department
Total Employees: 850
Average Entry-Level Hiring: 10-12
Opportunities: Advertising, Reporters, Clerks, Classified Advertising—All require a high school diploma and good communication skills, including typing, accurate spelling and simple math.

SAN FRANCISCO BAY GUARDIAN

2700 19th St.
San Francisco, CA 94110
415-824-7660

Employment Contact: Laura Bull, Editorial Asst.
Average Entry-Level Hiring: 1
Opportunities: Very little full-time, entry-level hiring, but interns often go on to become freelancers for this small weekly paper.

SAN FRANCISCO CHRONICLE

See listing for San Francisco Newspaper Agency

SAN FRANCISCO EXAMINER

110 Fifth Street
San Francisco, CA 94103
415-777-2424

Employment Contact: Tara Stevens, Director of
Human Resources
Total Employees: 255
Average Entry-Level Hiring: 0

SAN FRANCISCO NEWSPAPER AGENCY

925 Mission Street
San Francisco, CA 94103
415-777-1111

Newspapers Published: The San Francisco
Chronicle
Employment Contact: Betty Cutter, Personnel
Manager
Total Employees: 300
Average Entry-Level Hiring: 7-8
Opportunities: Clerks, Sales, Reporters—High
school graduates, no experience.

THE SAN JOSE MERCURY NEWS

750 Ridder Park Drive
San Jose, CA 95190
408-920-5000

Employment Contact: Patty Fisher, Assistant
Managing Editor/Personnel (Editorial). Jim
Schoeber, Personnel Director (all other departments)
Total Employees: 1,500
Average Entry-Level Hiring: 12
Opportunities: Reporters—College degree,
demonstrated strong journalistic talents . Previous
internships or extensive school news experience or
freelance writing. Sales—College degree. No
other requirements specified for latter area.

THE SCHENECTADY GAZETTE

332 State Street
Schenectady, NY 12301
518-374-4141

Employment Contact: Personnel Department
Total Employees: 320
Average Entry-Level Hiring: 4-5
Opportunities: Editorial Department, Clerks,
Sales—College degree (prefer BA in journalism or
English)

SEATTLE TIMES

Fairview Avenue N, PO Box 70
Seattle, WA 98111
206-464-2400

Employment Contact: Tom Bryan, Personnel
Department
Total Employees: 2,000
Average Entry-Level Hiring: 6-10
Opportunities: Customer Service Clerks, Sales—
High school graduates.

SENIOR AMERICAN NEWS

See listing for Prime National Publishing
Corporation

SMITHFIELD HERALD

See listing for The News and Observer Publishing
Company

SODUF RECORD

See Listing for Empire State Weeklies

SOUTH BEND TRIBUNE

225 W Colfax Road
South Bend, IN 46626
219-233-6161

Employment Contact: Ed Henry, Personnel
Department
Total Employees: 500
Average Entry-Level Hiring: 7-10
Opportunities: Advertising Department,
Newsroom, Reporters, Advertising Sales—
College degree, good writing and spelling skills.

SPRINGFIELD NEWS LEADER

651 Boonville Avenue
Springfield, MO 65801
417-836-1100

Employment Contact: Jan Lowe, Human Resource
Director
Total Employees: 346
Average Entry-Level Hiring: 7-10
Opportunities: Reporters, Clerks, Sales—High
school graduates; college a plus.

THE STAR-NEWS

525 E Colorado Boulevard
Pasadena, CA 91109
818-578-6300

Employment Contact: Pamela Smaron, Personnel
Manager

Total Employees: 240
Average Entry-Level Hiring: 5-7
Opportunities: Reporters. Sales. Data Processing, Clerks—College degree, good spelling and writing skills.

THE STATE-TIMES

PO Box 588
Baton Rouge, LA 70821-0588
504-383-1111

Other Newspapers Published: Morning Advocate, Sunday Advocate
Employment Contact: Betty Jo Baker, Personnel Manager
Total Employees: 700
Average Entry-Level Hiring: 0
Opportunities: Clerks, Sales, Reporters—High school graduates; any college a plus.

THE SUDBURY TAB

See listings for the Tab Newspapers

THE SUNDAY ADVOCATE

See listing for the State-Times

THE SUN REPORTER

See listing for Reporter Publications

THE TAB NEWSPAPERS

1254 Chestnut Street
Newton, MA 02164
617-969-0340

Newspapers Published: The Brookline Tab, The Newton Tab, The Boston Tab, The Cambridge Tab, The Wellesley Tab, The Natick Tab, The Weston Tab, The Framingham Tab, The Wayland Tab and The Sudbury Tab.
Employment Contact: Bonnie Hooker, Office Manager; David Lubdoff, Editor; Laurie Nordman, Art Director, Wendy Maxfield, Production Manager; Jonathan Brickman, Sales
Total Employees: 140
Average Entry-Level Hiring: 3-4
Opportunities: Clerks, Circulation Assistants—High school graduates, college a plus; Paste-up—Minimum high school diploma (prefer college). Sales Assistant, Sales—High school graduates, some college a plus.

THE TALLAHASSEE DEMOCRAT

277 N Magnolia Drive, PO Box 990
Tallahassee, FL 32302
904-599-2100

Employment Contact: Doris Dunlap, Director of Employment
Total Employees: 300
Average Entry-Level Hiring: 5-6
Opportunities: News Clerks, Mail Room Inserters, Advertising Assistants, Account Clerks, Salkes—High school grads; any college a plus.

TAMPA TRIBUNE-TIMES

202 Parker Street
Tampa, FL 33601
813-272-7711

Employment Contact: Sandra Sheffiled, Personnel Manager
Total Employees: 1,200
Average Entry-Level Hiring: 7-8
Opportunities: Reporters, Clerks Advertising Sales Representatives—College degree required; no experience.

TOLEDO BLADE

541 Superior St.
Toledo, OH 43660
419-245-6163

Employment Contact: Cheryl Lutz, Assistant Managing Editor
Total Employees: 140
Average Entry-Level Hiring: ?
Opportunities: Reporters, Photographers—College degree (BA or BS), 2-3 years experience required.

TRENTONIAN

Southard at Perry Street
Trenton, NJ 08602
609-989-7800

Employment Contact: Emile Slaboda, Editor
Total Employees: 380
Average Entry-Level Hiring: 3-5
Opportunities: Reporters. Clerks, Sales, Desk People—High school graduates; any college a plus.

THE TRIBUNE

See listing for Newspaper Printing Corporation

THE TRIBUNE (Salt Lake City, UT)
See Listing for Deseret News Publishing Co.

USA TODAY
See listing for Gannett Co., Inc.

VICTOR HERALD
See Listing for Empire State Weeklies

THE VILLAGE VOICE
842 Broadway
New York, NY 10003
212-475-3300
Employment Contact: Terry West, Head of Personnel
Total Employees: 200
Average Entry-Level Hiring: 6-8
Opportunities: Clerks, Sales—High school graduates, no experience.

THE VIRGINIAN-PILOT
150 W Brambleton, PO Box 449
Norfolk, VA 23501
804-446-2090
Other Newspapers Published: The Ledger Star
Employment Contact: Ken Wyatt, Head of Personnel
Total Employees: 1,250
Average Entry-Level Hiring: 6-8
Opportunities: Advertising Services. Clerks. Typists, Sales—High school graduates, no experience.

THE WALL STREET JOURNAL
A subsidiary of Dow Jones
200 Liberty Street
New York, NY 10281
212-416-2000
Employment Contact: Personnel Department
Total Employees: 7,000
Average Entry-Level Hiring: 0

THE WASHINGTON POST
1150 15th St NW
Washington, DC 20071
202-334-6000
Employment Contact: Molly Martin, News Personnel Administration
Total Employees: 4,000
Average Entry-Level Hiring: 6-8

Opportunities: Salespeople, Reporters, Clerks—College degree, no experience.

THE WASHINGTON TIMES
3600 New York Avenue NE
Washington, DC 20002
202-636-3100
Employment Contact: Carole An Belle, Personnel Manager
Total Employees: 1,000
Average Entry-Level Hiring: 5-6
Opportunities: Sales, Clerks—High school graduates, no experience.

THE WAYLAND TAB
See listing for The Tab Newspapers

WAYNE COUNTY MAIL
See Listing for Empire State Weeklies

WEBSTER HERALD
See Listing for Empire State Weeklies

THE WELLESLEY TAB
See listing for The Tab Newspapers

THE WESTON TAB
See listing for The Tab Newspapers

WICHITA EAGLE-BEACON
825 E Douglas, PO Box 820
Wichita, KS 67201
316-268-6000
Employment Contact: Jim Spangler, Head of Personnel
Total Employees: 750
Average Entry-Level Hiring: 5-6
Opportunities: Advertising Sales Representatives, Circulation —College degree, no experience.

THE WORLD
See listing for Newspaper Printing Corporation

YORKVILLE INQUIRER
See listing for News and Observer Publishing Co.

ZEBULON RECORD
See listing for News and Observer Publishing Co.

CHAPTER THIRTY ONE

Internship And Training Program Listings

Many of the publishers listed in the previous chapter also provided us with information about internships and training programs at their papers. We have included that important information in this chapter.

The listings are pretty self-explanatory. Following the name, address and telephone number of the publisher, we listed the data as follows:

Internship Contact: The person in charge of internships, often *different* from the one indicated in the previous chapter as *employment contact*. If there are different contacts for different departments—or for different offices—we've indicated them.

Internships Offered: Salaried, non-salaried or some of each ("Both").

Average Number Per Year: Just a note here—a "?" means they have internships available, but couldn't (or wouldn't) hazard a guess as to an exact number.

Internship Departments: in which internships are offered (not training)

Training Available: Their own words—what kinds of training they offer entry-level hirees.

Departments: in which training is offered (not internships)

If any of the above entries is missing from a particular paper's listing, that's because we were unable to confirm that entry with the publisher itself. Rather than give you wrong or misleading information, we simply omitted it.

One final note: In order to make available the most extensive and pertinent information on publishing internships—more than space would allow us to include in this volume—we have just published a brand-new volume, **Internships, Volume 2: Newspaper, Magazine and Book Publishing**. Additional data—application procedure, number of applications received, duties and responsibilities of the intern and more—is included for each of the publishers listed in this volume (and all the book and magazine publishers included in our Book Publishing Career Directory and Magazines Career Directory).

With the exception of only this new Internships volume, here are *more* listings of *more* newspapers offering *more* internships than you'll find in any other publication...anywhere.

ABILENE REPORTER-NEWS
PO Box 30
Abilene, TX 79604
915-673-4271
Internship Contact: Glenn Dromgoole, Advertising Editor
Internships Offered: Salaried
Average Number Per Year: 3-4

AKRON BEACON JOURNAL
44 Exchange Street
Akron, OH 44328
216-375-8751
Internship Contact: Barbara Dean, Head of Personnel
Internships Offered: Both
Average Number Per Year: 6

ALBUQUERQUE JOURNAL
ALBUQUERQUE TRIBUNE
Listings deleted at Publisher's request

ANCHORAGE DAILY NEWS
PO Box 149001
Anchorage, AK 99514
907-786-4200
Internship Contact: Lou Ann Hennig, Personnel Manager
Internships Offered: Non-Salaried
Average Number Per Year: 3-4

ANN ARBOR NEWS
340 E Huron Street
Ann Arbor, MI 48104
313-994-6989
Internship Contact: Brian Malone, Editor
Internships Offered: Both
Average Number Per Year: 3-4

ARIZONA DAILY SUN
PO Box 1849
Flagstaff, AZ 86002
602-774-4545
Internship Contact: Rick Velotta, Managing Editor
Internships Offered: Non-Salaried
Average Number Per Year: 2

ASSOCIATION FOR EDUCATION IN JOURNALISM
New York University Summer Internship Program for Minorities
Institute of Afro-American Affairs
New York University
269 Mercer St.
New York, NY 10003
212-998-2130
Internship Contact: Sidique A. Wai, Program Coordinator
Internships Offered: Salaried ($200.00/week minimum
Average Number Per Year: 10-15+

Internship Departments: Newspapers, Magazines, Broadcasting
Note: Interns are placed with various publications. Summer term—10 weeks, 35 hours per week.

ATLANTA JOURNAL
ATLANTA MORNING CONSTITUTION
72 Marietta Street
Atlanta, GA 30303
404-526-5151
Internship Contact: Cheryl Bingham, Employment Manager
Internships Offered: Both
Average Number Per Year: 3-4
Training Available: Yes, but no details available
Departments: Advertising (Classified, Display)

AUGUSTA CHRONICLE
Box 1928
Augusta, GA 30913
404-724-0851
Internship Contact: Howard Eames, Executive Editor
Internships Offered: Salaried
Average Number Per Year: 4

BALTIMORE SUN
501 N Calvert Street
Baltimore, MD 21278
301-332-6000
Internship Contact: Barbara Scott Jones, Personnel Manager
Internships Offered: Salaried
Average Number Per Year: 4

THE BATESVILLE GUARD
PO box 2036
Batesville, AR 72503
501-793-2383
Internship Contact: Jo Cargill, Vice President
Internships Offered: Salaried
Average Number Per Year: 1

BEE PUBLICATIONS
5564 Main St.
Williamsville, NY 14221
716-632-4700
Internship Contact: Donald J. Goreham, Executive Editor
Internships Offered: Non-Salaried
Average Number Per Year: 2

BOCA RATON NEWS
34 SE 2nd Street, PO Box 580
Boca Raton, FL 33432
305-395-8300
Training Available: Yes, but no details available
Departments: Pressroom

THE BRADENTON HERALD
102 Manatee Avenue W, PO Box 921
Bradenton, FL 33506
813-748-0411
Internship Contact: Barbara Cashion, Personnel Director
Internships Offered: Both
Average Number Per Year: 2-3

BUCKS COUNTY COURIER TIMES
8400 Route 13
Levittown, PA 19057
215-752-6701
Internship Contact: Joe Halberstein, Assoc. Editor
Internships Offered: Salaried
Average Number Per Year: 6
Internship Departments:

BUFFALO NEWS
1 News Plaza, PO Box 100
Buffalo, NY 14240
716-849-3434
Internship Contact: Richard Feather, Senior VP-Human Resources
Internships Offered: Salaried
Average Number Per Year: 14-22
(Editorial—up to 14; Advertising—up to 8)
Training Available: Yes, but no details available
Departments: Editorial

CAPITOL NEWS SERVICE
1113 H Street
Sacramento, CA 95814
916-445-6336
Internship Contact: Verma Kline, Bureau Chief
Internships Offered: Non-Salaried
Average Number Per Year: 12

CEDAR RAPIDS-MARION GAZETTE
500 Third Avenue SE
Cedar Rapids-Marion, IA 52401
319-398-8211
Internship Contact: Michelle Wiebel, Employment Assistant
Internships Offered: Salaried
Average Number Per Year: 3-4

CENTER FOR COMMUNICATION, INC.
30 Rockefeller Plaza, 53rd Floor
New York, NY 10020
212-265-9130
Internship Contact: Kim Gantz, Program Director
Internships Offered: Salaried (Travel money paid)
Average Number Per Year: 12
Internship Departments: Journalism, Advertising, Public Relations, Broadcasting

CENTER FOR INVESTIGATIVE REPORTING, INC.
54 Mint St., 4th Floor
San Francisco, CA 94103
415-543-1200
Internship Contact: Dan Noyes, Managing Editor
Internships Offered: Salaried
Average Number Per Year: 4-5

CENTRAL NEWSPAPERS, INC.
307 N. Penn
Indianapolis, IN 46204
317-633-9208
Internship Contact: Harvey C. Jacobs
Internships Offered: Salaried
Average Number Per Year: 20

CENTRE DAILY TIMES
3400 E College Avenue
State College, PA 16804
814-238-5000
Internship Contact: Karen Lobeck, Managing Editor
Internships Offered: Non-Salaried
Average Number Per Year: 4-5

CENTURY PUBLICATIONS, INC.
3 Church St.
Winchester, MA 01890
617-729-8100
Internship Contact: William Finucane, Executive Editor
Internships Offered: Non-Salaried
Average Number Per Year: 15

CHARLESTON GAZETTE
1001 Virginia St E
Charleston, WV 25301
304-348-5105
Internship Contact: John Bowyer, Hd of Personnel
Internships Offered: Salaried
Average Number Per Year: 6-8

CHARLOTTE OBSERVER
600 S Tryon Street, PO Box 32188
Charlotte, NC 28202
704-379-6660
Internship Contact: Paul Connelly, Personnel Services Manager
Internships Offered: Salaried
Average Number Per Year: 10-12
Training Available: Yes, but no details available

CHATTANOOGA NEWS-FREE PRESS
400 E 11th Street
Chattanooga, TN 37401
615-756-6900
Internship Contact: Ray Marler, Director of Personnel
Internships Offered: Salaried
Average Number Per Year: 2-3

CHICAGO SUN-TIMES
401 N Wabash Avenue
Chicago, IL 60611
312-321-3000
Internship Contact: Don Kopriva, Assistant Managing Editor
Internships Offered: Salaried
Average Number Per Year: 6-8

CHICAGO TRIBUNE
435 N Michigan Avenue
Chicago, IL 60611
312-222-4571
Internship Contact: Ronald Williams, Employment Manager
Internships Offered: Salaried
Average Number Per Year: 3-5
Training Available: Sales training and product knowledge
Departments: Advertising/Marketing

CINCINNATI ENQUIRER
617 Vine Street
Cincinnati, OH 45201
513-721-2700
Internship Contact: Dennis Doherty, Deputy Managing Editor
Internships Offered: Salaried
Average Number Per Year: 3-4

CINCINNATI POST
125 East Court Street
Cincinnati, OH 45202
513-352-2000
Internship Contact: Carole Philipps, Assistant
Managing Editor Administration
Internships Offered: Salaried
Average Number Per Year: 3-4

CLEVELAND PLAIN DEALER
1801 Superior Avenue NE
Cleveland, OH 44114
216-344-4970
Internship Contact: Russ Pinzone, Managing
Editor—Personnel
Internships Offered: Both
Average Number Per Year: 8-10

COLUMBUS LEDGER
17 W 12th Street, PO Box 711
Columbus, GA 31994
404-324-5526
Internship Contact: Jack Swift, Managing Editor
Internships Offered: Salaried
Average Number Per Year: 4-6

COURIER-JOURNAL
525 W Broadway
Louisville, KY 40202
502-582-4011
Internship Contact: Larry Vonderhaar, VP-
Human Resources
Internships Offered: Salaried
Average Number Per Year: 8
Training Available: Yes, but no details available
Departments: Circulation

THE DAILY DISPATCH
1720 Fifth Ave.
Moline, IL 61265
309-764-4344
Internship Contact: Russell A. Scott, Managing
Editor
Internships Offered: Salaried
Average Number Per Year: 4
Internship Departments: Editorial, Advertising
Training Available: Yes, but no details
available.
Departments: Editorial

THE DAILY JOURNAL
8 Dearborn Square
Kankakee, IL 60901
815-937-3300
Internship Contact: Marx Gibson, Managing Editor
Internships Offered: Salaried
Average Number Per Year: 3-4

THE DAILY REVIEW
116 Main St.
Towanda, PA 18848
717-265-2151
Internship Contact: Dennis Irvine, Editor
Internships Offered: Non-Salaried
Average Number Per Year: 3
Internship Departments: Reporting, Editorial
Training Available: Yes—no details available.
Departments: Editorial

DALLAS MORNING NEWS
Communications Center
Dallas, TX 75265
214-977-8222
Internship Contact: R.E. Hass, Assistant
Managing Editor
Internships Offered: Salaried
Average Number Per Year: 20

DALLAS TIMES HERALD
1101 Pacific Avenue
Dallas, TX 75202
214-720-6111
Internship Contact: Tom Rice, Sr. VP-Human
Resources
Internships Offered: Salaried
Average Number Per Year: 4-5

DAYTONA BEACH JOURNAL
901 Sixth Street
Daytona Beach, FL 32015
904-252-1511
Internship Contact: Richard Kearley, Personnel
Director
Internships Offered: Salaried
Average Number Per Year: 3-4

DECATUR HERALD AND REVIEW
601 E. William St., Box 311
Decatur, IL 62525
217-429-5151
Internship Contact: Terri Kuhle, Personnel
Manager
Internships Offered: Salaried

Average Number Per Year: 2
Internship Departments: Reporting

DELAWARE COUNTY DAILY TIMES
500 Mildred Ave.
Primos, PA 19018
215-284-7200
Internship Contact: Linda DeMeglio, Managing Editor
Internships Offered: Salaried
Average Number Per Year: 3
Internship Departments: Editorial (Reporters—two in news, one in sports)

THE DESERET NEWS PUBLISHING CO.
30 East First South St., PO Box 1257
Salt Lake City, UT 84110
801-237-2800
Internship Contact: Jay Livingood, Personnel Director
Internships Offered: Salaried ($5.00/hour)
Average Number Per Year: 3
Internship Departments: City Desk

DES MOINES REGISTER
PO Box 957
Des Moines, IA 50304
515-284-8000
Internship Contact: Martha Glehaus, Personnel Manager
Internships Offered: Salaried
Average Number Per Year: 3
Training Available: Yes, but no details available
Departments: Advertising, Circulation

DETROIT FREE PRESS
321 West Lafayette
Detroit, MI 48231
313-222-6490
Internship Contact: Kathy Warbelow
Internships Offered: Salaried (union wages)
Average Number Per Year: 12
Internship Departments: Editorial

DETROIT NEWS
615 Lafayette Boulevard
Detroit, MI 48231
313-222-2000
Internship Contact: Marcia Hart, Administrative Supervisor
Internships Offered: Salaried
Average Number Per Year: 5

DOW JONES NEWSPAPER FUND
Box 300
Princeton, NJ 08543
609-520-5927
Internship Contact: Tom Engleman, Personnel Dept.
Internships Offered: Salaried (and payment at end of program—$1,000 scholarship)
Average Number Per Year: 60*
*Interns are placed with major papers nationwide; paper participation varies from year to year, but examples are the Chicago Tribune, Los Angeles Times, Washington Post, etc.

DURHAM HERALD COMPANY, INC.
115 Market St.
Durham, NC 27702
919-682-8181
Internship Contact: Sandra Gainey, Personnel Director
Internships Offered: NA
Average Number Per Year: 1-2
Internship Departments: Library

EMPIRE STATE WEEKLIES
2010 Empire Blvd.
Webster, NY 14580
716-671-1533
Internship Contact: James J. Gertner, Managing Editor
Internships Offered: Non-Salaried
Average Number Per Year: 2
Internship Departments: Editorial, Advertising

FAYETTEVILLE OBSERVER
458 Whitfield Street, PO Box 849
Fayetteville, NC 28302
919-323-4848
Internship Contact: John Holmes, Personnel Director
Internships Offered: Salaried
Average Number Per Year: 1-2
Training Available: Yes, but no details available
Departments: Production

FLORIDA TIMES-UNION
1 Riverside Avenue, PO Box 1949F
Jacksonville, FL 32231
904-359-4111
Internship Contact: Ron Martin, Assistant Executive Editor
Internships Offered: Both
Average Number Per Year: 1-2

FORT WAYNE NEWSPAPERS
600 W Main Street
Fort Wayne, IN 46802
219-461-8444
Internship Contact: Tim Harmon, Managing
Editor Journal Gazette
Internships Offered: Both
Average Number Per Year: 1-2
Internship Departments: All

FORT WORTH STAR TELEGRAM
PO Box 1870
Fort Worth, TX 76101
817-390-7400
Internship Contact: Jim Mason, Personnel
Department
Internships Offered: Both
Average Number Per Year: 3-4
Internship Departments: All

GAINESVILLE SUN
2700 SW 13th Street, Drawer A
Gainesville,d FL 32608
904-378-1411
Internship Contact: Virginia Rhodes, Office
Manager
Internships Offered: Both
Average Number Per Year: 1-3
Training Available: Yes, but no details available
Departments: All

GANNETT COMPANY, INC.
1100 Wilson Boulevard
Arlington, VA 22209
703-284-6000
Internship Contact: Sheila Gibbons, Manager of
Public Affairs (Also contact each newspaper for
opportunities.)
Internships Offered: Both
Average Number Per Year: 1-3

GARY POST-TRIBUNE
1065 Broadway
Gary, IN 46402
219-881-3000
Internship Contact: Al Johnson, Executive
Managing Editor
Internships Offered: Salaried
Average Number Per Year: 2-3

GRAND FORKS HERALD
120 N 4th Street
Grand Forks, ND 58201
701-780-1100
Internship Contact: Mike Jacobs, Editor
Internships Offered: Both
Average Number Per Year: 2
Internship Department: Reporters

GREENSBORO NEWS AND RECORD
200 East Market St.
Greensboro, NC 27420
919-373-7000
Internship Contact: Ned Cline, Managing Editor
Internships Offered: Salaried ($275/week)
Average Number Per Year: 8
Internship Departments: Photography, News,
Copy Desk, Production, Sports

HARRISBURG EVENING NEWS
812 Market Street, PO Box 2265
Harrisburg, PA 17105
717-255-8100
Internship Contact: Mary Runkle, Personnel
Manager
Internships Offered: Both
Average Number Per Year: 2-4

HOUSTON CHRONICLE
801 Texas Avenue
Houston, TX 77002
713-220-7171
Internship Contact: Beverly Lumberg, Manager of
Records
Internships Offered: Both
Average Number Per Year: 2-3
Internship Departments: All

HOUSTON POST
4747 Southwest Freeway
Houston, TX 77001
713-840-5600
Internship Contact: Ernie Williamson, Managing
Editor
Internships Offered: Salaried
Average Number Per Year: 1-3

INDIANAPOLIS STAR AND NEWS
307 N Pennsylvania Street
Indianapolis, IN 46206
317-633-9000
Internship Contact: Harvey C. Jacobs
Internships Offered: Salaried

Average Number Per Year: 3-4
Training Available: Yes, but no details available

THE JERSEY JOURNAL
30 Journal Square
Jersey City, NJ 07306
201-653-1000
Internship Contact: Steven Newhouse, Editor
Internships Offered: Salaried
Average Number Per Year: 2-3
Internship Departments: All

THE JOURNAL OF COMMERCE
Listing deleted at Publisher's request

KALAMAZOO GAZETTE
401 S Burdick Street
Kalamazoo, MI 49003
616-345-3511
Internship Contact: James Mosby Jr., Editor
Internships Offered: Non-Salaried
Average Number Per Year: 1-2
Internship Departments: Circulation

KENT GROUP
PO Box 30
Chestertown, MD 21620
301-778-2011
Internship Contact: H. Hurtt Deringer, Publisher
& Editor
Internships Offered: Salaried
Average Number Per Year: 1

LA CROSSE TRIBUNE
401 N 3rd Street
La Crosse, WI 54601
608-782-9710
Internship Contact: David Offer, Mnging Editor
Internships Offered: Salaried
Average Number Per Year: 1

LAS VEGAS REVIEW-JOURNAL
Box 70
Las Vegas, NV 89125
702-383-0289
Internship Contact: Charles Zobell
Internships Offered: Salaried
Average Number Per Year: 3-4
Internship Departments: 1 in Features, 2 in News, 1 in Photo.

THE LEADER-TELEGRAM
701 S Farwell
Eau Claire, WI 54701
715-834-3471
Internship Contact: E. Ringhand, Editor
Internships Offered: Salaried
Average Number Per Year: 2-3
Internship Departments: Editorial

THE LEDGER
Box 408
Lakeland, FL 33802
813-687-7820
Internship Contact: Bruce Giles, Managing Editor
Internships Offered: Salaried
Average Number Per Year: 4
Internship Departments: Newsroom

LONG BEACH INDEPENDENT VOICE
320 East Park Ave.
Long Beach, NY 11561
516-432-0065
Internship Contact: Terry Kohn, Managing Editor
Internships Offered: Non-Salaried
Average Number Per Year: 4
Internship Departments: Writing, Photography

LONG ISLAND JOURNAL
Box 697
Long Beach, NY 11561
516-889-1822
Internship Contact: John Gold
Internships Offered: Salaried
Average Number Per Year: 4
Internship Departments: All

LOS ANGELES HERALD-EXAMINER
1111 S Broadway, PO Box 2416
Los Angeles, CA 90015
213-744-8000
Internship Contact: Grace Gonzalez, Personnel
Manager
Internships Offered: Salaried
Average Number Per Year: 1-2

LOS ANGELES TIMES
Times Mirror Square
Los Angeles, CA 90053
213-655-8810
Internship Contact: Human Resources Department
Internships Offered: Salaried
Average Number Per Year: 1
Internship Departments: Publishing (Reporters)

MACON TELEGRAPH & NEWS
120 Broadway, PO Box 4167
Macon, GA 31213
912-744-4200
Internship Contact: Ron Woodgeard, Managing
Editor
Internships Offered: Salaried
Average Number Per Year: 8
Internship Departments: Editorial

MIAMI HERALD
1 Herald Plaza
Miami, FL 33132-1693
305-350-2111
Internship Contact: Mary Jean Connors, Managing
Editor
Internships Offered: Both
Average Number Per Year: 15-20
Internship Departments: Editorial (Reporters)

MILWAUKEE JOURNAL
Box 661
Milwaukee, WI 53201
414-224-2355
Internship Contact: Paul Salsini, Staff Editor
Internships Offered: Salaried ($250/week)
Average Number Per Year: 10
Internship Departments: Sports, News Reporting,
Copy Editing, Retail Advertising, Classified
Sales, Promotion

MOBILE BEACON
2311 Costaries Street
Mobile, AL 36617
205-479-0629
Internship Contact: Ms. Blackman, Ms. Thomas
Internships Offered: Salaried
Average Number Per Year: 1-2
Internship Departments: Publishing

NATCHEZ DEMOCRAT
503 N Canal Street, PO Box 1447
Natchez, MS 39120
601-442-9101
Internship Contact: Editorial—John Mathews,
Managing Editor; Advertising—Jim Elsberry,
Associate Publisher
Internships Offered: Both
Average Number Per Year: 2
Internship Departments: Advertising, Editorial

NATIONAL NEWS BUREAU
2019 Chancellor St.
Philadelphia, PA 19103
215-569-0700
Internship Contact: Harry J. Katz
Internships Offered: Both
Average Number Per Year: 16

NEWARK STAR LEDGER
Star Ledger Plaza
Newark, NJ 07101
201-877-4141
Internship Contact: Mark Herrick, Personnel Dept.
Internships Offered: Salaried
Average Number Per Year: 2
Internship Departments: Advertising

**THE NEWPORT NEWS DAILY PRESS AND
TIMES HERALD**
7505 Warwick Boulevard, PO Box 746
Newport News, VA 23607
804-244-8424
Internship Contact: Margaret Simonson, Personnel Mgr.
Internships Offered: Both
Average Number Per Year: 4

NEWS AND COURIER
134 Columbus Street
Charleston, SC 29402
803-577-7111
Internship Contact: Howard McDougal
Internships Offered: Salaried
Average Number Per Year: 6
Internship Departments: 4 in revisions, 1 in
sports, 1 in features.
Training Available: Yes, but no details available

**THE NEWS AND OBSERVER PUBLISHING
COMPANY**
2155 S McDowell Street, PO Box 191
Raleigh, NC 27602
919-829-4500
Internship Contact: Hunter George, Assistant
Managing Editor
Internships Offered: Salaried
Average Number Per Year: 6

NEWSDAY
235 Pinelawn Avenue
Melville, NY 11747
516-454-2020
Internship Contact: Barbara Sanchaz, Editorial
Personnel Manager

Internships Offered: Both
Average Number Per Year: 40

NEWSPAPER PRINTING CORPORATION
315 S Boulder Avenued, PO Box 1770
Tulsa, OK 74102
918-583-2161
Internship Contact: Edward Knighten, Director of Personnel
Internships Offered: Salaried
Average Number Per Year: 6-8

NEWS PRESS
2442 Anderson Ave.
Fort Myers, FL 33902
813-335-0280
Internship Contact: Lou Brancaccio, Managing Editor
Internships Offered: Salaried ($250/week)
Average Number Per Year: 6
Internship Departments: All

OMAHA WORLD-HERALD
World Herald Square
Omaha, NE 68102
402-444-1000
Internship Contact: Gene Overman, Personnel Manager
Internships Offered: Salaried
Average Number Per Year: 6

OREGONIAN
1320 SW Broadway
Portland, OR 97201
503-221-8280
Internship Contact: Frank Lesage, Personnel Director
Internships Offered: Salaried
Average Number Per Year: 2

ORLANDO SENTINEL
633 North Orange Ave.
Orlando, FL 32801
305-420-5000
Internship Contact: James C. Clark, Deputy Managing Editor
Internships Offered: Salaried ($300/week)
Average Number Per Year: 15
Internship Departments: Business, Photography, Graphic Arts, Editorial

THE PENINSULA DAILY NEWS
Box 1330
Port Angeles, WA 98362
206-452-2345
Internship Contact: Steve Boyer, Managing Editor
Internships Offered: Salaried ($200/week)
Average Number Per Year: 1
Internship Departments: News

PENSACOLA NEWS JOURNAL
1 News Journal Plaza
Pensacola, FL 32501
904-435-8591
Internship Contact: James Barnett, Director of Human Resources
Internships Offered: Both
Average Number Per Year: 3-4

PHILADELPHIA DAILY NEWS
North Broad St.
Philadelphia, PA 19101
215-854-5851
Internship Contact: Carole Carmichael, Business Office
Internships Offered: Salaried ($450/week)
Average Number Per Year: 7
Internship Departments: News, Photography, Features, Sports, Graphics, Copy Desk, Business

PHILADELPHIA INQUIRER
400 N Broad Street
Philadelphia, PA 19101
215-854-2000
Internship Contact: Cynthia Murphy, Employee Programs
Internships Offered: Both
Average Number Per Year: 1

PHOENIX NEWSPAPERS
120 E Van Buren, PO Box 1950
Phoenix, AZ 85004
602-271-8000
Internship Contact: Mary Lou Bessette
Internships Offered: Salaried
Average Number Per Year: 10

PITTSBURGH POST GAZETTE
566 Boulevard of the Allies
Pittsburgh, PA 15222
412-263-1524
Internship Contact: John G. Craig, Jr., Editor
Internships Offered: Salaried ($359/week)

Average Number Per Year: 6
Internship Departments: Editorial (Reporting, Copy Desk, Editorial)

THE POST BULLETIN
18 First Street SE
Rochester, MN 55904
507-285-7640
Internship Contact: Robert Retzlaff, Managing Editor
Internships Offered: Both
Average Number Per Year: 1

THE PRESS-TELEGRAM
604 Pine Avenue
Long Beach, CA 90844
213-435-1161
Internship Contact: David Whiting
Internships Offered: Salaried
Average Number Per Year: 3

PRIME NATIONAL PUBLISHING CORPORATION
470 Boston Post Road
Weston, MA 02193
617-899-2702
Internship Contact: William Haslam, General Manager
Internships Offered: Both
Average Number Per Year: 1-2

PROVIDENCE BULLETIN/JOURNAL
75 Fountain Street
Providence, RI 02902
401-277-7200
Internship Contact: Donald Zimmerman, Assistant Director of Personnel and Labor Relations
Internships Offered: Salaried
Average Number Per Year: 23
Internship Departments: News, Computer Systems, Advertising

REPORTER PUBLICATIONS
1366 Turk Street
San Francisco, CA 94115
415-931-5778
Internship Contact: Amelia Ashley-Ward, Managing Editor
Internships Offered: Salaried (Stipend)
Average Number Per Year: 4 (2 in summer, 2 in winter)

Training Available: Printing: training in Web Press operation. Editorial: Training in writing for newspapers and use of camera. Production: Training in all aspects of newspaper layout.
Departments: Printing, Editorial, Production

REPORTERS COMMITTEE FOR FREEDOM OF THE PRESS
800 18th St. NW, Ste. 300
Washington, DC 20006
202-466-6312
Internship Contact: Rebecca Dougherty
Internships Offered: Salaried (Stipend)
Average Number Per Year: 2
Internship Departments: Reporting/Editing

RICHMOND NEWS LEADER-DISPATCH TIMES
333 E Grace Street, PO Box C-32333
Richmond, VA 23293
804-649-6000
Internship Contact: Personnel Department
Internships Offered: Salaried
Average Number Per Year: 12

ROANOKE TIMES & WORLD-NEWS
201-09 W Campbell Avenue, PO Box 2491
Roanoke, VA 24010
703-981-3100
Internship Contact: News—William K. Warren, Managine Editor; Advertising—Judy Perfater, Advertising Manager
Internships Offered: Salaried
Average Number Per Year: 4

ROCHESTER DEMOCRAT & CHRONICLE
55 Exchange Street
Rochester, NY 14616
716-232-7100
Internship Contact: Pat Rissberger
Internships Offered: Salaried
Average Number Per Year: 7
Training Available: Yes, but no details available

ROCKY MOUNTAIN NEWS
400 W Colfax Avenue, PO Box 719
Denver, CO 80204
303-892-5000
Internship Contact: Dave Butler, Personnel Department
Internships Offered: Both
Average Number Per Year: 1-2

ST. LOUIS GLOBE-DEMOCRAT
Paper no longer published

ST. LOUIS POST-DISPATCH
900 N Tucker Boulevard
St Louis, MO 63101
314-622-7000
Internship Contact: David Lipman, Managing
Editor
Internships Offered: Salaried
Average Number Per Year: 1-2

ST PAUL PRESS DISPATCH
345 Cedar Street
St. Paul, MN 55101
612-222-5011
Internship Contact: Editorial—Wayne Hassell,
Assistant to the Executive Editor; Advertising
and Circulation—Mary Ann Thomas, Personnel
Department
Internships Offered: Salaried
Average Number Per Year: 4-6

ST. PETERSBURG TIMES INDEPENDENCE
PO Box 1121
St Petersburg, FL 33701
813-893-8111
Internship Contact: Margaret Johnson, Staffing
Services Administrator
Internships Offered: Salaried
Average Number Per Year: 7-10
Training Available: Yes, but no details available

SAN ANTONIO EXPRESS/NEWS
PO Box 2171
San Antonio, TX 78297
512-225-7411
Internship Contact: Willis Moss
Internships Offered: Salaried
Average Number Per Year: 1-2

SAN ANTONIO LIGHT
420 Broadway
San Antonio, TX 78205
512-271-2971
Internship Contact: Ted Warmbod, Executive
Editor; Larry Wynn, Advertising Director
Internships Offered: Salaried
Average Number Per Year: 2-3
Training Available: Training program conducted
by supervisor.
Departments: Classified Advertising,
Circulation Quality Control

SAN FRANCISCO BAY GUARDIAN
2700 19th St.
San Francisco, CA 94110
415-824-7660
Internship Contact: Laura Bull, Editorial Assistant
Internships Offered: Non-Salaried
Average Number Per Year: 6-8
Internship Departments: Editorial, 1 publishing
assistant

SAN JOSE MERCURY NEWS
750 Ridder Park Drive
San Jose, CA 95190
408-920-5000
Internship Contact: Patty Fisher, Asst. Managing Ed.
Internships Offered: Salaried
Average Number Per Year: 3-4
Training Available: On-The-Job with series of
special lunches and meetings
Departments: All

SEATTLE TIMES
Fairview Avenue N, PO Box 70
Seattle, WA 981211
206-464-2400
Internship Contact: Rene Follett, Training Manager
Internships Offered: Salaried
Average Number Per Year: 1-2

SOUTH BEND TRIBUNE
225 W Colfax Road
South Bend, IN 46626
219-233-6161
Internship Contact: Ed Jenry, Personnel Manager
Internships Offered: Salaried
Average Number Per Year: 10-15
Training Available: Yes, but no details available

SPRINGFIELD NEWS LEADER
6512 Boonville Avenue
Springfield, MO 65801
417-836-1100
Internship Contact: Jan Lowe, Hmn Resources Dir.
Internships Offered: Non-Salaried
Average Number Per Year: 3-4

STAR-NEWS
525 E Colorado Boulevard
Pasadena, CA 91109
818-578-6300
Internship Contact: Jackie Knowles, City Editor
Internships Offered: Both
Average Number Per Year: 3-5

THE STATE-TIMES
PO Box 588
Baton Rouge, LA 70821-0588
504-383-1111
Internship Contact: Betty Jo Parker, Personnel
Manager
Internships Offered: Non-Salaried
Average Number Per Year: 2-3

THE TAB NEWSPAPERS
1254 Chestnut Street
Newton, MA 02164
617-969-0340
Internship Contact: Bonnie Hooker, Office
Manager
Internships Offered: Both
Average Number Per Year: 5-6

TALLAHASSEE DEMOCRAT
277 N Magnolia Drive, PO Box 990
Tallahassee, FL 32302
904-599-2100
Internship Contact: Doris Dunlap, Director of
Employment
Internships Offered: Both
Average Number Per Year: 3-4

TAMPA TRIBUNE-TIMES
202 Parker Street
Tampa, FL 33601
813-272-7711
Internship Contact: Sandra Sheffield, Personnel
Manager
Internships Offered: Salaried
Average Number Per Year: 3-4

TOLEDO BLADE
541 Superior St.
Toledo, OH 43660
419-245-6163
Internship Contact: Cheryl Lutz, Assistant
Managing Editor
Internships Offered: Salaried ($445/week)
Average Number Per Year: 6
Internship Departments: City Desk

TRENTONIAN
Southard at Perry Street
Trenton, NJ 08602
609-989-7800
Internship Contact: Emil Slaboda, Editor
Internships Offered: Non-Salaried
Average Number Per Year: 2-4

THE VILLAGE VOICE
842 Broadway
New York, NY 10003
212-475-3300
Internship Contact: Marilyn Savino, Asst. to
Editor
Internships Offered: Salaried
Average Number Per Year: 2-4

VIRGINIAN-PILOT
150 W Brambleton, PO Box 449
Norfolk, VA 23501
804-446-2090
Internship Contact: Ken Wyatt, Head of
Personnel
Internships Offered: Salaried
Average Number Per Year: 10

THE WALL STREET JOURNAL
No longer offers internships

THE WASHINGTON POST
1150 15th Street NW
Washington, DC 20071
202-334-6000
Internship Contact: Molli Martin, News
Personnel Administrator
Internships Offered: Salaried
Average Number Per Year: 4-5

THE WASHINGTON TIMES
3600 New York Avenue NE
Washington, DC 20002
202-636-3100
Internship Contact: Carol Ann Belle, Personnel
Manager
Internships Offered: Salaried
Average Number Per Year: 12

THE WICHITA EAGLE BEACON
825 E Douglas, PO Box 820
Wichita, KS 67201
316-268-6000
Internship Contact: Jim Spangler, Head of
Personnel
Internships Offered: Both
Average Number Per Year: 3-5

SECTION V

Appendices

APPENDIX A

Industry (And Allied) Trade Organizations

AMERICAN ASSOCIATION OF SUNDAY AND FEATURE EDITORS
The Houston Chronicle
801 Texas Avenue,
Houston, TX 77002
713-220-7500

AMERICAN JEWISH PRESS ASSOCIATION
c/o Robert A. Cohn
St. Louis Jewish Light
12 Millstone Campus Drive,
St. Louis, MO 63146
314-432-3353

AMERICAN NEWSPAPER PUBLISHERS ASSOCIATION
And ANPA FOUNDATION
Box 17407, Dulles Airport,
Washington, DC 20041
703-648-1000

AMERICAN NEWS WOMEN'S CLUB
1607 22nd Street, NW,
Washington, DC 20008
202-332-6770

AMERICAN PRESS INSTITUTE
11690 Sunrise Valley Drive,
Reston, VA 22091
703-620-3611

AMERICAN SOCIETY OF JOURNALISTS AND AUTHORS
1501 Broadway, Suite 1907,
New York, NY 10036
212-997-0947

AMERICAN SOCIETY OF NEWSPAPER EDITORS
PO Box 17004, Dulles Airport,
Washington, DC 20041
703-648-1145

AMERICAN SOCIETY OF PICTURE PROFESSIONALS
c/o Jane Kinney
Comstock
30 Irving Place,
New York, NY 10003
212-353-8600

ASSOCIATED PRESS MANAGING EDITORS
50 Rockefeller Plaza,
New York, NY 10020
212-621-1552

ASSOCIATED PRESS SPORTS EDITORS
c/o Jack Sims
PO Box 1129,
Auburn, AL 36831
205-826-4607

ASSOCIATION OF AMERICAN EDITORIAL CARTOONISTS
c/o Ed Stein
Rocky Mountain News
400 W. Colfax,
Denver, CO 80204
303-892-5000

ASSOCIATION OF NEWSPAPER CLASSIFIED ADVERTISING MANAGERS
Box 267
Danville, IL 61834
217-442-2057

CANADIAN DAILY NEWSPAPER PUBLISHERS ASSOCIATION
890 Young St., Ste. 1100
Toronto, Ontario, Canada M4W 3P4
416-923-3567

CAPITAL PRESS CLUB
PO Box 19403,
Washington, DC 20036
301-559-3381

GAY AND LESBIAN PRESS ASSOCIATION
PO Box 7809,
Van Nuys, CA 91409
213-877-1045

INTERNATIONAL CIRCULATION MANAGERS ASSOCIATION
PO Box 17420, Dulles Airport,
Washington, DC 20041
703-648-1150

INTERNATIONAL NEWSPAPER ADVERTISING & MARKETING EXECUTIVES
PO Box 17210, Dulles Airport,
Washington, DC 20041
703-648-1178

INTERNATIONAL NEWSPAPER FINANCIAL EXECUTIVES
PO Box 17573, Dulles Airport,
Washington, DC 20041
703-648-1159

INTERNATIONAL NEWSPAPER MARKETING ASSOCIATION
PO Box 17573, Dulles Airport,
Washington, DC 20041
703-648-1094

INTERNATIONAL SOCIETY OF WEEKLY NEWSPAPER EDITORS
Department of Journalism
Northern Illinois University
DeKalb, IL 60115
815-753-1925

INVESTIGATIVE REPORTERS AND EDITORS
Box 838
Columbia, MO 65205
314-882-2042

NATIONAL ASSOCIATION OF BLACK JOURNALISTS
PO Box 1712
Washington, DC 20041
703-648-1270

NATIONAL ASSOCIATION OF HISPANIC JOURNALISTS
National Press Bldg., Ste. 634
Washington, DC 20045
202-783-6228

NATIONAL CONFERENCE OF EDITORIAL WRITERS
6223 Executive Blvd.,
Rockville, MD 20852
301-984-3015

NATIONAL FEDERATION OF PRESS WOMEN
Box 99
Blue Springs, MO 64015
816-229-1666

NATIONAL NEWSPAPER ASSOCIATION
1627 K Street, NW,
Washington, DC 20006
202-466-7200

NATIONAL PRESS CLUB
National Press Building
529 14th St, NW, 13th Floor
Washington, DC 20045
202-662-7500

**NATIONAL PRESS PHOTOGRAPHERS
ASSOCIATION**
3200 Croasdaile Dr., Ste. 306
Durham, NC 27705
919-383-7246

**NATIONAL SPORTSCASTERS AND
SPORTWRITERS ASSOCIATION**
Box 559
Salisbury, NC 28144
704-633-4275

NEWSPAPER ADVERTISING BUREAU
1180 Avenue of the Americas,
New York, NY 10036
212-921-5080

NEWSPAPER ASSOCIATION MANAGERS
PO Box 17407, Dulles Airport,
Washington, DC 20041
703-648-1123

**NEWSPAPER PERSONNEL RELATIONS
ASSOCIATION**
PO Box 17407, Dulles Airport,
Washington, DC 20041
703-648-1069

NEWSPAPER RESEARCH COUNCIL
601 Locust, Suite 1000
The Two Ruan Cut,
Des Moines, IA 50309
515-245-3828

PUBLIC RELATIONS SOCIETY OF AMERICA
33 Irving Place
New York, NY 10003
212-995-2230

THE SOCIETY OF ILLUSTRATORS
128 East 63rd Street,
New York, NY 10021
212-838-2560

THE SOCIETY OF NEWSPAPER DESIGN
PO Box 17290, Dulles Airport,
Washington, DC 20041
703-648-1027

**WHITE HOUSE CORRESPONDENTS
ASSOCIATION**
National Press Building
529 14th St., NW, Room 1067,
Washington, DC 20045
202-737-2934

**WHITE HOUSE NEWS PHOTOGRAPHERS
ASSOCIATION**
PO Box 7119, Ben Franklin Station,
Washington, DC 20044
202-634-7940

WOMEN IN COMMUNICATIONS, INC.
Box 9561
Austin, TX 78766
512-346-9875

APPENDIX B

Industry (And Allied)
Trade Publications

The following trade publications are primarily or substantially concerned with the art, science and business of newspapers and newspaper publishing. There are numerous others particular to areas of professional specialization (i.e., public relations, finance, etc.) but not to *newspapers*—we have omitted all but the most important of these. If you are interested in a particular specialization, ask your professor, boss or co-workers about the magazines that cover that specialization.

ADVERTISING AGE
Crain Communications
740 North Rush Street,
Chicago, IL 60611
312-649-5200

One of the two "bibles" of the industry (the other being *Adweek)*. Available at most New York newsstands and, more than likely, at your local public and/or college library. Special issue: "100 Leading Media Companies" (June).

ADWEEK
A/S/M Communications
49 East 21st Street, 11th floor,
New York, NY 10010
212-529-5500

The other "bible," consisting of six regional editions (East, New England, Southeast, Midwest, Southwest and West) plua a national marketing edition. Reports on agencies and all media.

AMERICAN PRINTER
MacLean Hunter Publishing Company
29 North Wacker Dr.
Chicago, IL 60606
312-726-2802

For members of the publishing, printing and graphic arts industries. Especially helpful for aspiring manufacturing and distribution professionals.

ART DIRECTION
10 East 39th Street, 6th floor,
New York, NY 10016
212-889-6500

COLUMBIA JOURNALISM REVIEW
Columbia University
School of Journalism, Room 700,
New York, NY 10027
212-280-2716

A national media "monitor," helpful in defining standards of journalism and calling attention to the profession's strengths and weaknesses.

EDITOR & PUBLISHER
11 W 19th Street
New York, NY 10011
212-675-4380

The bible of the newspaper industry -- spot news and features on all aspects of the business, plus regular columns covering most departments. And, of course, publishers of the Editor & Publisher International Yearbook, the primary reference resource you should be utilizing in addition to this Newspapers Career Directory.

THE EDITORIAL EYE
Editorial Experts, Inc.
85 S. Bragg St., Suite 400
Alexandria, VA 22312-2731
703-642-3040

Focuses on publication standards and practices, including information on grammar, usage, style and editorial standards.

FOLIO: THE MAGAZINE FOR MAGAZINE MANAGEMENT
Folio Publishing Corp.
6 River Bend, PO Box 4949,
Stamford, CT 06907-4949
203-358-9900

The absolute "must read" for anyone interested in a career in magazine publishing, but includes occasional articles helpful to newspaper pros. Covering every area, from editorial and ad sales to production and circulation.

GRAPHIC ARTS MONTHLY
Technical Publishing
249 West 17th St.
New York, NY 10011
212-645-0067

For both graphic artists and production professionals. Focuses primarily on methods and techniques of lowering costs and enhancing productivity.

MARKETING AND MEDIA DECISIONS
Decisions Publications, Inc.
1140 Avenue of the Americas,
New York, NY 10036
212-725-2300

Each issue, planned with the aid of a "guest editor," examines, evaluates and chronicles the factors involved in deciding who gets what share of a client's advertising dollar. Covers all media.

MIN: MEDIA INDUSTRY NEWSLETTER
MIN Publishing Inc.
145 East 49th St., Suite 7B
New York, NY 10017
212-751-2670

Expensive ($175) newsletter covering current events in media. Primarily read by executives, but invaluable (if you can get a free copy) to learn the business.

NEWS PHOTOGRAPHER
National Press Photographers Association
School of Journalism
Bowling Green State University
Bowling Green, OH 43403
419-372-0308

Covering all aspects of still, motion picture and TV news photography.

PHOTO DESIGN
Billboard Publications
1 Park Ave.
New York, NY 10016

For creative professionals who commission and/or produce photo/illustrations for newspapers, magazines and other media.

PRESSTIME
American Newspaper Publishers Association
11600 Sunrise Valley Drive
Reston, VA 22091
703-648-1074

Regular reports on news editorial and readership, press freedoms, circulation, training, products, promotion, etc.

PRINT & HOW
R.C. Publications, Inc.
104 Fifth Ave., 9th Floor
New York, NY 10011
212-463-0600

For design and, especially, production professionals.

PRINTING IMPRESSIONS
North American Publishing Co.
401 North Broad St.,
Philadelphia, PA 19108
215-238-5300

For adminsitrative, production and supervisory management in graphic arts, newspaper publishing and commercial printing fields; emphasizes printing management/finance, marketing and technology.

PUBLIC RELATIONS JOURNAL
Public Relations Society of America
845 Third Avenue, 12th floor,
New York, NY 10022
212-826-1757

Official publication of the PRSA and, as such, must reading for anyone considering the specialized world of newspaper PR.

PUBLISHERS AUXILIARY
National Newspaper Association
1627 K Street, #400
Washington, DC 20006
202-466-7200

News of the newspaper printing and publishing business, including changes of ownership, etc., re: 8,000 weekly, daily and Sunday newspapers in U.S. and Canada. Also covers the activities of the state, regional and local trade associations and journalism schools.

THE QUILL
Society of Professional Journalists
(Sigma Delta Chi)
53 W Jackson Blvd., Suite 731
Chicago, IL 60604
312-922-7751

For journalists, teachers of journalism and students of journalism. Features on newspaper and broadcast news production, reporting and photography.

QUILL & SCROLL
(International Honorary Society for High School Journalists)
School of Journalism and Mass Communications
University of Iowa
Iowa City, IA 52242
319-335-5795

Most helpful if you're in high school (or a little younger or older, for that matter); so is the group.

THE ST. LOUIS JOURNALISM REVIEW
8606 Olive Blvd
St. Louis, MO 63132
314-991-1699

Primarily covers St. Louis, but many features on regional, national and international issues. In addition to evaluating news and editorial, covers advertising, public relations and communication.

SELLING SPACE
JB & Me
PO Box 480311,
Los Angeles, CA 90048
213-546-1255

"The newsletter of the advertising space sales field." (They also have a book—The Guide To Selling Advertising Space). Both are very oriented to people already out there selling (and, perhaps, especially to independent reps specializing in magazines, not staff salespeople at magazines or newspapers—not surprising since the publisher is himself an independent magazine space rep) but may be a helpful introductions to space sales.

STANDARD RATE & DATA (SRDS)
Standard Rate & Data Service, Inc.
3004 Glenview Rd.,
Wilmette, IL 60091
312-256-6067

Two volumes particular to newspapers -- "Newspaper Rates & Data" and "Newspaper Circulation Analysis." Includes separate listings for weeklies and dailies.

STEP-BY-STEP GRAPHICS
Dynamic Graphics, Inc.
6000 North Forest Park Drive,
Peoria, IL 616144
309-688-2300

Resource to aid professional visual communicators in developing new and existing skills—design, illustration, typographic, photographic, composition, etc.

TYPEWORLD
Blum Publications
15 Oakridge Circle,
Washington, MA 01887
617-658-6876

Articles on the application and development of word processing and typesetting devices, systems and peripherals.

TYPOGRAPHIC JOURNAL
International Typographers Union of North America
PO Box 2341
Colorado Springs, CO 80901

UPPER AND LOWER CASE (U&lc)
International Typeface Corporation
2 Dag Hammarskjold Plaza, 3rd floor,
New York, NY 10017
212-371-0699

For aspiring art directors and designers. Deals primarily with typeface selection, design and use.

WASHINGTON JOURNALISM REVIEW
2233 Wisconsin Avenue NW, #442
Washington, DC 20007
202-333-6800

Analyzes the press in all its forms.

THE WRITER
120 Boylston Street,
Boston, MA 02116
(617)423-3157

AND

WRITERS DIGEST
1050 Dana Ave.
Cincinnati, OH 45207
513-531-2222

The two key publications for professional writers (and certainly helpful to aspiring editors). Long on technical tips and training, but also important information on where and how to sell your work.

C

D

E

F

G

MAIL ORDER COUPON

Name: _____

Mailing Address: _____

City, State, Zip Code: _____

Telephone:_____ ❑ **CHECK HERE FOR CATALOG**

Quantity	Binding	Title	Price
SERIES TITLES (Add postage and handling)			
_____	Paper	Internships, Vol 1.	$11.95
_____	Paper	Internships, Vol. 2	$11.95
_____	Paper	Advertising Career Directory	$26.95
_____	Paper	Book Publishing Career Directory	$26.95
_____	Paper	Magazines Career Directory	$26.95
_____	Paper	Marketing & Sales Career Directory	$26.95
_____	Paper	Newspapers Career Directory	$26.95
_____	Paper	Public Relations Career Directory	$26.95
_____	Hardcover	Advertising Career Directory	$34.95
_____	Hardcover	Book Publishing Career Directory	$34.95
_____	Hardcover	Magazines Career Directory	$34.95
_____	Hardcover	Marketing & Sales Career Directory	$34.95
_____	Hardcover	Newspapers Career Directory	$34.95
_____	Hardcover	Public Relations Career Directory	$34.95
NON-SERIES TITLES (Prices include postage and handling)			
_____	Paper	College Comes Sooner Than You Think!	$11.95
_____	Paper	Your First Resume Book	$11.95
_____	Paper	High Impact Resumes & Letters	$13.95
_____	Paper	Interview for Success	$11.95
_____	Paper	Complete Guide to Public Employment	$15.50
_____	Paper	Public Schools USA	$14.95
_____	Paper	International Careers: An Insider's Guide	$11.95
_____	Paper	After College: The Business of Getting Jobs	$11.95
_____	Paper	Parenting Through the College Years	$11.95
_____	Paper	What's Next? Career Strategies After 35	$11.95
_____	Paper	Complete Guide to Social Security	$11.95

Total number of Series volumes ordered: _____   Amount : $_____

$2.50 per order plus $1.00 per volume shipping charges $_____

Total number of non-Series volumes: _____   Amount: $_____

Total amount of order. <u>This must be enclosed.</u> $_____

NON-SERIES TITLES

- [ ] **COLLEGE COMES SOONER THAN YOU THINK! The College Planning Guide For High School Students And Their Families,** by Jill Reilly and Bonnie Featherstone. ISBN 0-934829-24-1, Paper, 6 x 9, 176 pp. $11.95 postpaid.

- [ ] **YOUR FIRST RESUME: The Comprehensive Preparation Guide for High School and College Students** by Ronald W. Fry. ISBN 0-934829-25-X, Paper, 8 1/2 x 11, 160 pp. (approx.). $11.95 postpaid.

- [ ] **HIGH IMPACT RESUMES AND LETTERS: How to Communicate Your Qualifications to Employers,** 3rd Edition, by Dr. Ronald L. Krannich and William J. Banis. ISBN 0-942710-20-7, Paper, 8 1/2 x 11, 180 pages. $13.95

- [ ] **INTERVIEW FOR SUCCESS: A Practical Guide To Increasing Job Interviews, Offers and Salaries,** by Drs. Caryl & Ron Krannich. ISBN 0-942710-19-3, Paper, 6 x 9, Indexed & Illustrated, 165 pages. $11.95 postpaid.

- [ ] **THE COMPLETE GUIDE TO PUBLIC EMPLOYMENT,** by Drs. Ron and Caryl Krannich. ISBN 0-942710-05-3, Paper, 6 x 9, 512 pages. $15.50 postpaid.

- [ ] **PUBLIC SCHOOLS USA: A Guide To School Districts,** by Charles Harrison ISBN 0-913589-36-5, Paper, 6 x 9, 256 pages. $14.95 postpaid.

- [ ] **INTERNATIONAL CAREERS: An Insiders Guide,** by David Rearwin. ISBN 0-913589-28-4, Paper, 6 x 9, 192 pages. $11.95 postpaid.

- [ ] **AFTER COLLEGE; The Business of Getting Jobs,** by Jack Falvey ISBN 0-913589-17-9, Paper, 6 x 9, 192 pages. $11.95 postpaid.

- [ ] **PARENTING THROUGH THE COLLEGE YEARS,** by Norman Giddan and Sally Vallongo ISBN 0-913589-37-3, Paper, 6 x 9, 192 pages. $11.95 postpaid.

- [ ] **WHAT'S NEXT?/Career Strategies After 35,** by Jack Falvey. ISBN 0-913589-26-8 Paper, 6 x 9, 192 pages. $11.95 postpaid.

- [ ] **THE COMPLETE & EASY GUIDE TO SOCIAL SECURITY AND MEDICARE,** by Faustin F. Jehle. ISBN 0-930045-02-5, Paper, 8 1/2 x 11, 175 pages. $11.95 postpaid.

TO ORDER ANY OF THESE TITLES—OR TO REQUEST A CATALOG—SIMPLY FILL OUT THE ORDER FORM ON THE OPPOSITE PAGE OR CALL **1-800-CAREER-1** TO USE YOUR MASTERCARD OR VISA.

GREAT BOOKS FROM THE CAREER PRESS

TO ORDER ANY OF THESE ACCLAIMED VOLUMES or request a catalog, **CALL 1-800-CAREER-1**. For your convenience, we accept MASTERCARD and VISA.

Or simply check the titles you would like on the coupon on the preceding page, fill out the required information completely, tear out the entire page and send (with full payment if you are ordering books) to: The Career Press, 62 Beverly Rd., PO Box 34, Hawthorne, N.J. 07057.

<u>SERIES TITLES:</u>

❑ **INTERNSHIPS, VOL. 1: ADVERTISING, MARKETING, PUBLIC RELATIONS & SALES,** edited by Ronald W. Fry. ISBN 0-934829-27-6, Paper, 6 x 9, 320 pages (approx.). $11.95.

❑ **INTERNSHIPS, VOL 2: NEWSPAPER, MAGAZINE AND BOOK PUBLISHING,** edited by Ronald W. Fry. ISBN 0-934829-28-4, Paper, 6 x 9, 320 pages (approx.). $11.95.

ADVERTISING CAREER DIRECTORY, 3rd edition, 320 pages, 8 1/2 x 11
❑ Paper — ISBN 0-934829-30-6, $26.95.
❑ Hardcover (cloth) — ISBN 0-934829-40-3, $34.95.

MARKETING & SALES CAREER DIRECTORY, 2nd edition, 320 pages, 8 1/2 X 11.
❑ Paper — ISBN 0-934829-34-9, $26.95.
❑ Hardcover (cloth) — ISBN 0-934829-44-6, $34.95.

PUBLIC RELATIONS CAREER DIRECTORY, 3rd edition, 320 PAGES, 8 1/2 X 11.
❑ Paper — ISBN 0-934829-33-0, $26.95.
❑ Hardcover (cloth) — ISBN 0-934829-43-8, $34.95.

MAGAZINES CAREER DIRECTORY, 3rd edition, 256 pages, 8 1/2 X 11.
❑ Paper — ISBN 0-934829-31-4, $26.95.
❑ Hardcover (cloth) — ISBN 0-934829-41-1, $34.95.

BOOK PUBLISHING CAREER DIRECTORY, 3rd edition, 224 pages, 8 1/2 X 11.
❑ Paper — ISBN 0-934829-32-2, $26.95.
❑ Hardcover (cloth) — ISBN 0-934829-42-X, $34.95.

NEWSPAPERS CAREER DIRECTORY, 2nd edition, 240 pages, 8 1/2 X 11.
❑ Paper — ISBN 0-934829-35-7, $26.95.
❑ Hardcover (cloth) — ISBN 0-934829-45-4, $34.95

Please enclose $2.50 per order and $1.00 per title for each series volume ordered.

* * * MORE BOOKS AND MAIL ORDER COUPON ON PRECEDING PAGES * * *